ADAPTIVE COUNSELING IN SCHOOLS

PRENTICE-HALL COUNSELING AND GUIDANCE SERIES

NORMAN R. STEWART, *Editor*

Changing Children's Behavior
JOHN D. KRUMBOLTZ *and* HELEN B. KRUMBOLTZ

ADAPTIVE COUNSELING IN SCHOOLS

JOHN W. M. ROTHNEY

University of Wisconsin

PRENTICE-HALL, INC., *Englewood Cliffs, N.J.*

© 1972 by Prentice-Hall, Inc.
Englewood Cliffs, New Jersey

ISBN: C 0–13–003954–3

Library of Congress Catalog Card Number: 73–167908

10 9 8 7 6 5 4 3 2 1

Prentice-Hall International, Inc., *London*
Prentice-Hall of Australia, Pty. Ltd., *Sydney*
Prentice-Hall of Canada, Ltd., *Toronto*
Prentice-Hall of India Private Ltd., *New Delhi*
Prentice-Hall of Japan, Inc., *Tokyo*

Printed in the United States of America

To Ruth Betty Rothney
source of health, strength, and tranquility
this book is gratefully dedicated

contents

1

individual differences in counselees, 1

2

two samples of counseling techniques, 31

3

foundations of adaptive counseling, 53

4

techniques of adaptive counseling, 74

5

procedures in adaptive counseling, 102

6

evaluation of counseling, 118

7

synthesis for adaptability, 152

Appendix
use of case studies, 161

references, 182

subject index, 189

author index, 191

preface

The two following quotations, one from the French philosopher Montaigne and the other from the first chapter of this volume, introduce the two themes which have governed preparation of the text. Individual variability, and the need for adaptation of counseling procedures by school counselors to serve each individual, are stressed throughout.

> Not only does the wind of chance move me according to its bent, but also I move and trouble myself by instability of my position; and whoever observes very attentively will hardly find himself twice in the same state. I give my soul sometimes one face, sometimes another, according to the side to which I turn it. If I speak variously of myself, it is because I look at myself variously. All contradictions are to be found in me in some shape or other.
>
> Montaigne, 1533–1592

> The vast accumulation of information about how persons differ from each other, and even differ in their own behavior at various times and under varying circumstances, seems to have been minimized by those who advocate a one-best-way to counsel. . . . [I]t is suggested that limiting oneself to one method of counseling while working with the variety of persons and circumstances met in educational institutions is likely to be a futile exercise.

The book is directed to those who counsel and those who are in preparation for counseling in educational institutions. Workers in other counseling settings may find the discussion of some interest, since some principles are common to all counseling endeavors, but educational settings present restrictions and opportunities which make counseling a special challenge. It is to persons who would undertake the tasks in such settings that the concepts, suggestions, and cautions in this volume are addressed. Since it is important that such persons do not align themselves too firmly too soon with one school of thought and thereby reduce their flexibility in adjusting to individual differences, this text should be used primarily in a second course in counseling, often called counseling techniques, procedures, or strategies. The author has attempted to present issues in a manner which encourages thought and discussion by students.

Throughout the author's professional career he has arranged his work so that he could counsel frequently with adolescents in schools, their parents, and their teachers, while he was also conducting large-scale experimental studies in guidance. The realities of school circumstances recognized in the former activity have served as cautions in the interpretation of results of the latter. It is suggested that experimental studies have their place in providing generalizations about counselors and counselees, but that when the counselor works with an individual all generalizations must be modified. With considerable knowledge about each counselee, and with the adaptibility that freedom from disciplehood to particular schools of thought allows, it appears that counseling can come into its own as a democratic process for helping youth to know themselves better and find suitable and rewarding places in current and future environments. It has been suggested that some evidence of counselors' effectiveness must be obtained to insure continuous attempts to improve procedures, and to justify their place in schools.

The purpose of the University of Wisconsin seems to be well-described in a report of an Interdisciplinary Studies Committee on the Future of Man, and the Purpose and Function of a University. The committee reported as follows: "The primary purpose of a University is to provide an environment in which faculty and students can discover, examine critically, preserve, and transmit the knowledge, wisdom, and values that will help ensure the survival of the present and future generations with improvement in the quality of life." It is in the setting described in this quotation that the author has studied and tried to practice counseling and guidance for many years. It is in the spirit of that statement, particularly the terms "discover," "examine critically," "preserve" and "transmit" that this volume has been prepared. The opportunity to attempt to serve such purposes in an institution devoted to them is deeply appreciated.

John W. M. Rothney

Madison, Wisconsin

CHAPTER

individual differences

in counselees

The persistent search for and advocacy of a single method for the counseling of individuals despite increased evidence of differences among and within them is one of the many strange contradictions in the field of guidance and counseling. The vast accumulation of information about how persons differ from each other, and even differ in their own behavior at various times and under varying circumstances, seems to have been minimized by those who advocate a one-best-way to counsel. There is a tendency to offer would-be counselors a set of packaged procedures based on single learning or personality theories which are said to be suitable with only minor modifications in any counseling circumstance. Those who make these offers seem not to recognize the contradictions involved in the employment of unvarying methods in complex situations. In the pages which follow it is suggested that limiting oneself to one method of counseling while working with the variety of persons and circumstances met in educational institutions is likely to be a futile exercise.

The extent of differences among counselees in educational institutions is well documented and summarized, and is too voluminous to report in detail here. The reports are presented in statistical charts and tables which, while they tend to obscure the individual, reveal the wide distribution of all the characteristics studied.[1] However, each characteristic is

[1] Leona E. Tyler, *The Psychology of Individual Differences* (New York: Appleton-Century-Crofts, 1965).

1

reported separately, which reduces their significance to the counselor working with the whole individual in whom differences in many characteristics are merged, and with a developing person whose behavior may vary from time to time. The general findings of variability of separately measured characteristics take on increased importance when they are combined in one person. A particular counselee may vary upward or downward from his group average in height, mental alertness, adjustability, interests, performances, attitudes, knowledge, health, home background, or any of the characteristics studied, and these deviations and their interrelationships make for more complexity than is revealed by studies of single characteristics. It is these combinations which make individuals unique and which must lead to the employment of various procedures in dealing with them.

"Individual differences" may mean different things to different persons. To the administrator it may mean distributions from which overall averages can be computed and provision made for groups with average deviations from those averages. To a teacher of one of the latter groups it may mean provision for differences among student performances when the group is working toward common school goals for various grade and developmental levels. For example, although the administrator is aware of differences in physical size of third graders, he can order desks or chairs of certain dimensions which will be generally acceptable. The teacher, aware of differences in reading performances, may still find that textbooks of certain vocabulary levels can be used effectively. The words "provision for individual differences," which are so commonly used in education, have really meant classification of students so that certain kinds of *group* instruction may be employed. It would seem appropriate in such cases to substitute the term "provision for groups with obvious *similarities*."

In view of the above, it is difficult for those who have talked about providing for individual differences to think of counseling and guidance as a process of working with one person at a time. Schools are, and are likely to remain, organizations committed to group processes. Like many other assemblages in our society (church, scouts, teams, clubs, and the recently developed confrontation groups), they emphasize clusters to the point where counselors who insist on dealing with individuals are suspect. In such groups, despite statements about attention to individuals, concern for individuality within the communality is rare. To the counselor, the individual must predominate.

A counselor tries to assist *individuals;* if he nurtures any pattern of behavior, it is an *individual pattern.*[2] He knows that each counselee will

---

[2] This is not to deny the desirability of conformity. The following statement by I. A. Berg in *Counseling News and Views,* XVI, No. 1 (1964) needs consideration by those who would push the concept of individuality too far: "What's wrong with conforming? Sure, one can chuckle at the surface elements of conformity, like men

deviate in thousands of ways from hypothetical averages, and that individuality is not just a total but a product of mutual interaction of the deviations. He may find averages and variances of distributions of individual differences essential as background settings, but a counselee will not conform precisely to any of the averages. Counseling, therefore, becomes a very personal affair.

General descriptions of individual differences become relevant to a counselor only if there is a demonstrable relationship between them and a particular counselee's personal concerns. The remainder of this chapter contains samples of relevant conditions which the writer has observed as causes of differences in students' vocational, educational, and personal-social decision-making behavior. The lists of conditions provide merely a small sampling of those a counselor may meet when he works with a cross section of students. School counselors who do not have the freedom of private clinicians or university experimenters in choosing their counselees must be prepared to work with some of the conditions and kinds of persons described in this chapter. The reader is reminded that their placement into vocational, educational, and personal-social categories is only for convenience in presentation. Do not assume that they are not interrelated; it is the total individual, and not a single or diverse aspect of him, which is involved in every decision he makes.

INDIVIDUAL VARIABILITY

Reports of individual differences indicate clearly that the range of variation among groups is great, but the amount of differences within individuals over periods of time has not been given enough consideration. Perhaps this situation is due to the scarcity of longitudinal studies; their paucity, in turn, is caused by the difficulty in making them. Study of existing data makes it clear that differences in individual development must become as much a matter of concern to a counselor as the extent of variation within groups.

---

in gray flannel suits or like the popular song that satirizes suburbia with its houses all "made of ticky-tacky." Such aspects are the superfluities, the froth of conformity. But the heart of conformity is the gyroscope of our society. The conforming person is the one who sees to it that we have electricity and heat, gasoline for our cars, water in the faucets, planes flying, trains running. The conforming person feeds the baby, stocks the grocery shelves, builds our roads, arrests robbers, fights fires, delivers the mail and a thousand other things. The conforming person is responsible—he does what he is supposed to do when he is supposed to do it. He may not be highly creative; few people are. But he makes it possible for the creative person to create and he makes it possible for the rest of us to live as we do."

Differences in the mental growth (as measured by tests labeled as measures of mental ability or intelligence) of five girls over a nine-year period are presented in Figure 1–1. Although all five had reached the same level at age 16, they arrived there by widely different routes. Case *A* scored below the average at age 8, reached her greatest height considerably above it at age 14, and dropped precipitously toward it at age 16. Case *E* did not rise to the average until she was 15 years old, while Case *B* maintained a quite regular course always slightly above the average.

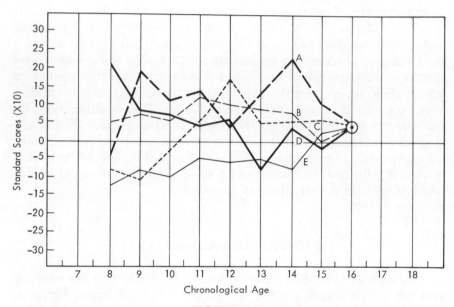

FIGURE 1–1

Differences in Mental Growth

The patterns of cases *C* and *D* are unlike each other, and both differ significantly from *A*, *B*, and *E*. The range of standard scores from −1.2 to +2.2 at age 8 is reduced to zero at age 16.[3]

Variability in rates of physical development as measured in units of standing height is illustrated in Figure 1–2. All five girls were of equal stature at age 12, but variation from the average at all other ages is readily observable. Differences such as those described above have been extensively documented, but their significance for counselors has rarely been considered.

[3] See W. F. Dearborn and J. W. M. Rothney, *Predicting the Child's Development,* 2nd ed. (Cambridge, Mass.: Sci-Art Publishers, 1963).

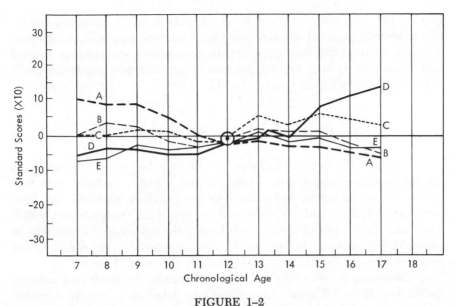

FIGURE 1–2

Variability in Rate of Physical Development

Variations from common physical and mental development patterns are sometimes closely associated with a counselee's behavior. A girl who reaches puberty early is likely to be considerably taller at that time (though not necessarily at end points of growth) than others of her chronological age, and will show concomitant changes in her physical appearance because of the development of secondary sex characteristics. She may worry that she will grow to an excessive height, may become intolerant of what she calls the childish behavior of her peers, and her interests may become more womanly than girlish. On the other hand, the girl for whom the advent of the menarche is delayed beyond the usual age may be disturbed about her lack of development. She may be ignored by contemporaries who think that she is not "grown up," and she may resort to various kinds of compensatory behavior. (It should be noted that the word "may" has been used because the correlation of physical status and certain kinds of behavior is not high enough for the latter to be predicted certainly from the former.) It is, of course, possible that the mental and physical patterns described above may not be accompanied by any unusual behavior on the part of a particular counselee.

These illustrations have been presented to emphasize the point that counselors must be concerned not only with individual differences in groups, but also with intraindividual variations as counselees develop.[4] Observation of personal differences suggests that continuous study of counselees is essential. As they get older, their problems may change in kind and increase in number, and the solution of one does not negate the possibility of the unanticipated occurrence of others.

DIFFERENCES WITHIN SPECIAL GROUPS

Members of certain subgroups within such larger populations as all the students in a school system meet so many similar circumstances that many common likenesses and differences are apparent. Regional and demographic variations and current social or economic circumstances which often accentuate differences and similarities do not require alterations in counselors' ultimate goals, but they do demand considerable adaptation of practices to meet the exigencies of members of special groups.[5]

There can be little doubt that school counselors in affluent suburbs spend their time differently from those who labor in culturally deprived areas. For example, although students in the former situation might profit from participation in a work-study program, and counselors might suggest that they give serious consideration to such activity, they are less likely to do so than the students in deprived areas.[6] In the latter case, the demand from students for such participation may be as much a matter of economics as of self-development, since their earnings may be required to supplement a family's scanty budget.

Provision for the 2 to 3 per cent of students in school populations who have serious mental or physical handicaps is not a prime responsibility of counselors. Most states have made accommodations for them at a greater than average expense, and their teachers are given special training and better salaries.[7] But handicapped persons need counseling, too, and when there are significant numbers of them in a particular population the coun-

---

[4] One of the most common arguments offered in support of counseling in elementary schools is that, if children are helped when they are very young, they will have fewer problems in later years. There may be some justification for the argument (although there are no conclusive studies on the subject), but it must be recognized that new and personal problems of adjustment must inevitably rise when a student reaches puberty. They will occur despite efforts at sex education in preparation for that development.

[5] P. M. Smith, Jr., ed., "What Guidance for Blacks?" *Personnel and Guidance Journal*, XLVIII (1970); W. H. Sewell, "Community of Residence and College Plans," *American Sociological Review*, XXIX (1964); *idem*, "Community of Residence and Occupational Choice," *American Journal of Sociology*, LXX (1965).

[6] J. B. Conant, *Slums and Suburbs* (New York: McGraw-Hill Book Company, 1961).

[7] C. W. Telford and J. M. Saurey, *The Exceptional Individual: Psychological and Educational Aspects* (Englewood Cliffs, N.J.: Prentice-Hall, Inc., 1967).

selor may be required to spend considerable time with them. The ultimate goals to which he strives will be similar to those he sets when working with the less handicapped, but the adaptation of his methods becomes greater. Just the reduced mobility of the physically handicapped, and the lack of highly developed verbal facility of those who have mental handicaps, make for differences in counseling procedures.

Despite the common criticism that counselors spend too much time with academically superior students, there is reason to believe that not enough real counseling is done with them. Since most such students plan to enter post-high school education, much time is spent on selection of the "right" college. There is more involved in the counseling of academically superior students than simply helping them make this one choice, as those who have attempted to really counsel such students have found.[8] Their greater verbal facility and multipotentiality, and the particular pressures which they encounter, present very special challenges to counselors.[9]

Many pathways to satisfactory adolescence and adulthood may be opened, but some of them are largely shaped by particular demographic and economic circumstances. When such circumstances are highly influential in restricting or enlarging choice behavior of students, the counselor is required to adapt his usual practices (but not his ultimate purposes) to meet them. However, it is essential that he does not lose sight of the fact that no two members of even any subpopulation are alike. He must resist the notion that there is one best way to counsel all persons who are put in such classifications as handicapped, alienated, talented, or delinquent, or even that there is one best method for those who do not fall into special categories. Similarity of group membership must not be confused with identity. Description of subgroup provides only general background against which the individuality of each counselee is to be recognized.

CLASSIFICATION OF INDIVIDUAL DIFFERENCES

Classification of the many kinds of individual differences which concern counselees is a hazardous procedure because it suggests separation into mutually exclusive categories. Thus the classification of such concerns into the widely-used educational, vocational, and personal-social categories may suggest that, for example, educational counseling could be carried on

[8] E. Ginzberg and J. L. Herma, *Talent and Performance* (New York: Columbia University Press, 1964). See some of the special counseling procedures described in J. W. M. Rothney and M. P. Sanborn, *Identifying and Educating Superior Students in Wisconsin High Schools* (Madison: University of Wisconsin Research and Guidance Laboratory for Superior Students, 1967).

[9] Joyce S. Mitchell, "Social Visibility and College Choice," *Personnel and Guidance Journal*, XLVIII (1970).

without attention to the other two. Acceptance of that suggestion would be unfortunate. Because there are so many indications of differences, however, some classification seems essential, and therefore some categories are used in this section. In order to indicate their relationships, the categories are supplemented by case studies and brief sketches. The sample items have been accumulated by the writer in his counseling of youth over the past three decades, but they have been documented by others in the literature of psychology, sociology, guidance, and counseling, and in general writings about human beings. Their universality and similarity suggest that they are common concerns, but their individuality within the greater universality, their irregularity of occurrence, and their variability in intensity for a particular individual at different times make them matters of prime concern to a counselor.

Vocational Preferences

The thinking of counselees about vocational choices ranges from some who have "no idea of what I want to do after high school" to those who make choices before entering secondary school, persist in them throughout the school period, and actually enter the occupation after graduation. The range of interest in career choices extends from subjects who suggest apathetically that "something will turn up" to almost neurotic anxiety about "choosing the right thing right now." Without forcing the issue or implying that a specific choice is desirable immediately, counselors are expected to raise questions about what the counselee plans to do after completing his training. The counselees need to be reminded that a choice based on self-analysis and study of available opportunities will probably be better than a hurried, unconsidered one at the time of graduation.

In cases where general post-high school training seems certain and suitable, postponement of choice by some counselees until they explore vocations further would be desirable. In most cases, however, selection of a first job or a place of training is essential before graduation from high school. Although the multipotentiality of counselees for achievement in many different kinds and levels of jobs or training is recognized, and the desirability of considering broad areas rather than specific jobs is acknowledged, it is essential that each counselee choose some place from which to start.

Samples of the differences among individuals in the area of career preferences, and illustrations of some of the situations which counselors meet, are presented below.[10]

[10] Names (pseudonyms) in parentheses following each situation are those of students described in the vignettes, case studies, and sketches found later in this chapter. The situations and circumstances were important factors in the counseling of the students named throughout the text and in the appendix.

1. *Counselees tend to have inadequate information about the advantages and disadvantages of occupational opportunities they choose, are considering, or should consider.* Students' knowledge about occupations, even those well represented in their own communities, vary from almost complete naïveté to a high level of sophistication. Some know very little about even their fathers' occupations, while others know much because they have participated in them. (Peter, Jim, Teddy, but also applicable in most cases)

2. *Counselees give a wide variety of reasons for making vocational choices.* The reasons often reflect such factors as ignorance of occupations, glorification of unusual vocations with impressive-sounding names, attractiveness of the remote, admiration of persons whom they are not like, pressures of ill-informed persons, lack of realism in considering themselves and opportunities, too-high ambitions, and morbid fear of failure. (Jim, Sandy, Caspar, Sonia)

3. *Opportunities for work experience, visits to places of business or training, and conferences with persons who could inform them about openings, vary widely.* Many counselees take advantage of the opportunities available and even develop some of their own. Others neither seek them out, nor use what is available. (Sonia, Brent)

4. *Knowledge about training for careers varies greatly.* The impatience of some youth to be independent of adult supervision, and the desire to take a job that provides higher initial pay, means that some students reject the long-term benefits of apprenticeship, or even short-term training courses, so that they can take immediate advantage of current high rates of pay for unskilled labor. (Common in almost all cases)

5. *Current economic conditions are variable in their effect on youths' career planning.* In prosperous times, jobs may be plentiful and pay so high that employment immediately after completion of high school seems much more attractive to many students than several years in training with its consequent delay in drawing a paycheck and getting an automobile. (Clark, Jim, Teddy)

6. *While some girls plan for careers, others want only temporary jobs.* Some may be engaged to men serving in the armed forces and want to work only until their fiancés are released from service. The occupations chosen, and entered immediately after graduation, are often stopgaps for which they have previously shown neither interest nor fitness. Others want to plan for careers that require many years of education. (Vera, Sonia, Martha)

7. *Required service in the armed forces affects the planning of youth in many different ways.* It is necessary for healthy boys to weigh the possi-

ble effects of volunteering immediately, beginning a job and waiting for the draft, or seeking deferments. Some can do this without assistance, but others seek varying amounts of counseling before making decisions. (Teddy, Roundy, Peter, Sandy)

8. *Some students who do not have enough financial resources to begin college need to develop plans for working their way through.* For others, financial matters need little consideration. Many youth need to decide whether to work a year before starting college, to try to raise the funds by part-time and summer work while in training, or to plan to work and study in alternate years. (Mike, Brent, Philip)

9. *Combinations of such factors as those mentioned above produce varying degrees of conflict for many youth.* One boy reported in his senior year of high school that he wanted to avoid military service, would like to go to college, and wished to marry soon after graduation. His father wanted him to remain on the farm and, if he did so, he could be assured of early marriage, a good income, and possible agricultural deferment from military service. If he went on to college it might mean delay in marriage and probable postponement of military service. Since his father and fiancée were trying to influence his choice, and many of his teachers were urging him to attend college, he wanted to talk over his dilemma with someone who could understand his problem. Some of his classmates worked out their answers to similar problems without consulting anyone. (Mike, Roundy, Donnie)

The samples above reveal some individual differences among counselees in the career preference area, and some of the differences in their circumstances which require the counselor to perform a diversity of tasks. It should be noted that they are only samples and that no attempt has been made to cover the great variability of individual reactions found even within the sample categories.

Educational Problems and Plans

Complete elaboration of all the educational problems that are met and the issues raised by counselees is not possible here. A list of some of the general problems is given below, with occasional elaboration. Reading of the latter will show that the grouping of problems under general headings does outline an area of concern, but does not indicate the nuances and subtleties involved, or the real complexity of the problems faced by particular individuals.

Although there has been much discussion of educational guidance, it has never been made quite clear just what should be subsumed under that heading. Reports about educational guidance of high school students usually reveal that counselors are concerned primarily with helping them to decide whether or not they should elect college preparatory courses. If the student does not propose to go to college, his choice among electives is often governed by what a counselor *thinks* may be a wise choice. If he chooses cabinetmaking as a vocation, it is usually suggested that he elect woodworking, and if he chooses to go into mechanical work, the election of shop courses is encouraged. Actually, the requirement for entrance into many such vocations is only a high school diploma without specification of courses. If a counselor suggests election of specific courses, then, it is usually on the basis of his *belief* rather than knowledge that the courses are required for particular occupations.

If a student has chosen the college preparatory course, the selection of electives is rarely difficult. Unless he wishes to enter one of the few colleges that require long lists of specific courses for matriculation, there is little restriction on his choices. If, however, the counselee has definitely made up his mind that he will enter a certain college of engineering, the counselor must point out to him that specific sequences in mathematics are required. Only in such relatively rare cases can educational guidance, in the sense of selection of courses, be specifically based upon stated requirements.

With the above statements in mind, the reader may now look at a sample of problems in educational guidance.

1. *Selection among various broad curricular groupings offered by the schools.* Choice of one program from the college preparatory, business, trade, or general groups involves consideration of such matters as a student's post-high school training plans and the generally greater prestige value for parents and students of college preparatory courses. (Leslie, Sandy, Larry)

2. *Selection among electives within or without broad curriculum groupings.* Consideration must be given to such matters as possible vocational and avocational values of courses. Such selection is generally limited to a curriculum group, as in the case of a boy in the college preparatory program who wants to take a machine shop course. Parents' insistence on certain kinds of training needs consideration. A farmer, for example, insists that his son take only academic work in school since he thinks he can teach him the practical aspects of agriculture and machine work at home. (Peter, Larry, Joan)

3. *Arrangement for taking university correspondence courses not offered by a school in order to meet specified requirements or to provide for a student's interests.* In smaller schools where curricular offerings are

limited, students are often advised that they may take correspondence courses and get full credit toward graduation. (Peter, Joan)

4. *Consideration of students' course loads.* Such factors as health, desire to finish school in less than the usual time, enrichment, opportunity to work for pay, correlation of work in the local vocational school, and participation in work experience programs are given consideration. (Roundy, Mike, Joan, Sandy, Marilyn)

5. *Selection of courses designed particularly to prepare for marriage.* Some girls are engaged to be married soon after graduation and want to elect combinations of courses that will prepare for homemaking as well as for the work they plan to do outside the home. (Sonia, Vera, Martha)

6. *Provision of special help with study habits or with difficulties in particular courses.* Occasionally counselors help students to work out study schedules and give assistance with study techniques. Some counselees are referred to the services provided by the schools; in other cases conferences are held with the students' teachers. (Diana, Brad, Jim)

7. *Arrangement of special summer courses or experiences.* These provide enrichment, permit make-up work, or offer special preparation for a planned experience. (Lena, Peter, Joan)

8. *Interpretation of educational data.* When analyses of data about test scores and educational records or requirements seem necessary, counselors provide and interpret them. (Provided to all students)

9. *Information is given about availability and methods of obtaining scholarships and other aids for post-high school training.* (Available to all students)

Many of the students' problems seem to be caused by rigid, narrow, and antiquated curricular requirements. Counselors who may not approve of them and who may be working to get them revised must still face the realities of their existence in working with counselees.

Personal-Social Adjustments

Solution of problems in the areas described above require the counselees to make adjustments, so it seems almost unnecessary to add another category devoted to them. However, some special problems do not fit into those areas and are commonly discussed under the heading of personal-social adjustments. In general, they deal with youths' problems in getting along with other persons, particularly their peers. These do not fall into neat categories. If they are forced into such classifications for statistical manipulation, the categories conceal the fact that similarity of behavior does not mean equivalency. The following samples indicate some of the problems in adjustment encountered in a cross section of high school students.

1. *Some youth are extremely shy, reserved, and withdrawn.* They find it difficult to mix with other youth, to volunteer in class, or to offer their services for school activities. Many are unhappy, others seem unconcerned, and still others are definitely worried about their lack of status in peer groups. Some eagerly seek help in solving their problems, some try procedures planned cooperatively with the counselor, and others reject all invitations to discuss their problems. (Elsie, Marilyn, Rosie, Jean)

2. *Problems of grooming and related problems of presenting an acceptable appearance trouble many youth.* When this problem is considered with a counselee, a counselor can use grooming charts as a basis for discussion of the condition, or refer them to persons known to be interested in such matters (Rosie, Jean)

3. *Development of strong interests and enthusiasms produces changes in usual behavior.* Some youth who participate in many group activities withdraw to pursue new interests alone and sometimes the reverse of that situation develops. When a counselor discusses such enthusiasms and the possible outcomes of their pursuit, some students seem to develop new personal insights. (Diana, Larry, Roundy, Jim)

4. *Some rural youth seem never to become assimilated to city high schools.* Limited in opportunities to participate in extracurricular activities by having to meet bus and commuting schedules, they have few chances to make friends. For some of them school is not a particularly friendly place and they seem to appreciate the opportunity to talk things over with persons interested in them. Plans for improving their situations are sometimes worked out during interviews. (Caspar, Jean)

5. *Violent temper tantrums create difficulties for some students.* Momentary lapses that result in swearing at a teacher, refusing to follow instructions, criticizing school personnel publicly, and "walking out" on teachers seem, at times, to bring consequences out of proportion with the behavior. Discussion of such events with counselors sometimes helps the counselee. (Jim, Sonia)

6. *Outstanding performances in athletics, dramatics, music, and other activities bring special problems to some students.* The hero of the football team is in so much demand seasonally that his marks drop, but his ego-satisfactions are raised high. The leading lady in the school play enjoys a brief period of high prestige. At times the letdown after a large build-up

raises serious problems of adjustment. Occasionally jealousies that develop during competition produce very unhappy consequences. Many of the students who meet such problems appreciate the opportunity to discuss them with counselors. (Diana, Teddy, Vera, Larry)

7. *Some brighter students who can achieve high academic records do not want to earn reputations of being "grinds."* In order to avoid them, some try to pose as regular fellows, and their behavior thus shows considerable variability. (Marilyn, Lena, Peter)

8. *Physical development with consequent increase in masculinity and femininity produces problems for many counselees.* Although most counselees take their development in stride, marked differences in behavior can be seen. Rejection of the feminine role by some girls and failure of some boys to develop masculinity produce peer reactions that range from indifference to rejection, and in some cases extend even to ridicule. Extremes in expression of the sexual role results in similar reactions by peers, but occasionally can produce temporary periods of great popularity. Problems of sex are seldom raised by the counselees, but there is little doubt that they are present. (Leslie, Brent, Sonia)

Family Circumstances

Since most counseling is done with minors, their parents, who are legally and financially responsible for them and who usually care about them, must be involved in the counseling process. The items listed below are samples of problems raised by family circumstances. Although they are grouped for convenience in presentation, it must not be assumed that they have similar effects upon the youthful members of the families. As in the lists above, there are great individual differences in response to the situations.

1. *Some youth are required to contribute to the support of their families.* Their activities, performances, and plans are seriously affected by this situation. One boy, for example, was faced with the alternative of holding two part-time jobs or withdrawing from school to take a full-time job. (Mike, Brent, Brad)

2. *Some families cannot provide any financial support for post-high school training.* Youth who want to continue their education are often forced either to give up their ambitions or find a way to raise the money that is needed. (Elsie, Marilyn, Nancy, Brent)

3. *Both parents in some families are employed outside the home.* Their children are forced to perform so many household tasks that recrea-

tional pursuits and academic achievements are seriously curtailed. (Brent, Jean, Sonia)

4. *Some parents choose to spend limited financial resources for their own benefit.* A counselee may be deprived of the financial support that had been promised for post-high school training when the parents buy a new automobile. (Brent, Mike)

5. *Occasionally parents offer money rewards for their children's school accomplishments.* By doing so they encourage students to get high marks by *any* means. (Leslie)

6. *A few parents give their children too much money.* Counselees who receive generous allowances may yield to temptations to buy liquor or drugs and to engage in other nonacceptable activities. (Clark, Leslie)

7. *Significant changes in the family financial circumstances can seriously affect the student's plans.* A home that has been rated very high in socioeconomic status is reduced to poverty when the father defaults on his financial obligations. A boy who has enjoyed considerable prestige, and who has made elaborate plans for training that require much financial support, may find that the family is now in disgrace and his plans are impossible of realization. Another may suffer because his father loses income as a result of a prolonged strike. Still another is required to change his plans when the coming of a new baby requires the use of money that had been saved for him. A counselee may meet new problems when his father enters bankruptcy proceedings, and another's attitudes may be seriously altered when the family receives a substantial inheritance. (Nancy, Sandy)

8. *Prolonged illnesses of parents may present difficulties for youth.* Some students are required to drop out of school, others' activities and performances are curtailed, and others are required to change plans which had seemed sound at the time they were made. (Teddy, Elsie)

9. *Alcoholism of one or both parents brings problems that are difficult for some students to cope with or understand.* They tend to think of their parents' alcoholism as disgraceful behavior rather than as a symptom of illness. They reject their parents and seek escape from unhappy situations by behavior that is disruptive rather than adjustive. (Elsie, Brent, Brad)

10. *Some parents insist that their children take their post-high school training in sectarian schools and colleges.* Despite the youth's preferences, the lack of particular curricula, and even the cost, parental pressure to attend a sectarian college is sometimes so strong that youth are forced to give up well-conceived plans. (Does not appear in vignettes)

11. *Some parents make it very clear to their children that they do*

not trust them. By constant surveillance of their activities, including extreme invasion of privacy, they develop attitudes of suspicion, raise doubts in the youths' minds about their own competence, and unwittingly encourage the development of deceitful practices. (Rosie, Sonia, Nancy, Philip)

12. *Sometimes two parents disagree on disciplinary or regulatory practices.* Caught in the conflict of parents' opinions, some youth feel insecure and resentful. Occasionally they reject all parental counsel or control. (Marilyn, Clark, Rosie)

13. *One or both parents are sometimes oversolicitous about their child's progress.* Their strenuous efforts to assure high performance and acceptable behavior often produce embarrassment and conflict. (Leslie, Nancy)

14. *Some parents neglect their offspring.* Seemingly unconcerned about their child's progress, they provide little supervision, encouragement, or assistance. They become concerned only when the youth gets involved in academic or disciplinary difficulties. Even in those circumstances the action they take is just enough to clear up the current difficulty. When it is settled they revert to their previous apathetic behavior. (Brent, Rosie, Philip)

15. *Some parents do not participate in the recreational, academic, or vocational interests of their children, while others go to great lengths to support them.* The range of participation extends from those who share interests with their children and abet their development to those who tend to discourage or prohibit any development of interests. One parent burns a manuscript of a story her daughter has written. Another provides a large sum of money for the development of a collection that interests his son. Others study the subject of their children's interests so that they may participate jointly in them. (Leslie, Donnie, Rosie, Lena)

16. *Some fathers are determined that their sons enter their occupations, and some mothers insist that their daughters follow the vocations in which they have been employed before marriage.* When sons or daughters reject the occupations chosen for them by either or both parents, they are often subjected to pressures which make them depressed, confused, or apathetic. (Roundy, Leslie, Donnie)

17. *Mothers and fathers sometimes disagree about the wisdom of a youth's choice of vocation.* The result is usually confusion and conflict at home. One boy wants to be an actor, the father is determined that he enter his plumbing business, the mother applies pressures to have him enter church work, and the counselors think that none of these is a suitable choice. (Marilyn, Philip)

18. *Strong father-son relationships sometimes bring subtle pressures on the son to enter the father's vocation.* Under such circumstances a son may resist all efforts to have him consider opportunities in, or fitness for, other vocations. Subtle pressures include such things as taking the boy on frequent hunting and fishing trips, to tournaments, and to conventions of members of an occupation. These are sometimes offered to the youth despite the fact that they require long absences from school. (Donnie)

19. *Some parents are willing to provide financial support for the post-high school education of their sons but not of their daughters.* A girl cannot get a scholarship that she seeks because it is awarded on the basis of merit *and* need. Since her family has considerable financial resources, she cannot qualify under the need criterion. Because her family will not approve of college for girls, she is faced with the choice of giving up plans to go to college or earning enough to pay her expenses. (Does not appear in vignettes)

20. *Some parents are unwilling to provide support for the education of their children because they do not have enough faith in the value of education.* In some cases parents encourage their sons to leave school before graduation because they cannot see any value in obtaining a high school diploma. (Brent, Philip)

21. *A few parents go to ridiculous and even embarrassing lengths to assure their child's success in school.* Some parents plague school personnel for special permissions and additional homework. Others attempt to curry favor, or use their influence to raise their children's marks. (Leslie, Lena)

22. *Some parents publicly criticize school practice and personnel.* Such behavior sometimes results in acceptance by the students of their parents' attitude toward education, and they do not put forth their best efforts. (Clark, Brent, Rosie)

23. *Location of family homes may influence some youths' choice of activities, occupations, and training.* A neighbor who is very successful and who flaunts his success may influence a boy to choose that occupation, though it seems particularly unsuitable and unlikely of accomplishment. (Diana, Larry)

24. *Families that move frequently create some problems for their children.* Changes in commuting arrangements, the loss of part-time jobs, and changes in availability of companions may result in alterations of behavior or performance. (Mike)

25. *The behavior and performance of younger siblings are sometimes appreciated more than those of older children.* At times this may result in

jealousy, resentment, and the feeling that the older one's merits are not appreciated. Occasionally satisfaction with the younger child's performance results in desirable reduction of pressure on an older child. (Philip, Donnie, Leslie)

26. *Some parents fail to challenge their children.* Occasionally a son knows that he will always be well received and that the family will take good care of him regardless of misbehavior or failure. Having a "cushion" to rely on, he sees no need for striving to accomplish at a high level, or for behaving in an acceptable manner. (Donnie)

Health and Physical Development

The influences of family situations on the behavior and performances of youth have been spelled out in considerable (but not complete) detail to illustrate how they operate. If each of them operated independently and could be isolated and recognized, they would be difficult enough for a counselor to cope with, even if he had unlimited time to work with his counselees. But problems seldom come singly. They are usually associated with other problems that arise at home or in school. Nothing short of complete case histories can ever portray the hazards that youth meet in the process of coming of age. Samples of the hazards of family situations have been given in the previous section; the area of health provides additional problems.

Descriptions of the health status of counselees may be obtained from records kept in schools and from interviews with counselees, their parents, and their teachers. A summary of health problems of counselees, made by tabulating the entries on school cumulative records, is presented in Table 1–1. Some subjects have several of the handicaps or problems. The categories in the table do not always represent common medical classifications, but they are descriptive of health problems as a nonmedically trained counselor must meet and deal with them. An appendix operation, for example, may mean only a short period of absence from school, but if it comes at a critical time it may be a very important factor in the decisions a youth must make. A visual defect that can be corrected by the wearing of glasses is a problem quite different from a pronounced squint. A persistent case of acne may be a matter of great concern to a girl who plans to be a waitress, but the common adolescent acne that clears up at the usual time may present only a temporary period of distress to the youth who has begun dating.

In addition to the health difficulties diagnosed and reported by competent medical personnel, the counselor must take into consideration health problems, real or imagined, which students report. One counselee, for example, claimed that he suffered greatly in cold weather. He wanted

TABLE 1-1

Numbers and Percentages
of 344 High School Students Reporting
One or More Health Problems and Physical Handicaps

PROBLEM OR HANDICAP	NUMBER	PER CENT [a]
Wearing glasses	102	29.6
Serious skin blemishes (acne, boils, warts, scars, eczema)	34	9.9
Short-term diseases, injuries, operations (appendicitis, broken bones, chicken pox, mastoids, mumps, muscle strains, throat troubles, tumors)	33	9.6
Extended illnesses and injuries (anemia, diabetes, female troubles, hearing handicaps, hemophilia, kidney trouble, polio, ruptures, thyroid malfunction, tuberculosis)	28	8.2
Allergies (asthma, food allergies, hay fever)	19	5.5
Physical difficulties		
Severe dental problems	14	4.1
Back, ankle, and joint difficulties	14	4.1
Minor ear troubles	13	3.8
Visual handicaps (not correctable by glasses)	12	3.5
Serious speech handicaps	9	2.6
Recurring headaches (other than associated with other health conditions and including one migraine case)	6	1.7
Unclassified (car sickness, epilepsy, easily fatigued, posture problems, very unusual height or weight)	9	2.6

Source: J. W. M. Rothney, *Guidance Practices & Results* (New York: Harper & Row, Publishers, 1958).

[a] Percentages do not total 100 because some of the subjects reported more than one of the conditions.

to sit near a radiator while in school and he felt that, since he wanted to do outside work, he would have to move to a warmer climate after he finished high school. A girl who exhibits such violent temper tantrums at the beginning of each menstrual period that she has to be excluded from classes needs special counseling even though the medical report is negative. A student who wants to enter training for the nursing profession but who has special food allergies needs more than the usual help in her vocational planning, and the girl with epilepsy who wants to become a teacher requires special consideration. In dealing with some counselees who have health or physical handicaps, there is the special problem of use of their handicaps as alibis for not doing as well as they might. Special treatment is required in other cases for those who are spurred on to extreme over-compensatory behavior.

Counselors are not specialists in the field of health, but they are forced to be concerned with health problems during counseling. They refer cases to medical personnel or suggest that counselees seek professional advice. They inform teachers about some of the less obvious health difficulties of their students and consider procedures for making adjustments in their classes. In addition, they discuss the educational and vocational implications of health handicaps with counselees and others concerned.

Illustrative Vignettes

If the reader has sampled the excerpts given above, he must be impressed with the extent of the differences in behavior and circumstances of counselees. They are awesome when noted one at a time, but in combination in a particular counselee they present what may seem insurmountable difficulties which require the counselor to use many procedures in assisting his counselees. Consider, for example, the counseling needed by the following subjects.

> The huskiest boy in his class, *Teddy* was known for his prowess as one of the solid blockers on the football team. Uninterested in matters academic and unhappy about "sitting still as much as they want you to do in school," Teddy almost became a dropout. His friends wanted him to go out west with them and forget about school. His marks were just above the failure level and he scored low on all tests. His parents did not care whether he finished school and would really have applauded if he had left, taken a job, and helped to pay for his father's medical bills. He had fear of the armed forces and was afraid that if he dropped out of school he might be drafted and sent to the air force. He disliked all his classes, even his elective of woodwork, because his marks were determined by written tests. He wanted to leave but he saw that leaving had its disadvantages. Each day he arose to face his problems and he wanted so much to solve them.

> *Joan* loved to learn. While still a sophomore she wrote as well as the ablest seniors, analyzed problems with a high degree of skill, verbalized very effectively, and scored at a high level on all tests. She was tall for her age and exhibited that vague attribute which

is commonly called maturity. She was very popular among her classmates, but frequently sought out older students as friends. She carried a full load of courses and supplemented them with correspondence courses and summer study. Her hobbies and activities were many and varied. She wanted to work out plans for even greater academic challenges, including the possibility of completing school in less than the usual time.

All who talked about *Brent* used superlatives. He was the *shortest* boy in his grade, the *best* wisecracker among his peers, the student who behaved *worst* in school assemblies, the *most* consistent in his test scores, the one who did the *least* homework, the *most* financially self-supporting of all his age mates, and the one who came from the *worst* home as far as stimulation to academic achievement was concerned. To some teachers he was their *most* interesting student; to others he was their *most* difficult problem.

Jim described himself when he was a junior in high school. With enough editing to prevent identification, his description follows:

I am about sixteen years old, weigh one hundred thirty pounds and have a hell of an Irish temper, which cools off in a short time. This description fits me.

My interests are hunting, fishing, sports and girls. Hunting and fishing take up my weekends. Friday nights I go to the games. Saturday nights I go to dances.

To say I have no faults would be a big lie. I am bull headed and have a temper. I have a rather tight grip on money but when I spend the sky is the limit.

The family interests and mine run along the same lines. My father is a white collar worker. My mother and father are very liberal and fair with me.

We live in a rural district of the county.

As far as friends go I am rather fussy. They have to be rather easy going and not angels or sinners. I used to follow others but now I follow myself.

I was going through northern Wisconsin seeing the wild, which gave me the idea of being a forest ranger. I would like to get a job out in the open. After coming back I read a lot about forestry which made me even more interested in forestry. I wanted to be a doctor but grades foiled that idea. Now I have planned to go to the University of Michigan for my training in forestry.

Some friends of mine and I have started a band. We practice every Monday and Wednesday nights. I play the trumpet but not too well.

I like school but have a hard time with my spelling. I take five subjects which include chemistry, band, English, history and geometry. This course will prepare me for college.

My spare time has been occupied with outdoor things such as hunting and fishing. This I think had much to do with my choosing forestry as my life work.

I'd have liked to have gone out for football but I was too

light. Being five-five and only a hundred and thirty pounds makes a lot of difference.

After I finish college I hope to get a job as a forest ranger. This is a government job and pays well so I think I am really well fitted for this job. You get a cabin, a horse, and salary in God's country. I really have not changed my plans much as my only other choice was medicine. As far as I am right now and what I hope to be are quite different. I plan to be in the north woods and in a very densely populated area. I hope to be in the forest six years from now.

By her own description, *Marilyn* was "anxious, dependable, sort of slow." Her teachers felt she was a perfectionist who drove herself too hard in school. Her parents reported that she spent from four to six hours per day on homework. They frequently had to command her late at night to stop working and go to bed. Marilyn—even as early as grade nine—was worried about how to finance college. Besides having an intrinsic value that required her to be at the top of her class, Marilyn wanted to be sure that her high school record would warrant scholarship aid to college. "My limitations may slow me down," she said, "but only a catastrophe could prevent me from completing college with a good record."

In addition to her strong academic motivation, Marilyn was concerned about her social position with her fellow students. Because she was considered a "brain" she felt she had to go an extra mile to become involved with age mates in nonclass activities. She became a working participant in a variety of school organizations which took many hours of her time. No one convinced her that she was taking on too much, and because of her dependability she was in demand for many jobs. By the time she was halfway through the tenth grade her parents and teachers became concerned about her health. They did not see how she could continue at her current pace, but they were aware of her determination to attain a broad experience of classes and activities.

Philip seems to pull himself along in life by his own bootstraps. Handicapped by apparently insuperable difficulties, he plods stalwartly ahead and succeeds when all the evidence cries out that he should fail. He scored far below the college average in mental tests, his home was broken early in his life, and his childhood was riddled with traumatic experiences. Coming to college in the face of strong family opposition, he was forced to rely upon small grants-in-aid supplemented by his own earnings throughout his four years there. Nor did he feel a strong confidence in himself to compensate for the doubts expressed by members of his family regarding his ability to go through college; he came up "very much afraid" and reported that, even during his senior year, "that feeling is still with me—'I can't.'" Nevertheless, he succeeded in winning the respect and encouragement of the Dean for his "conscientiousness" and "serious purpose," and he graduated with a point average in the thirty-second percentile of his class.

When he was a high school senior *Peter* wrote the following paragraphs:

The main stumbling block in my path to decision has not been simple procrastination. I have been unable to decide because I do not know where my best abilities and strongest interests lie.

I have found, that if I apply myself I can do almost anything. I don't seem to have a serious lack of aptitude in any field. I find an English assignment equally as difficult as a physics problem. I find them also to be equally as challenging and equally as interesting. The same goes for math, social studies, music, speech, or any other subject area.

As I say, everything is possible *if I apply myself.* Nothing is so simple for me that I can do a perfect job without effort, but nothing is so hard that I can't do it, given enough time.

This is why I find it so difficult to decide on my place in the future. Many people don't consider this much of a problem, but to me, this lack of one area to stand out in is very grave indeed.

Individual Differences in a High School Class

The challenge to counselors presented by individual differences among students in an American high school may be observed in the brief sketches of a random sampling of students which follow. The details behind the general descriptive statements are too elaborate to present here, but a scanning of the sketches suggests that any counselor who would serve the diverse individuals they represent would need to be highly adaptable.

Sandy   Sandy loved to talk. A chummy sort during conferences with teachers and counselors, he leaned over and talked about himself in a very confidential manner, as though he were letting his listener in on a secret. He would confidently outline ambitious plans and then, when he had reached a peak, would stop and say, "But I'll never make it. I couldn't do it." Eager to learn more about himself, he would almost climb on the counselor's desk to get a better view of his records. It was in such conferences that one gained the impression that he might be a better thinker than his school record suggested.

Caspar   Caspar was a quiet farm boy with a shy smile who did what he was told, spoke only when he was spoken to, completed minimum assignments, and felt relieved at the end of the school day when he could leave his books and get back to the farm, where there would "always be important things to do." Farming was Caspar's life and things rural were his domain. His best marks in school were earned in agriculture; the Future Farmers of America was his only club; square dancing in the neighboring village hall on Saturday nights was his greatest pleasure; agricultural subjects were the ones on which he could converse best; and the only goal he ever stated was that of having a farm of his own. "I have the ability to do farm work and I like to be out in fresh air."

Clark Clark had begun to think of all adults, except his father, as persons whose chief activities consisted of berating youth and telling them what was good for them. Teachers, he felt, were people who flunked students and fussed about such unimportant things as homework, credits, and grades, but who knew nothing about such important things as driving a truck, drinking beer, riding around the city in a big car, and dressing up in a fancy suit for a date.

Diana Preference for physical over mental activity was evident in Diana's life. When encouraged to talk about herself she spoke about sports, hiking, camping, making things with her hands, cheerleading, and always dancing—tap dancing, dancing to jukebox music, dancing at school and at community affairs, and practicing dancing at home.

Helen Helen was an enigma because she was so variable in her performances and moods. Some teachers said she was lethargic, but others had never observed this behavior and questioned it when it was brought to their attention. Her friends, she said, would describe her as "funny," and at the same time as "older than her age," because she was so serious. She could do good school work when she wished to, but she refused to do homework in some courses even when she knew that failure was inevitable.

Nora Everyone liked Nora. Her sunny smile was always there, and everyone seemed to feel that it was a pleasure to know her. She said she liked "everyone and everything." Life was interesting to Nora and her zest for living was high. Her high degree of responsibility and her enthusiasm for school produced an excellent academic record, even though her test scores were not high. She said she wanted to be a stenographer for a little while after graduation and then get married.

Rosie Rosie was a large plump girl with thick glasses and a serious case of acne that did not clear up at the usual time. She had not learned enough about personal grooming to make the most of her possibilities and her plain appearance resulted in rejection by most of her classmates. Withdrawing from them, she became listless and apathetic to the point where no assignments were done. It appeared that she would follow the pattern set by many of her contemporaries of dropping out of school as soon as she became of age.

Leslie Charming and chic Leslie was a striking blonde whose fashionable coiffure and clothes made her appear more mature than most high school girls. Extremely feminine in manner, she was often described as a "personality girl." Driven by her parents' ambition and pushed by them to flaunt their newly acquired wealth and to rise to the social status that their financial success demanded, Leslie had many problems in school, at home, and in the community.

Donnie   Everyone called Donnie a "nice guy." Teachers generally agreed that he could have done much better work if he had limited his activities enough to get school work done, but they said it without malice. His father thought he was an ideal son and wanted him to become a partner in his trade. Donnie had developed a kind of composure and balance that seemed likely to serve him well in troubled times. His home situation seemed ideal, but it also produced a feeling that he need not strive hard, because no matter how bad things were he could always return to the comfort of his home.

Brad   Brad was one of three students who were not graduated with their high school class of 220. A stuttering, confused lad whose unshaven face, greasy clothes, grimy hands, and dirty fingernails made him the worst-groomed boy in school, Brad began losing contact with reality, lapsed into periods of incoherent speech, and deteriorated rapidly in the last two years of high school. Needing sympathy and encouragement, Brad received only abuse, threats, and failing grades until he felt so bitter about "this educational clambake" that he wanted to leave school. When he tried to do so in order to begin an apprenticeship in his chosen work, he found that a high school diploma was needed. Forced back into the school that he hated and into the classes of teachers who, he hoped, might "approach me with something a little bit less deadly than a double-bit axe," Brad stuck out four years of misery in high school.

Lena   Lena was a neat, well-scrubbed little girl from a farm who was exceptionally enthusiastic about things agricultural. Nothing in Lena's behavior was put on for effect—nothing was pretense. She was a genuine "take-me-as-I-am" person, wholesome, well organized, highly adjustable, poised, and confident about the future. Her two greatest disappointments were that she had not done as well in high school as she had in a rural school ("because I spent too much time reading") and that the study of veterinary medicine seemed impossible for her. She was the youngest student in her class, but the adjustments which that situation required were made easily.

Nancy   Nancy was crippled. When the high school commencement exercises were over, the parties began. Pairs, cliques, groups, and gangs had made their plans to celebrate. Diplomas in hand, they cut loose and expressed, whether they believed it or not, great joy that school was over. Only Nancy hobbled downtown alone. The freedom and independence that graduation meant to her was not a thing to rejoice about. It was a very serious matter, an emotional experience that she did not choose to share. There had been long periods of her life, even after she had grown to young womanhood, during which she was carried by her father from room to room because she could not walk and her mother was too frail to carry her. From these and other experiences Nancy seemed to derive a strong need for independence—to be free from the ministrations and solicitousness of others, to literally "stand on her own feet."

Vera   Vera had a twinkle in her eyes and a smile that radiated enthusiasm for life and living. Nothing, it seemed, would bother her for long, and everything seemed to interest her. Immaculate in grooming, confident, poised, and mature, Vera was pleasant to meet. "A swell girl," one teacher said. "There seems little more to say."

Life was wonderful to Vera, and school was one of the wonderful things about life. She liked every subject she took, and only once did she indicate even a least-liked course. She was an enthusiast about her English classes because she thought they helped her; she spoke enthusiastically about her chorus and home economics (clothing) courses in her senior year; and she genuinely enjoyed every course except history and German. She made it plain, however, that she did not *dislike* even these two subjects.

Music played a very important part in Vera's life. She took piano lessons for six years and private voice lessons for one year, but these interests are not apparent from the school record. She had been advised that school music courses would confuse her because different methods were used in private and public school music instruction; consequently, she did not elect any in school. She practiced one or two hours daily, sang in church choirs, and was a member of highly selective choirs and triple trios in her senior year. She wanted to sing in choirs after she was graduated, and she read biographies of composers. Her closest friend, the man who later became her fiancé, majored in music at the state university while Vera was still in high school.

Elsie   "If she would just relax once—if she would just laugh, or at least smile—I'd feel that I was doing something for Elsie."

"Elsie is a sphinx if there ever was one."

"She's pleasant enough to have in class but she seldom smiles."

"She seems aloof and remote."

These are comments of teachers and counselors about Elsie. What was she really like, and what could teachers who really cared have done for her?

When Elsie came to senior high school, her teachers knew that she had been a good student and that her test scores were high. They did not know that her mother had a "nervous condition" or that Elsie was already bored with education. Since she continued to earn good grades and did her work conscientiously, most of her teachers apparently saw no reason to inquire about her lack of the usual adolescent zest for living. Those who did remark upon her manner were content to note, as in the comments above, that she was sphinxlike, shy, withdrawn, aloof and remote. They also noted that her grooming was always immaculate and that her health record was perfect.

Larry   Larry was never antagonistic, but he was usually too exuberant to sit still in classes. He was skilled enough in machine-shop work to qualify, while still in high school, for a job in a machine tool plant of high standards, but he could not inhibit the tendency to disturb others working at neighboring machines. He could annoy teachers by his groans and hoots, nearly, but not quite up to, the breaking point of their tolerance. When trouble seemed finally to be coming to a head, handsome Larry knew how to calm the situation with a disarming smile. He was a thorn in a prim teacher's flesh, but he had not a mark against him in the disciplinary black book. He seemed to have an array of talents and potentialities, mechanical and political if not academic.

Jean   Jean and her twin were shy little country girls who could never quite get adjusted to the city high school. When called on in class, Jean blushed and kept her eyes glued to the floor. She ended her sentences uncertainly and pleadingly, as if to ask whether what she had said was acceptable and that she was sorry if it was not. Her grooming and speech improved steadily throughout four years of high school, but at the time of graduation both were still rather unfinished. She had not yet found, for example, a happy medium between too much and too little make-up, or a satisfactory balance between extremes of too gaudy and too plain dresses. Her speech still showed a heavy accent from the use of German at home, and her conversation revealed her rural background. She wanted, when she finished high school, to get a job in the city that would permit commuting to her parents' farm every night.

Sonia   Sonia was a difficult person to find in school. She stayed home the equivalent of 51 days in half-day sessions during her years in senior high school, and when she was there she was so expert at evading school regulations that she just never seemed to be in the place to which she was assigned. She flitted about the halls with permission slips to go to the library, the nurse's office, the typing laboratory, or any other spot in the building. She failed to do assignments and often arranged to be absent from classes on the days when they were due so that she had an alibi for work not done. Only one teacher followed through sufficiently to recognize what she was doing, and in that class she received her only failing grade.

That Sonia had physical assets was freely admitted by everyone. She was generally described as good-looking of face and figure, and she had learned to make the best of these features. Her grooming was immaculate and she used very good judgment in make-up, coiffure, and dress. Her general visual impression called up such words as slender, petite, pretty, glamorous, and chic. Her choice of modeling as a vocation seemed possible of accomplishment.

Roundy   Farming, football, and father were the important factors in Roundy's post-high school life, as they had been while he was in high school. Examination of his record indicates that the rank of 70 in a graduating class of 100 was due largely to his grades in agriculture and physical education, taught by the football coach. Academic courses for Roundy were the fillings he was forced to accept if he was to enjoy the two layers of icing—football and agriculture. "Those verbs and stuff get me. I don't understand them," he said when talking about English. He did not dislike courses in which definite and specific assignments were laid out as much as he disliked the subjects in which, as in woodwork, students were given more freedom in choice of activities.

No one was quite sure what Roundy might have done in school if he had kept up a sustained effort. At times, particularly when his friends suggested that he go on to college to become a football star, Roundy put forth great effort and seemed to be near the point of solid achievement, but the spurts were not sustained enough to achieve a high academic record.

Mike   Mike had always been required to work hard at part-time jobs. He did farm work, clerked in a store, and, during his senior year, worked as a houseman at a neighboring city hotel three or four evenings a week and all day on Saturdays and Sundays. Since he did not get home until one o'clock in the morning on the evenings he worked, he was often sleepy in class and seldom got his homework done. As the result of an accident in which he suffered a concussion, Mike had frequent headaches. This condition and the lack of sleep resulted in the description of him by his teachers as the "epitome of apathy and lethargy." Despite these handicaps, he made a creditable record in school.

Martha   The favorable impression she made carried over beyond the school situation when Martha was sent out on a work-experience program during her senior year. The employer reported that she could come to work in his office "part-time, full-time or any time" that she chose.

Despite this impression, Martha lacked confidence in herself, and her greatest trials in school were the oral exercises in English. She dreaded them but forced herself to carry through because she thought that they would be good for her. In an attempt to overcome shyness before groups, she elected a speech course during her senior year, but dropped it when it did not provide the opportunities that she had expected. Her difficulty in appearing before groups made her give up the choice of teaching as a career.

THE CHALLENGE TO COUNSELORS

Those who would counsel individuals who differ so greatly and are as diverse in background as those described above undertake a very complex task. The array of genetic and environmental influences upon behavior are awesome in their frequency, potency, and variety. Although they seem to produce an overall pattern of behavior that is distinctive for each person, significant variations from such patterns appear as development occurs and situations change. Understanding of such patterns and variations becomes more difficult as the counselee learns new skills in adaptation and increasingly obscures his underlying motives. New experiences influence the way that situations were managed formerly, and complexity expands. Inner feelings become increasingly more potent in their influence on a subject, and a person's skill in working out a truce between those inner feelings and the demands of the outside world may be hidden so well that surface observations must be suspect. Thus the adjustments of the individual to new experiences and the degree of complexity increase to the extent that one must wonder if even multiple approaches to the counseling task, much less a channeled single method of attack, can ever be effective.

Despite evidence about the uniqueness, complexity, and variability of individuals, and the consequent need to make adjustments for them in counseling, many suggestions of one-best-ways to accomplish the counseling task have appeared. Some of those who advocate the use of a single method reject all other approaches as less than helpful. Thus the leader of the client-centered school writes: "The person who attempts to reconcile them [opposing points of view] by compromise will find himself left with a superficial eclecticism which does not increase objectivity and which leads nowhere." [11] Although a leader in the behavior counseling group writes that he wants to find new and better ways to be of service to counselees, he makes it clear that he believes that the best way to counsel is to condition counselees in problem-solving by the methods of the behavioristic school of psychology, and that no other procedure is acceptable. [12] In taking such single and simple approaches to the counseling task, these advocates must reject, ignore, or minimize the extent of differences among and within persons.

The devising of simple systems for dealing with complex and variable persons living in complicated environments has been carried on through the ages, and the practice seems likely to be continued. There are certain personal satisfactions, frequently accompanied by monetary rewards, for those who announce a presumably new theory or technique that will revolutionize current beliefs and practices. Such satisfactions and rewards come more surely if they appeal to persons who go beyond sentiment to sentimentality, or, at the other end of the scale, to those who are fascinated by the words "science" or "scientist" and seem to believe that if something is labeled as scientific it must be accepted without question. [13]

[11] C. R. Rogers, *Client-Centered Therapy* (Boston: Houghton Mifflin Company, 1951), p. 8.

[12] J. D. Krumboltz, ed., *Revolution in Counseling: Implications of Behavior Science* (Boston: Houghton Mifflin Company, 1966), Chap. I.

[13] C. E. Thoresen, "The Counselor as an Applied Behavior Scientist," *Personnel and Guidance Journal*, XLVII (1969).

The history of causes in the counseling field reveals that they follow a common pattern. They are promoted by a series of speeches, conference reports, papers, and books which assure their listeners and readers that a new day has dawned.[14] They enjoy a relatively short period of popularity before critics ask crucial questions that remain unanswered. The fervor begins to ebb as research exposes the fallacies. The disciples then begin to defect to another revolutionary approach which will go through a similar cycle. The cyclic phenomenon can be depressing unless one finds some comfort in the fact that strong advocacy of a theory or method results in its comparison with others, and the final conclusion that what had seemed to be *the only* explanation or technique has become just one of many. In Chapter 2 two of the one-best-way approaches are examined.

The reader must not assume that all counselors of a given theoretical orientation walk in single file and imitate their master exactly. Variability in practice is much greater than one might anticipate from reviews of statements made by those whose theories are described.

Selected References

ALDRIDGE, J. W. "In the Country of the Young," *Harper's Magazine* (October and November 1969), Parts I and II. Observations on differences in the behavior of youth by a professor of English. Comments and criticism of the establishment and the youth who are against it. One of the best among the many commentaries on youth today. Highly recommended.

DEARBORN, W. F. aud J. W. M. ROTHNEY. *Predicting the Child's Development* (2nd ed.). Cambridge, Mass.: Sci-Art Publishers, 1963. This is a description of the first longitudinal study of children and youth. Some 3,000 students' mental and physical development were studied during the 12 years they attended school. Demonstrations of differences between groups and changes within individuals are illustrated by tables and charts.

GORDON, E. W., ed. "Education for Socially Disadvantaged Children," *Review of Educational Research*, XL (1970). Timely information about a topic of great current concern. The extent of individual differences within a special group is reported.

MILLARD, C. V. and J. W. M. ROTHNEY. *The Elementary School Child: A Book of Cases.* New York: Holt, Rinehart and Winston, Inc., 1957. Detailed descriptions of the development of children from kindergarten to junior high school years.

ROTHNEY, J. W. M. *The High School Student.* New York: Holt, Rinehart and Winston, Inc., 1953. Twenty-seven case studies of secondary school students which demonstrate the amount of variability in performances and behavior that may be found in a high school class.

TYLER, Leona E. *The Psychology of Individual Differences.* New York: Appleton-Century-Crofts, 1965. Perhaps the best description of the range of individual differences in humans now available.

---

[14] Even the titles suggest great change. See, for example, Krumboltz, *Revolution in Counseling, op. cit.*

CHAPTER 2

two samples
of counseling techniques

Within the recent history of the counseling movement several one-best-way approaches have appeared. They have been described by their advocates and reviewed by others in several volumes.[1] Many of these approaches are primarily suitable for work with persons who exhibit serious maladjustments, and are of greater concern to clinical psychologists and psychiatrists than to those who work in the field of counseling and guidance in educational institutions. The two approaches which have been most commonly advocated for the use by the latter are *client-centered therapy* [2] and *behavioral counseling*.[3] A distillation of what appears to be the basic concepts of these approaches is presented below. It must be recognized that the statements are interpretations of the writer and of others with whom he has discussed the subject, and that their sponsors may not agree with them in all respects. The rejection of these approaches which appears later in this volume is not based on their inadequacies for use with specific individuals, but on their shortcomings when prescribed as generally applicable in all counseling circumstances.

[1] B. Stefflre, *Theories of Counseling* (New York: McGraw-Hill Book Company, 1965); C. H. Patterson, *Theories of Counseling and Psychotherapy* (New York: Harper & Row, Publishers, 1966).
[2] C. R. Rogers, *Client-Centered Therapy* (Boston: Houghton Mifflin Company, 1951).
[3] J. D. Krumboltz and C. E. Thoresen, *Behavioral Counseling: Cases and Techniques* (New York: Holt, Rinehart and Winston, Inc., 1969).

BEHAVIORAL COUNSELING

Some Basic Concepts

Behavioral counselors [4] differ from others because they are linked more closely with a single learning theory, its related laboratory experimentation, and models built on the results of the experiments. They accept without question the learning theory known as conditioning, and particularly that phase of it called operant conditioning. The behavioral application to counseling is said to be part of a highly technical system, "based on laboratory investigations of the phenomena of conditioning for describing behavior and specifying the conditions under which it is acquired, maintained and eliminated." [5]

It is assumed that readers of this volume will be familiar with the concept of conditioning, so no attempt is made to review it here. Those who need to refresh their memories or to learn about recent developments are referred to the writings of Hilgard [6] and Michael and Meyerson [7] for technical details and to Ullman and Krasner,[8] Krumboltz and Thoresen, and Bandura [9] for applications of the theory. It should be noted that despite variations in the procedures employed in what behavioral counselors choose to call counseling, there is complete commitment to some form of conditioning. That full commitment makes behavioral counseling unpalatable to those aware of the great gaps in our knowledge of what takes place when learning occurs, and who recognize that no theory of learning yet devised is invulnerable to criticism.

Study of the literature of behavioral counseling reveals that the following concepts are basic to it:

1. The only subject matter of importance is overt observable behavior. There is no need to hypothesize any inner-determining agents such as ego, superego, or id. Introspection is eliminated. There is no place in the behavior model for the concept of symptoms.

[4] Choice of the label "behavioral counseling" seems unfortunate. All counselors are concerned about behavior and changes in it. The word "behavior" has so many connotations that its attachment to one specific process is unjustified.

[5] J. D. Krumboltz, ed., *Revolution in Counseling* (Boston: Houghton Mifflin Company, 1966).

[6] E. R. Hilgard, *Theories of Learning* (New York: Appleton-Century-Crofts, 1966).

[7] J. Michael and L. Meyerson, "A Behavioral Approach to Counseling and Guidance," *Harvard Educational Review*, XXXII, No. 4 (Fall 1962).

[8] L. P. Ullman and L. Krasner, *Case Studies in Behavior Modification* (New York: Holt, Rinehart and Winston, Inc., 1965).

[9] Krumboltz and Thoresen, *Behavioral Counseling, op. cit.;* see also A. Bandura, *Principles of Behavior Modification* (New York: Holt, Rinehart and Winston, Inc., 1969).

2. All behaviors except those which are genetically and constitutionally determined, or drug and surgically induced, are learned by conditioning processes. Learning is inferred from a subject's behavior.
3. Behavior is a function of the interaction of hereditary and environmental variables.
4. The only channel open to counselors for influencing human behavior is through systematic changes in the environment to alter a subject's responses to stimuli or responses to responses.[10]
5. Counselors do not find it necessary to spend much time in reconstructing original causes of behavior. Concern is with the here and now. Counselors must be concerned about specific, precise, and current problems.
6. Applications of conditioning theory in counseling can be made through such techniques as reinforcement, modeling, role playing, cognitive structuring, simulation, confrontation, counter-conditioning, and combinations of any of the above. Practitioners of behavioral counseling must limit their applications to solution of problems which can be solved only by the conditioning process.

The essentials of behavior counseling can be indicated by use of the *if-then* approach.

IF THE COUNSELOR:

Helps a counselee to establish his goal precisely and specifically.
Communicates his understanding of the goal to see if he is perceiving the counselee's thoughts and feelings accurately.
Is willing (after considering his own ethics, interests, and competencies) to help the counselee to achieve the designated goal.
Conceives all counselee's problems to be learning problems.
Places responsibility for decisions and resulting action squarely on the counselee, after making sure that the counselee is aware of all the consequences.
Establishes his place as an important person who may be viewed as a social model and whose verbal responses may be effective reinforcers.
Provides reinforcement at suitable times.
Focuses on specific behaviors that will assist the counselee to accomplish his highest goals.
"Brainstorms" with his counselee.
Gives frank personal opinions when asked to do so.

[10] A behavioral counselor is said to have no vested interest in any single technique; if one technique does not work, it is suggested that he try something else. The implication is clear, however, that the something else must be another application of the same theory. He must not, for example, postulate that any inner-determinants might be operating. That would require departure from the system. See Krumboltz and Thoresen, *Behavior Counseling, op. cit.*

Helps the counselee learn how to decide.

Encourages his counselee to engage in activities which will test the feasibility of each alternative course of action.

THEN THE COUNSELEE WILL:

State his goals in terms of specific changes that he desires.[11]

Learn to use sequences of problem-solving steps in the solution of personal, educational, and vocational decisions.

Learn more adaptive ways of coping with difficulties.

Indulge in more information-seeking activities.

Engage in behavior that will enable him to solve conflicts.

Feel increased responsibility for his own actions.

Take constructive steps to reach his highest goals, developing alternative plans if necessary.

Learn that frustrations and setbacks have always accompanied great accomplishments.

Make final decisions based on his own goals and values.

Solve current and future problems more independently and effectively.

It is assumed that good rapport between the counselor and the counselee will be developed and maintained; that the counselor is genuinely concerned about the welfare of his subjects; that he will communicate his ideas well; and that the counselee will respect him enough to accept some direction. Such assumptions are not unique to the behavioral counseling school of thought.

Some of the basic tenets of the school incorporated in the if-then model used above are illustrated by some of the comments of its sponsors. Thus we find statements such as the following:

The counselor's job is to help the client [12] consider the alternatives and to make sure the client is aware of the consequences for each alternative.

The counselor must discover ways to help his client take constructive steps to accomplish his highest goals, develop alternative plans if necessary, and learn that frustrations and setbacks have always accompanied great accomplishments.

[11] Illustrations of specific changes include such behavior as breaking habits of procrastination, speaking up in class, making good academic records, avoiding disturbing behavior in school, eliminating excessive fears, and reducing test anxiety.

[12] Use of the word "client" seems particularly unfortunate when considering counseling in education settings. A *student* doesn't change to a *client* just because he enters the counselor's office. Lawyers, real estate workers, and prostitutes may have *clients*. Counselors meet *counselees*. The language of the marketplace seems ill suited to the school.

The counselor's task is to help the client engage in a type of behavior that will enable him or her to resolve the conflict.

The counselor must help the client describe how he would like to act instead of the way he currently acts. The counselor must help the client translate his confusions and fears into a goal that the client would like to accomplish and which would begin to solve the client's problems.

The purpose of counseling is to help people become self-sufficient and effective problem solvers.

Selection of Subjects

Throughout the literature of this school of thought there is recurring evidence that its main purpose is the salvage and repair of subjects with shortcomings, breakdowns, or other severe problems.[13] The counselor, it seems, sits in his office and waits for those who soil their clothes, procrastinate, fail in school, are afraid to speak up in class, make chronic classroom disruptions, have excessive fears, express sexual, interpersonal, or test anxieties, or have become hyperactive and aggressive. Just what the school counselor will do if there is no such remedial work to be done, or if a clinical psychologist, school psychologist, or remedial worker does it, is never stated.[14] One is tempted to use the analogy of the teacher of developmental reading and the remedial reading instructor, with the latter playing no part in the reading program until some pupils have failed to make satisfactory progress. Those who consider counseling and guidance to be a developmental process essential for all children and youth in the process of coming of age in America must dismiss the behavioral counselor's almost complete emphasis on salvage and repair. If the desirable outcomes usually ascribed to counseling (better problem solving, decision making, development of realistic self-concepts, better self-understanding) are possible of accomplishment, it does not seem desirable to limit counseling to the kinds of students described by members of the behavioral counseling school.

Self and Society

Those who are concerned about the extent to which guidance and counseling can contribute to the accomplishment of the broad objectives of society

---

13 Ullman and Krasner, *Case Studies, op. cit.;* Krumboltz and Thoresen, *Behavioral Counseling, op. cit.*

14 There is some reference to helping students to learn about vocations by playing games with commercially produced problem-solving career kits. It is indicated, however, that "carefully designed studies to examine the long-term effects, still need to be conducted." See Krumboltz and Thoresen, *Behavioral Counseling, op. cit.*

and its educational institutions must be distressed by the behavioral counselors' emphasis on correction of shortcomings and the almost complete lack of any clear-cut statements about social concerns.

The literature of behavioral counseling seldom contains any suggestion that a counselor's work might be guided by social goals broader than helping counselees to attain specific and precise behavior changes. There are occasional references to improved understanding of how behavior is formed and maintained, and to improved technologies for the deliberate building of a better world, but one is left to infer the nature of that better world. There is a tendency to leave social decisions to others and to offer technological aids in support of whatever decision they make. This point of view is illustrated in the following quotation:

> *If* the drop out problem is a serious one; *if* we really believe that our society and economy require an educated population; and *if* the monetary and social costs of large numbers of uneducated or undereducated persons are great; there should be no hesitancy in taking advantage of scientific principles of learning to apply effective reinforcers to help shape desirable behavior. [Italics added] [15]

Krumboltz refers to "producing a heightened sense of responsibility" which is assumed to be a desirable outcome of counseling, but he doesn't define the statement further. He leaves the term as vague as do those whom he criticizes for using "to achieve self-actualization" without further definition. He makes it clear that "goals of counseling must be stated in terms of specific behavior desired by each individual client and agreed to by his counselor." Some pages later one finds a behavioral counselor's concern about social problems in a statement to the effect that counselors do have some responsibility for the prevention of marriages that go on the rocks, inappropriate curricula and teaching methods, undesirable child-rearing methods, and the development of persons who feel rejected and unwanted.[16] The lack of elaboration of this statement suggests that social issues take a secondary place in the behavioral counselor's thinking. One is left to guess what kind of a world, or even a particular educational institution, he would envisage when the remedial work was completed. It hardly seems desirable to try to shape individuals without consideration of what the social outcomes may be. As Shoben has indicated, the person who leaves ends to be assumed by means may be a scientist, but he is not one who lives up to the fundamental responsibility of educator or counselor.[17]

If counselors are to meet their responsibilities, they must be con-

[15] Meyerson and Michael, "A Behavioral Approach to Counseling and Guidance," *op. cit.*

[16] Krumboltz, ed., *Revolution in Counseling, op. cit.*

[17] E. J. Shoben, Jr., "Personal Worth in Education and Counseling," in Krumboltz, ed., *Revolution in Counseling, op. cit.*

cerned for the goals of the institutions in which they are employed and the objectives of the broader society in which the institutions reside.[18] To be otherwise might mean that they would be working at cross purposes with colleagues, and no counselor can be effective under such circumstances. When it appears that accomplishment of the precise and specific goals which a counselee sets for himself might be damaging to society and its educational institutions, there is very little mention of any obligation on the part of the behavioral counselor to help him change these goals. One condition that members of this school of thought require before counseling is that "the counselor must be willing to help the client achieve his goal." Apparently no limitations are set upon the nature of the goals, other than that they be acceptable to the counselor. If the goals don't please him he may choose not to work with the individual as a counselee. Society and its educational institutions have not delegated to the counseling profession the responsibility of determining to which goals an individual will be assisted in his striving, and such an occurrence seems unlikely.

There does seem to be some evidence that behavioral counselors have learned to use their techniques to help individuals reach a few precise and specific short-term goals. But this seems an unrealistic limitation of the responsibility of the counselor. When behavioral counselors indicate (by their limited consideration of the objectives of society) that they are technicians with borrowed tools, then counseling reverts back to its pioneering days, when the job was simply the fitting of square pegs to square holes. Good means do not necessarily define good ends. The de-emphasis on reaching other than very private and personal goals has the effect of accentuating the mistaken idea that, because counselors work with individuals, the broader goals of society can be ignored, rejected, or, at least, minimized.

Evaluation

In a strange statement, an advocate of behavioral counseling has suggested that counseling in its totality cannot be evaluated, and "It is as foolish to say that counseling is or is not effective as it is to say that medicine is or is not effective." [19] Medicine may have been effective or noneffective in particular cases, but there is no doubt that the practice of medicine has been generally effective. The almost complete elimination of polio, diphtheria, and other diseases, the reduction of childbirth deaths, and prolongation of the life span are evidence of the effectiveness of medicine. Since these seem to be goals of our society, it can be concluded that med-

---

[18] There is no implication here that society and its institutions will always be best served by maintenance of the status quo. Neither can it be implied that variation from it will usually be desirable.

[19] Krumboltz, ed., *Revolution in Counseling, op. cit.,* p. 32.

icine has helped to reach them. Would that counseling had some evidence that it has served society as well!

Since society and its institutions pay for counseling, they have a right to demand an overall evaluation of it as well as an accounting of what was done to help specific subjects. Their demands cannot be answered by the response that society will be well served if each person reaches his specific goals. Counseling in its totality *will* be evaluated by the society which provides for it. Description of a process of getting students to look up items in a library will not be satisfactory. Society will want to know what happened as the result of such activity, for how long the searching habits were continued, and what social implications could be drawn from such behavior. The behavioral counselors, in their cursory treatment of social issues and overemphasis on satisfaction of individual desires, may have rendered a disservice to the field of counseling which could handicap it seriously and hasten its demise.

It must be noted again that all behavioral practitioners do not treat this topic lightly, even though they may seem to agree with published statements about it. Many incorporate social objectives in the evaluation of their own work.

Most of the following samples of evaluation by behavioral counselors are found in a volume which its authors describe as a cookbook for counselors and psychologists. In reading them one may note the short follow-up period (sometimes the length is not even stated), the use of telephone calls rather than depth interviews to collect data, reports by observers who are not adequately described and whose veracity is not checked, vague language, and very brief statements of a counselee's feelings.

Unless otherwise indicated the reports are taken from the work of Krumboltz and Thoresen.[20] Italics have been added to indicate the problems noted in the preceding paragraph. In studying these examples the reader will recognize the need for harder data and more careful selection of language, and he must wonder if the objectives implied by the reports of outcomes are those which counselors should espouse.[21] If one can judge behavioral counseling objectives by the stated outcomes, it seems clear that behavioral counseling is largely a salvage and repair process designed to eliminate annoying behavior.

Students completed a daily reporting form *for one week following their two model discussion sessions.* When compared with other

[20] From J. D. Krumboltz and C. E. Thoresen, *Behavioral Counseling: Cases and Techniques* (New York: Holt, Rinehart and Winston, Inc., 1969), by permission of the authors.

[21] Some longitudinal data are promised. See C. E. Thoresen, "Relevance and Research in Counseling," *Review of Educational Research*, XXXIX, No. 2 (1969).

students, those who met in the model reinforcement discussion session spent *considerably more time* in work areas than in the cafeteria. (p. 240)

A follow-up study *a year later* showed John to be making *good academic progress* and maintaining the friendship of *a few* other boys in his class. His hand-staring behavior had been eliminated and he had shown *significant improvement* in being *socially responsive* to many of his peers. (p. 264)

When *the therapy was terminated* there had been no domestic fights for six weeks—something of a record for the household. (p. 235)

Telephone calls in *September of the following year* indicated that both boys had been passed on to a combined first-second grade group and that they were performing *well.* The teacher of the class had not noted any particular *problem during the first three weeks of school.* (p. 160)

In summary the program of systematic exclusion was effective in modifying classroom behavior for *a period of five months. However behavior outside the classroom was unchanged.* (p. 123)

At *the end of the school year* the teacher planned culmination activities for each of the major teaching units. Mickey was among those who *volunteered to give an oral presentation* on what the class had done in social studies during the year. (p. 83)

The parents reported (*two months after treatment*) that Bill's soiling had decreased *but was still evident almost once a day.* (p. 46)

At *the end of the sessions* with Curt two changes were observed. First of all he was observed to approach several of the less active boys *much more often.* Second, on the less desirable side he was observed *to frequently stand* near the slide but not to climb on it. . . . The study did demonstrate, however, that it was possible *to significantly change* the behavior of this institutionalized autistic boy through the use in part of modeling techniques. (p. 199)

Several months later Tom reported that he had really worked on being more assertive with his father, culminating with his decision, announced to his father one evening, that he was moving to an apartment. . . . Finally he commented that during this time his pronounced fear of driving a car in freeway traffic had disappeared. Tom *observed that he felt* like a "new man." (p. 441)

A follow-up interview *three months later* revealed that there has been no setbacks and no substitute "symptoms" or additional problems. (p. 449)

During the week following termination of the counseling sessions the art, music, physical education and regular classroom teachers *were informally asked for their impression* as to [the subjects'] current school adjustment. Each of these teachers reported improving adjustment. . . . The teachers made *essentially the same reports* at the time of the *four-month informal follow-up interviews*. . . . This study lends support to the use of a behavior model in elementary school counseling.[22]

Within the first half hour of the first morning of reinforcing interaction with children, Ann *seemed* to react to the contingencies for getting teacher attention. . . . At times *Ann* even took and held a strong give-and-take role in play with *five or six* other children. *Occasionally* she defended herself *vigorously. In general,* her behavior indicated that she had become a *happy,* confident member of her group.[23]

Perhaps it is the lack of long-term and overall evaluation which gives a reviewer of the literature of behavioral counseling the feeling that it is a "quickie" process unconcerned with the longitudinal development of individuals long before or after they work with a counselor, and that it is a patching technique better suited to clinical and school psychologists, while counselors concern themselves with development of persons and their decision-making in important areas.

Summary

The insistence of behavioral counselors that there be specificity of tasks, goals, and outcomes has had a salutary effect on current counseling theory and practice. Their emphases on learning of social behavior, consideration of alternatives by counselees, assistance in helping counselees to engage in behavior that will enable them to resolve conflicts, and stress on the importance of counselee self-sufficiency are worthy contributions.

Such emphases do not, however, justify acceptance of behavioral counseling as the only useful practice in schools. Such practices are useful when remedial action is required, but remediation is not a prime function of school counselors. The lack of emphasis in behavioral counseling on developmental concepts and broad social goals, the almost complete restriction of populations to subjects who come to the counselor with serious problems, and the rejection of all but observable behavior seem likely to limit a school counselor's effectiveness.

In view of the above and the lack of longitudinal evidence of the effectiveness of behavioral counseling, the school counselor should consider it as one of the procedures which, as he adapts to meet the needs of

---

[22] D. A. Kennedy and I. Thompson, "Use of a Reinforcement Technique with a First-Grade Boy," *Personnel and Guidance Journal,* XLVI, No. 4 (1967).
[23] Ullman and Krasner, *Case Studies, op. cit.*

school populations, he may find useful for some counselees on some occasions.

CLIENT-CENTERED THERAPY

The publication in 1942 of *Counseling and Psychotherapy*,[24] followed in 1951 by *Client-Centered Therapy*,[25] probably resulted in more discussion of counseling procedures than had occurred in all the previous years of the movement. Although some doubts had been expressed about the value of the prescriptive practices of counselors, the author's suggestion of complete departure from them had a profound influence on the thinking and activities of counselors. In view of the continued failure of advocates of client-centered methods to provide convincing evidence of their effectiveness, the degree of influence now seems to be unwarranted, but there can be no doubt that the early pronouncements shook the guidance movement to its very foundations.[26]

It should be noted that the author of *Counseling and Psychotherapy* and *Client-Centered Therapy* was not concerned primarily with the preparation of school counselors who must work with subjects and conditions described in the first chapter of this volume. His experience and experimentation as a clinical psychologist had been in clinics serving volunteer or referred clients who displayed serious problems of adjustment. The time available for their treatment was much greater than a high school counselor (who serves some 300 students over a nine-month period of five-day weeks) could ever be expected to attain. High school counselors can seldom use more than 900 hours each year for individual counseling. If they were to use as many as the clinically recommended 50 hours of interviewing for each subject, their yearly populations would approximate only 18. No public school is going to provide financial support for a counselor with a load of that size, and college administrations seldom provide enough funds to staff counseling centers adequately. In view of differences between school and clinical subjects and the amounts of time available for each, attempts to extrapolate clinical theory and experimental findings to school circumstances must be questioned. However, since many such attempts have been made, it is necessary to consider the client-centered school of thought in any discussion of counseling in educational institutions.

[24] C. R. Rogers, *Counseling and Psychotherapy* (Boston: Houghton Mifflin Company, 1942).

[25] Rogers, *Client-Centered Therapy, op. cit.*

[26] C. H. Patterson et al., "A Current View of Client-Centered or Relationship Therapy," *Journal of Counseling Psychology*, I, No. 2 (Summer 1969).

Some Basic Concepts

The literature on client-centered therapy is so voluminous that it defies attempts at abridgment. Followers of the leader have added so many interpretations, modifications, and applications, and reported so many research findings, that one cannot escape references to the approach in any discussion of counseling. The quantity of words and the claimed universality of application make it almost impossible to make a condensed report, but the concept provides such a good illustration of an attempt to promote an all-inclusive one-best-way approach that it cannot be ignored.

The claim for universality of this school of thought is reflected in two statements of its chief supporter. First, it is said to be applicable to all customary classifications of persons according to age, normal or neurotic personality, dependence, socioeconomic status, intelligence, and health (the only two exceptions are mental defectives and delinquents); second, it is said that those who attempt to reconcile opposing points of view will be led nowhere, or into "superficial eclecticism." [27] For reasons given later, this writer suggests that such claims lack both sufficient theoretical foundation and adequate experimental justification. It is considered here as a technique in search of a theoretical base. Despite that limitation, it may be used occasionally by a counselor who has learned to adapt his procedures to varying conditions.

With the difficulty of abridging an extensive literature in mind, and with the caution that most counselors work with students in educational institutions rather than with patients in clinics and mental hospitals, the reader is invited to examine the following aspects of the client-centered approach. The essentials are presented employing the *if-then* procedure used in the previous section.

IF THE COUNSELOR:

> *Believes that an individual has sufficient capacity to deal constructively with all those aspects of his life which can potentially come into conscious awareness.*
> *Assumes the internal frame of reference of the individual (perceives the person and the world as the subject does).*
> *Lays aside all perceptions from the external frame of reference.*
> *Communicates something of this empathic understanding.*
> *Accepts the individual as a person of unconditional worth.*

[27] Rogers, *Client-Centered Therapy, op. cit.* p. 230.

Provides a permissive atmosphere for discussion of self (is congruent, empathic, and shows unconditional positive regard).

THEN THE COUNSELEE WILL:

Develop morale and confidence.
Learn to accept himself and others.
Develop responsible self-direction.
Reorganize his personality structure to cope with life more constructively.
Make a responsible and adequate analysis of his problem.

Obviously any such outline cannot describe the approach fully, nor can it reveal the nuances and implications of the words used. Much has been written in words whose special meanings to their authors are not conveyed to those who read them from different contexts. A case in point is the interchangeable use of the words *counseling* and *therapy*. Counseling requires mutual consultation and deliberation, but such processes do not necessarily imply curing or healing. It is stretching a point to suggest that a counselor who talks to a student about his choice of education or career is engaging in therapy. This student is not necessarily dissatisfied with himself or disturbed about his place in life. He may just have recognized that he has to begin thinking about making a living, and doesn't need curing or healing. When a counselor considers with a student the desirability of joining a protest movement or engaging in independent study, the help he may offer in considering alternatives could not be classified as healing or therapy. Adoption by school and college counselors of the language of clinical psychologists is unfortunate, particularly when the term *therapy*, one of the phases of counseling, is used to characterize the whole, or when therapy and counseling are used interchangeably.

Selection of Subjects

Since neither of the schools of thought described in this chapter is able to provide counseling for all persons, some criteria for selection of their counselees must be employed. Selective factors have operated in the guidance movement since its inception, apparently determined by such factors as personal characteristics of the counselor, locale and nature of the institution in which he is employed, preparation he has had for his work, and such other influences as counselor certification standards and current concerns of the nation (the talented after sputnik and the underprivileged during the sixties). The answer to the question of who gets counseled in educational institutions has changed over the past 60 years from initial concern with job-seeking adolescent males to inclusion of elementary school children and young adults enrolled in post-high school training.[28] Despite verbalizations about the need to serve all such students, there is still a tendency to let the problem student steal the show. Exhibiting extreme variation from usual behavior is one sure way to get the attention of the counselor, particularly if the counselor is of the client-centered therapy persuasion. Helping students to cope with day-to-day problems and selection of educational and vocational experiences becomes too mundane for such counselors.

Study of the cases used as illustrative materials and review of the literature in the field of client-centered therapy make it clear that this brand of counseling is concerned primarily with persons who come voluntarily to the counselor because they are emotionally disturbed, dissatisfied with themselves, or feel that there is a gap between what they are and what they want to be. Persons who need information, who need to make choices but are not emotionally disturbed, or who need to learn or unlearn a specific skill are not to be given client-centered therapy, but are to be subjected to remedial education and skill training. One of the chief spokesmen for this area, who tends to use the words "therapy" and "counseling" interchangeably, would exclude such activities from the counseling task. His clients would be those who lack facilitative interpersonal relationships conducive to self-actualization.[29]

In restricting their clientele to those subjects who fit into such a narrow classification, the client-centered therapists must limit the number they will counsel and thereby reduce their usefulness in educational institutions. Students who are seriously emotionally disturbed or who lack facilitative interpersonal relationships conducive to self-actualization (self-enhancement and self-realization are similar concepts) do come to school counselors' offices, but they are few compared to those who need information which only a counselor is likely to have, want to develop skills or embellish those they possess, and really want to talk about the choices they need to make. Few of these will exhibit unusual emotional disturbances, and are unlikely to accept any implications by the counselor that they have a deeper problem than the one for which they sought help.

Although several advocates of the client-centered approach have acknowledged its limitations for many counseling situations, some counselors have unfortunately attempted to use it for purposes for which it was

[28] See a more complete discussion of this matter in J. W. M. Rothney, "Who Gets Counseled and for What?" in the *1971 Yearbook of the Association for Supervision and Curriculum Development* (Washington, D.C.: The Association for Supervision and Curriculum Development, 1971).

[29] Patterson, "A Current View," *op. cit.*

never intended. Perhaps this was due to overselling by its first supporters; in any case, the guidance literature of the past two decades suggests that its universality has been overemphasized. Indeed, the emphasis was so strong and so pervasive that when a behavioral counselor offered an alternative procedure he used *Revolution in Counseling* as the title of the volume he edited.[30] But counselors in educational institutions are not usually clinical or counseling psychologists, and they cannot be expected to serve the same subjects. What may be helpful to the school counselor's wide variety of counselees may be unsatisfactory for the selected clientele of the most specialized practitioner.

Self and Society

Reports about subjects who have experienced client-centered counseling contain very brief statements about the family, or the society in which the subjects lived. Lengthy descriptions of the procedures employed are introduced by a brief statement, such as "She is a young married woman." In another report the readers are told simply that "She was a professional woman who had some psychological background [whatever that may mean], and had taken one course in psychotherapy. She was in the city temporarily with a friend and was to leave for a vacation shortly." In other examples, the reader learns simply that "She is a nursery teacher," "She is a teacher and part-time psychologist," "She is a guidance worker in a southern high school." The lack of information about the interactional situation becomes serious in view of recent studies that have brought out evidence of the importance of environmental contexts.

Although provision of further information about a subject's family and environment might encourage generalization about the individual, that risk must be balanced against having insufficient information for adequate interpretation of his statements. Lacking information about the society and the subsections of it (a southern high school, for example), and being insufficiently informed about the local mores and social conventions, one tends to make assumptions about them. Since these are personalized products of one's own experience, they may be highly misleading. It is impossible to decide whether a subject has made a considerable reorganization of personality (which certainly implies some sort of relationship with the society of which he is a part) unless one knows a good deal about that society.

Since there is little information about society, there is, of course, sparse comment about any social goals. Man is said to be a social animal who needs the group in order to exist. It is suggested that enhancement

---

[30] Krumboltz, *Revolution in Counseling, op. cit.*

of the self inevitably involves enhancement of other selves as well, and that self-actualization leads to socialization, broadly defined. It is also indicated that a well-counseled person will become free and responsible, will not become a self-aggrandizer, and will be more interested in, and concerned about, others. Presumably he will advance, or at least not hinder, the welfare of the social groups of which he is a member. He will not be manipulated by the counselor for the welfare of the state, but the state will profit as an incidental outcome of the person's self-actualization.

Perhaps it is assumed that if persons become more self-actualizing through therapy they will be more effective workers, better students, more constructive citizens who would develop a less neurotic society, more congenial, and better parents who would bring up more self-actualizing children. If such behaviors are implied in statements about improvement of the state through the development of persons, more evidence is needed to justify the implication. Without it, and without some rigorously defined statement of goals, there must be considerable doubt about the acceptability of client-centered counseling in public educational institutions.

The Longitudinal Picture

The client-centered therapist's lack of concern about a subject's history is disturbing. When that deficiency is combined with sparse and vague information about long-term follow-through after treatment, the disturbance often leads to rejection of the whole procedure as a brief intervention into the life of a person whose background is not known and whose future need not be ascertained.

Perhaps the failure to collect adequate information about a subject's history is due to rejection of diagnosis as a necessary step in counseling.[31] The rejection appears to be caused by the alleged tendency of those who do diagnose to classify persons into categories for which certain treatments must be prescribed, and lack of evidence that such treatments are particularly suitable for the persons so categorized. It is also argued that there may be only one cause of emotional disturbance (other than physical impairment) which stems from deprivation or inadequate personal relationships and resulting frustration, and hence no further diagnosis is necessary. More potent in the rejection of diagnoses may be, however, the questionable belief that all essential data about the person's difficulties may be obtained during interviews.

There can be little doubt that the interview, because of its flexibility, provides the opportunity to probe more deeply and more personally than

---

[31] Yet there seems to be a contradiction. Rogers uses a type of longitudinal case history to illustrate his concepts. See C. R. Rogers, *On Becoming a Person* (Boston: Houghton Mifflin Company, 1961).

any other instrument. It should be noted, however, that the subject is responding or reacting to *one* individual during the interview, and there might be great variation in his response to another interviewer. It is difficult to generalize about his behavior on the basis of his responses to only one person, and it is not even safe to assume that similar responses would be obtained by two interviewers who belonged to the same school of thought. While one interviewer might consciously or unconsciously encourage the subject to discuss his limitations, another might influence him to emphasize his strengths and play down his limitations.[32] For this reason, any extrapolation about a subject's behavior outside of the interview from the data obtained in it is a hazardous undertaking. But it is such common practice that it is almost heretical to suggest that interviews may not be as effective as they are commonly considered to be. The client-centered therapist's almost complete dependence on the interview must be seriously questioned.

Longitudinal data obtained from persons who have had sufficient opportunity to observe an individual, personal documents or other forms of expression by the subject before counseling begins, records of academic performances and health, and even a longitudinal pattern of test scores, questionable as many of these may be, seem to be essential supplements to faulty interview data. They need not result in classification into diagnostic categories, and might in fact serve the opposite effect—that of highlighting the individuality of the counselee. Sole use of the interview seems to put too much emphasis upon a relatively short interval in the life of an individual who has had a past which must have influenced his current condition, and perhaps has a long future to meet.

The client-centered therapy movement is some 25 years old. During that time no longitudinal studies (extending over 5 to 10 to 20 years) of subjects who experienced this form of counseling have been reported.[33] Perhaps such subjects have suffered irreparable damage, have become dependent persons, or have exhibited behavior which required that society confine them to institutions. Or perhaps they are free, responsible, self-actualizing persons who are aiding the enhancement of others. A movement which has claimed over the past 20 years that it could do so much for so many persons owes to its observers some evidence that there are positive lasting outcomes. Until it does provide such longitudinal evidence, observers must add skepticism about its long-term outcomes to the doubts they have about its short-term effectiveness.

[32] See J. W. M. Rothney, *Methods of Studying the Individual Child: The Psychological Case Study* (Waltham, Mass.: Ginn/Blaisdell, 1968).

[33] For evaluative comments by therapists of other persuasions, see *Journal of Counseling Psychology,* I, No. 2 (Summer 1969). Many are critical, but none of the critics raise the longitudinal issues considered here.

Evaluation

It has often been said that goals should be stated in terms which permit evaluation, and that the evaluation should be in terms of the stated goals. If this is to be accomplished in the evaluation of a counseling procedure, such broad terms as socialized maturity, self-actualizing, positive growth, and development of "a more broadly based structure of self, an inclusion of greater experience as a part of self, and a more comfortable and realistic adjustment to life" need to be restated so that they can be evaluated.[34] If these phrases were defined in terms of a person's behavior, which could be measured validly, they might permit evaluation, but as they appear in reports of client-centered therapy, where words are defined by words, they defy evaluation.[35]

Attempts at evaluation that go beyond the possibly biased reports of therapists, the opinions of the client himself, and shaky estimates by observers are sorely needed. This area requires studies in which effectiveness of treatment is appraised in terms of behavior other than the way the subjects respond to the Rorschach, drop check marks on so-called personality tests, engage in Q sorts, or fill out badly constructed rating scales. There is need for information about the extent of persistence of self-actualizing and reorganization of personality. We have no incontrovertible evidence that significant changes in persons who have undergone client-centered therapy persist over a period of years. But perhaps this is to be expected when no times, other than the vague use of the word "later," are stated when goals are given. Does reorganization of personality go on for years, or is it a reorganization which occurs during treatment and remains forever? Does self-actualizing continue throughout a lifetime following treatment? In the results of evaluative studies on client-centered therapy so far conducted, there is neither sufficient specificity of goals nor indications of the extent of time in which they are to be attained and retained.

It would be difficult for a school counselor to justify his use of client-centered counseling on the basis of evidence other than comments by probably biased reporters and obviously inadequate studies. When the client-centered therapists are asked for evaluation they tend to turn to description of their activities. One needs further evidence of effectiveness than a description of counselors as empathic, acceptant, and congruent. A question as to the effectiveness of the achievement of certain conditions is not answered by statements that such conditions were present. This simply raises further questions about what unbiased valid evidence can be pre-

---

[34] Rogers, *Client-Centered Therapy, op. cit.,* p. 195.
[35] See A. Lazarus, "Relationship Therapy: Often Necessary but Usually Insufficient," *Journal of Counseling Psychology,* I, No. 2 (Summer 1969).

sented to show that significant changes occurred in the behavior of the subjects, and over what period of time. Up to this time such questions have not been answered. There has been no adequate refutation of the statement that the conditions considered essential in client-centered therapy are *often* (implying not for *every* subject) necessary, but usually insufficient to accomplish its objectives.[36]

POSITIVE CONTRIBUTIONS

The introduction of new ideas by leaders of various schools of thought has contributed greatly to the revitalization of counseling. By retaining concepts promulgated by the originators of the guidance movement at the beginning of the century, and yielding to the demands of society to continue the process of placing square pegs in square holes, the counseling movement had become inflexible, stereotyped, and moribund. Not enough concern was being given to the individual as a whole person, and excessive direction and dictation was common. At the same time objectives were nebulous, theoretical bases were treated lightly, and evaluation was almost nonexistent.

The new schools of thought brought to this scene some rethinking about goals, theoretical bases, methods, and appraisals. Among their influences on the counseling movement, the following may be most significant:

1. Cautions to counselors to listen more, talk less, and provide for more empathy and warmth in the counseling relationship.
2. Emphasis on the development of the whole person rather than seeing him as simply a potential employee or student with particular aptitudes which demanded a specified type of placement.
3. Reduction of emphasis on the manpower utilization concept of guidance and greater stress on human development.
4. Increased attention to personal goals and concerns of counselees.
5. Encouragement of efforts to find better theoretical bases for counseling procedures.
6. Insistence on greater specificity of goals (particularly by behavioral counselors).
7. Beginning of evaluation (still short-term) in terms of specific goals.
8. Consideration of counseling as a learning experience rather than as primarily a diagnosis and placement procedure.
9. Greater emphasis on the development of decision-making skills in addition to the making of one decision at a crisis point.

[36] C. R. Rogers, "The Interpersonal Relationship: The Core of Guidance," *Harvard Educational Review*, XXXII, No. 4 (Fall 1962); *idem.*, "The Necessary and Sufficient Conditions for Therapeutic Change," *Journal of Counseling Psychology*, XXI (1957).

10. By raising issues about the nature and intent of counseling, and in recommending various practices, exponents of various schools of thought have stimulated thinking and have suggested that counselors need not limit their activities to those derived from any single system. By emphasizing several approaches they have increased the possibility that counselors may become truly adaptive in their work.

SUMMARY

Discussion of the two schools of thought presented in this chapter was designed to indicate the kinds of commitments made when counselors become members of a system. Membership seems to require acceptance of single all-explanatory theories, employment of certain prescribed techniques, and limitation of the population with whom counselors work. It should be noted, however, that variability in practice is probably much greater than one would assume from reading statements by the leaders of the schools of thought. Not all counselors of a given theoretical orientation imitate their leaders exactly.

There are some advantages for a counselor in associating himself with one school of thought, not the least of which are the invigorating influences of being part of a currently popular movement; becoming a follower of a well-publicized leader; finding mutual support for one's beliefs; and development of feelings that his work is significant because his colleagues offer their reinforcement.

Among the disadvantages of belonging, however, are tendencies to accept as truth that which seems plausible but which has not been firmly established; the reading into labels a distinctiveness which is not clearly evident in terms of techniques employed; persistence in beliefs or practices even when research evidence is nonsupportive; selection of counselees who seem most likely to profit from the application of particular techniques; avoiding long-term follow-up of subjects and thereby escaping consequences if results are not up to expectations; overgeneralizing from too few trials of a technique; and oversimplifying explanations of behavior of complex unique individuals living in a free dynamic society.[37]

Specific and frequent criticisms of each school of thought by members of opposing schools have been vigorously and sometimes arrogantly expressed. The procedures of client-centered therapy are most commonly described as essential but insufficient.[38] The behavioral counseling approaches are most frequently described as suitable for description of the

---

[37] M. R. Katz, "Theoretical Foundations of Guidance," *Review of Educational Research*, XXXIX, No. 2 (1969).

[38] Patterson, "A Current View," *op. cit.* Critical reviews of Patterson's presentation are included.

behavior of pigeons, dogs, and learners of typing and telegraphy, but inadequate for describing more complex processes, particularly reasoning, creative imagination, and inventiveness. In general, however, *the main criticism is that all theories are not wrong, but each is only partial.*

Despite assaults on each other by members of the various schools, one can find a good deal of agreement about some matters.[39] All of the proponents of systems agree that good rapport with counselees needs to be developed and maintained; the counselor must be respected and appreciated by counselees; counseling should provide an opportunity for the counselee to learn more about himself; some direction is always provided, either subtly or directly; there must be some desire on the part of the counselee to change; the counselee will become a freer, informed, and responsible person (though definitions of such terms vary considerably); and there will be transfer of learning from the confines of the counselor's office to real life situations.

In view of the number of common elements in various schools of thought and the lack of conclusive evidence that one system is better than any other, the school counselor would be well advised to avoid the restrictions imposed by alignment with a particular theory.[40] If he does reject such membership, he does not consign himself thereby simply to the role of an eclectic. He may do some borrowing from the various schools, but he may also, as an adaptable person, provide more for the individual differences in his counselees than any restrictive or eclectic system permits. But becoming an adaptable counselor does not just require the joining of another school of thought with another new label. The freedom that adaptability offers is indicated in the following chapter.

Selected References

ALLPORT, G. W. *Pattern and Growth in Personality.* New York: Holt, Rinehart and Winston, Inc., 1961. This classic volume is *must* reading for anyone who aspires to be a counselor. It provides a survey of the field, with great emphasis on individuality. Theory rather than application is stressed.

HOSFORD, R. E. "Behavioral Counseling," *Counseling Psychologist,* I (Summer 1969). Critics and questioners respond to a statement of one of the advocates of behavioral approaches to counseling.

[39] Krumboltz, *Revolution in Counseling, op. cit.;* W. H. Van Hoose and J. J. Pietrofesa, eds., *Counseling and Guidance in the Twentieth Century* (Boston: Houghton Mifflin Company, 1970); C. R. Rogers and B. F. Skinner, "Some Issues Concerning the Control of Human Behavior," *Science,* No. 124 (1956).

[40] There is no clear-cut evidence that any of the various schools of thought have ever had a strong influence on the work of school counselors. One suspects from conversations with many of them that they find the various systems either too restrictive or unrealistic for application in school situations. As they mature on the job, they recognize that the introduction of a new school is often only another example of the excessive faddism to which the counseling movement is addicted.

KRUMBOLTZ, J. D. and C. E. THORESEN. *Behavioral Counseling: Cases and Techniques.* New York: Holt, Rinehart and Winston, Inc., 1969. This is a "cookbook" illustration by the case method of the essentials of behavior counseling. Reports of the application of the procedures in varying circumstances and for several purposes are presented in considerable detail.

PATTERSON, C. H., *et al.* "A Current View of Client-Centered or Relationship Therapy," *Journal of Counseling Psychology,* I, No. 2 (Summer 1969). A retatement of the client-centered orientation and reactions by some who raise serious questions about it.

ROGERS, C. R. *Client-Centered Therapy.* Boston: Houghton Mifflin Company, 1951. Presentation of the essentials of this theoretical orientation. Subsequent publications by this author indicate that the basic premises were laid down in this volume and that they are still functional.

STEFFLRE, B. *Theories of Counseling.* New York: McGraw-Hill Book Company, 1965. This is the best book on counseling theory because it does not plead for a one-best-way to counsel. Very well written in a critical but constructive manner.

CHAPTER 3

foundations of
adaptive counseling

The two single approaches to counseling presented in the previous chapter were both seen as having made some contributions to counseling practice, but both were rejected as generally applicable techniques. In this chapter we shall be concerned with procedures for adapting counseling to meet the kinds of individual differences found among counselees in schools. Some of the procedures advocated by followers of the client-centered and behavioral counseling schools will be subsumed with others under the general heading of adaptive counseling.

The key to providing for individual differences is adaptation. Such techniques as modeling, reflecting, reinforcing, rephrasing, role playing, pouncing, and counterconditioning all have a place in counseling with some individuals some of the time. Some may be useful at one meeting with a counselee but wholly inadequate at the next session with him. Some which are suitable during the first half of an interview need to be discarded for the second half. The procedure that was adequate for a counselee in the morning may be unsuitable for a different one that afternoon. Slavishly following one procedure can result not only in failure to accomplish the objectives of counseling, but the setting back of the counselee so that he cannot profit from any counseling in the future.

ADAPTIVE COUNSELING

Definition

The activities of a counselor are determined by his definition of the counseling process, which will in turn be influenced by the situation in which he works. In view of the latter, it is unlikely that any definition of counseling will ever be universally accepted. For one who works in an educational institution, and who is not committed to salvage and repair operations, the following definition devised by the writer and restated in the language he uses with adolescent counselees may be suitable. When he meets a new counselee he tells him that *we will be working with you, your parents, and your teachers over a period of years to see if we can help you to understand yourself better than you otherwise might, so that when you have to make important decisions you will be better prepared to do so.* This definition contains many implications. It suggests that the process will be cooperative, and that there will be sharing of information. It does not suggest that the counselee will know himself fully (an impossible task), but that he may know himself better than he might if he had not been counseled. It states that there will be concern with major decisions rather than trivia, and it does not imply complete preparation for making them. It informs the subject that the counseling is not to be a short-term affair, and it implies that there will be follow-through. After the definition is given, some of the techniques to be employed, such as testing, inventorying, and interviewing, are described, and there is some indication of areas in which important decisions must be made. Time is provided for questioning by the counselee and counselor to see that the definition is fully understood. When the definition is grasped and the procedures described, the process of adaptive counseling can begin.

The essential aspects of adaptive counseling can be grasped by use of the *if-then* approach used in the discussion of other techniques in the previous chapter.

IF THE COUNSELOR:

> *Accepts the idea that learning can take place in many ways.*
> *Accepts the concept that various methods can be employed.*
> *Changes procedures as circumstances change.*
> *Offers opinions and information when they are sought.*

THEN THE COUNSELEE:

> *Recognizes that he is not being forced into a role chosen by the counselor.*

Feels free to be himself.
Can direct the interview in the direction he wants it to go.
Recognizes that he can get critical consideration of his ideas.
Learns about responsibilities as well as opportunities.
Hears the opinions of the counselor about what he proposes to do.
Recognizes that mere conversation will not provide enough help to meet his needs.

It is more difficult to put adaptive counseling into the *if-then* format simply because the adaptive counselor's behavior is not confined to a single theory or system, and may differ widely as counselees and circumstances vary. The number of verbs required to describe what adaptive counselors do has never been ascertained, but it must encompass almost all those that describe relationships (excluding the most personal, such as kissing, and such strongly censorial terms as berating) between two persons working on a common problem. In the first 16 pages of my dictionary, for example, there are 22 verbs (such as abet, abnegate, about-face, accede, accept, acknowledge, acquaint, admit) which might describe a counselor's behavior at any particular time. Any total listing would incorporate so many verbs with so many shades of meaning that it would become meaningless.[1] A sample of them in sentence context appears in the following list:

Arranges *conferences for the counselee with others.*
Asks *as many questions as necessary to understand a subject's situation and concern.*
Avoids *rephrasing or reiterating what subject has said unless it is unclear.*
Challenges *subject to undertake what seem to be desirable next steps.*
Commends *counselee when he thinks he has done something well.*
Cooperates *with counselee in planning next steps.*
Demonstrates *possible counselee behavior.*
Directs *counselee to sources of information.*
Disagrees *with a counselee when he feels he has misinterpreted information or made logical errors.*
Interprets *information (including test scores) to the counselee.*
Listens *to what the counselee says.*
Refers *counselee to additional sources.*
Reminds *subject that frequent verbal repetition of his problem does not necessarily increase the likelihood of its solution.*
Shows *genuine concern about counselee's problem.*

[1] Allport and Odbert have shown that there are 17,953 words in the English language that can be used to describe persons. See G. W. Allport and H. S. Odbert, "Trait Names: A Psycho-Lexical Study," *Psychological Monographs*, No. 211 (1936).

States *his opinions clearly when a counselee asks for them.*
Suggests *activities in which the counselee may participate.*
Teaches *counselee some steps in problem solving.*
Warns *subject about possible consequences of action he plans to
undertake.*

Adaptive Versus Eclectic Counseling

It would be unfortunate if adaptive counseling were considered identical
to what has been called eclectic counseling. In the sense that it is used in
this volume, *adaptation is to particular counselees, not selection from procedures* advocated by exponents of particular theories. Eclecticism signifies
simply the practice of selecting what seems best from various systems, but
dictionary synonyms for the word *adapt* include accommodate, adjust, arrange, attune, conform, fashion, fit, harmonize, and suit. Some of these
terms define the activities of an adaptive counselor, and if he did only
those, eclectic might well be used to describe him. To portray his activity
fully as adaptive, however, would require the addition of such terms as
innovate, go beyond (limitations imposed by adherence to a particular
system), redefine (goals), reject (some claims for universality and even
omnipotence), and individualize (his procedures). He is *not* just a borrower of techniques. He offers much of his own.

The adaptive counselor may carry on activities that are given scant
or no attention by proponents of various systems. Thus his practice of
making longitudinal case studies, which includes extensive search for patterns of individual development and long-term follow-up of counselees into
post-school periods, cannot be borrowed from either the behavioral or
client-centered schools simply because they do not advocate such procedures. The adaptive counselor's concern for helping educational institutions to achieve their broad objectives cannot be borrowed from any of the
several schools of thought because their sponsors tend to give scant consideration to such matters, reject any responsibility for working toward
goals other than meeting individuals' needs, or dismiss them as matters of
little consequence.

Procedures for counseling all students cannot be borrowed from either
the client-centered or behavioral counseling schools, since both tend to
restrict their services to subjects who exhibit maladaptive behavior or face
crisis situations. The adaptive counselor, unlike the eclectic and systems
counselors, plans his work with the conviction that the primary concern is
development rather than repair.

Adaptive counselors may use techniques similar to those employed
by members of various schools of thought, but such use does not imply
that they are based on identical concepts. Much time spent listening to their

counselees does not signify any belief that provision of a permissive atmosphere will necessarily result in responsible self-direction. It may mean simply that they are seeking cues that will help in providing direction for a counselee who currently seems to be aiming for unfortunate consequences. The counselor may provide reinforcement, not simply to assist a counselee to reach specific short-term goals, but to help him in greater understanding of how his behavior may affect others now and possibly in the future. Thus, though the surface manifestations may suggest alignment with a particular counseling system, the underlying concepts may differ significantly. The eclectic counselor, on the other hand, borrows both procedures and concepts.

Use of a test in the manner that will be described in Chapter 4 does not imply that a counselor accepts trait-factor theory. An adaptive counselor may use a test score to help a student to assess his current level of development without interpreting it as possession of an aptitude or ability, and justification for use of any other ethical technique can be found without reliance on a specific learning theory. If none of the theories seems to be appropriate, the counselor is free to disregard them so long as his counselee appears to be making progress in self-understanding and decision-making.

In all the above it has been implied that a counselor, like a counselee, is not an object to be manipulated for the maintenance of systems or the enhancement of their founders. Counselors are individuals with considerable freedom to choose, to reject or accept, to innovate, and to contribute much of their own. An adaptive counselor, not simply a borrower of concepts and techniques, can offer more than others because he is free to work out in his own way with each counselee what seem to be the best possibilities among the choices available.

A brief description of differences between counselors who are eclectic or systems followers and those who are adaptive (in terms of what the latter spurn) is presented in summary form below. Adaptive counselors reject:

1. Restrictions on their freedom to improvise as situations demand improvisation.
2. The concept of universal applicability of any procedure.
3. All-explanatory theories of human learning.
4. Too-simple analogies between human and animal learning.
5. Statements of objectives which ignore or minimize social implications of a counselee's behavior.
6. Procedures which do not require longitudinal studies of counselees.
7. Schools of thought which confine the activities of counselors to interviewing persons and leading groups.
8. Restriction of the persons whom he may serve to those who exhibit maladaptive behavior.

9. Exclusion of individual teaching, information giving, and essential skill development from descriptions of counseling.

Counselees of Adaptive School Counselors

It was noted in the previous chapter that advocates of particular psychological systems display a marked tendency to preselect their subjects, and that the selection techniques influence their thinking about processes they employ. Experimental behaviorists who reject introspection tend to work with animals from which no reports of introspective phenomena can be obtained, and, procuring none, they suggest that it does not exist. Client-centered therapists tend to select subjects who are verbally facile and who come to the therapist with problems for which they seek solutions. The danger in such selective processes lies in the tendency to generalize the applicability of their procedures to persons not represented in their selected populations.

School counselors seldom have as much freedom as clinicians or university experimenters in choice of subjects. They can avoid the task of counseling seriously disturbed students by making it clear to administrators that they are not competent to work in the field of serious maladjustment, and that their responsibility to disturbed persons ends with their recognition and referral to specialists. They can insist that they will not take part in disciplinary action, but they should indicate their willingness to work with a student before and after the disciplinary authorities have punished the offender.[2] They should refuse to spend long periods of time in providing remedial treatment in school subjects or in speech correction.[3] In all such cases they will work with the students up to the point where the need for remediation is recognized and the referral made. Except in such cases, however, the counselor is responsible for all the students to whom (after consultation with the administration about apportionment of students) he has been assigned. He will ordinarily counsel between four and five hundred students (and their teachers and parents) who constitute a representative sample of the school population. The challenge which this situation offers has been described in the writer's observation that a few counselors, individually different, will work with a larger number of teachers, all displaying individual differences; with an even larger number of students

---

[2] This does not mean that the counselor, as a member of a school staff, is not as concerned about the regulations of the institution as his colleagues. It simply means that he is not the person who metes out punishment for their infraction.

[3] There is, however, a marked tendency for counselors to undertake such tasks when specialists are not immediately available. Lacking special preparation for the task, they are likely to be unsuccessful, and their lack of achievement in such work tends to be generalized to lack of confidence in the counselor even when he is doing the work for which he is prepared.

exhibiting individual differences; and with twice that number of parents, each of whom differs from the other in many significant ways. This observation accentuates the claimed need for a high level of adaptability.

Some Backgrounds

Selective factors have operated in the guidance movement from its inception. Frank Parsons, who is generally credited with starting guidance in 1908, was concerned with youth who were about to seek employment, offered nothing for young children, and gave college-going youth only some general exhortation about behavior and good citizenship. All of these he hoped, would result in the development of a socialist state.[4] Anna Reid and Jesse Davis, who followed Parsons in the early part of the century, were concerned with the guidance of adolescents, the former to be sure that they secured employment which would enhance the profits of businessmen, the latter to develop what he called good moral character. John M. Brewer, the first man to hold a prestigious position as a professor of guidance at Harvard, advocated guidance as a means of making education more realistic for adolescents.[5] When the first group to promote guidance was organized in 1913, the members called it the National Vocational Guidance Association, implying by that title that counseling would be concerned primarily with persons who needed vocational guidance. In the depression years of the thirties determined efforts were made to help youth to find the kind of employment for which they seemed best fitted. The aptitude testing movement which began a few years earlier was designed primarily to offer assistance in that endeavor.

The advent of the progressive education movement in the thirties and early forties brought greater concern with the whole person as well as with his vocational aptitudes.[6] Interest in the early growth and development of individuals resulted in a limited amount of guidance being given to the preadolescent, although counseling had always been, and still is, primarily for youth. The efforts of the Veterans Administration after World War II to provide counseling for young adults, and the development of counseling centers in colleges and universities, expanded the age range. The emphasis in guidance really changed, however, when the provisions of the National Defense Education Act (NDEA), as originally conceived in 1957, were limited to secondary school youth.

Until very recently, then, most counseling was confined to adolescents

---

[4] F. Parsons, *Choosing a Vocation* (Boston: Houghton Mifflin Company, 1909).

[5] J. M. Brewer, *Education as Guidance* (New York: The Macmillan Company, 1932).

[6] L. A. Cremin, "The Progressive Heritage of the Guidance Movement," *Harvard Educational Review,* III (1964).

and young adults who were counseled primarily for vocational choice and placement. One didn't get counseled unless one had reached secondary school or beyond, and even in those stages one had to be preparing for or seeking employment, talented (NDEA prescription), or having adjustment problems. Some interest in counseling had developed in mental hygiene clinics and correctional institutions.

Although there has always been some interest in counseling of elementary school children, professional personnel did little about it until the current decade. Wrenn provided a great stimulus to elementary school guidance in 1964 by suggesting that counselors could do what had previously been done by school psychologists, family welfare workers, remedial specialists, curriculum consultants,[7] teacher educators, and good classroom teachers.[8] (The wide acceptance of this suggestion illustrates how some guidance workers are quick to use the filling station approach—if they think that something needs repair they rush in to make it, whether or not they are qualified or have the equipment to do it.) The recent amendment to the NDEA which permits and supports counseling and guidance in the elementary grades has stimulated a movement to place counselors in all schools. Without substantial evidence that they accomplish much, there is considerable current pressure on the public to employ them, and to pay well for a relatively unproven service.[9] For the first time in the history of the guidance movement, elementary school children in substantial numbers can be counted among those who get counseled.[10]

It seems clear from the above that the answer to who gets counseled in educational institutions has changed over the years from the initial concern with job-seeking adolescents to the current concern with elementary school children and young adults in post-high school educational programs. It is often proposed that there should be counseling for all the children of all the people but, in practice, the problem student steals the show. A student is more likely to get counseling if he is among the lame, the halt, the blind, the disadvantaged, the maladjusted, or the failures, or if he wants to get a scholarship and is a college admissions applicant.[11] In meet-

---

[7] It is often amusing to note the naïveté of many workers in elementary school counseling. They propose, for example, to add courses and units in occupational information to the curriculum. In doing so they seem to ignore the inability of small children to grasp the complex concepts involved, and fail to realize that good teachers have always done some work in this area at a level children can understand.

[8] C. G. Wrenn, The Counselor in a Changing World (Washington, D.C.: The American Personnel and Guidance Association, 1962).

[9] W. H. Van Hoose and M. Kurtz, "Status of Guidance in the Elementary School: 1968–69," Personnel and Guidance Journal, XLVIII, No. 5 (January 1970).

[10] V. Faust, History of Elementary School Counseling (Boston: Houghton Mifflin Company, 1968).

[11] V. F. Calia, "The Culturally Deprived Client: A Reformulation of the Counselor's Role," Journal of Counseling Psychology, XIII (1966).

ing such demands, the counselor tends to become more a salvage and repair man than a worker whose primary concern is development of all children. This is the way it has been in the past, but changes are coming about.

Unless selective factors such as residential restrictions, segregation practices, and student grouping policies are operating (and sometimes even when they are not), the differences in the population for whom the school counselor is responsible will run the gamut of human physiques, maturation levels, health performances, behavior, and environmental circumstances, and combinations of these characteristics. The counselor is expected to help all of these persons (some for only the short period before referral, as indicated above) to understand themselves better so that they will be better prepared to make important decisions. As great as the challenge is, the counselor who believes that he can assist persons to reach better (but not complete) self-understanding so that they can make better (but not necessarily perfect) decisions cannot restrict that assistance to those who come to him voluntarily because of a currently serious problem, and those who are at or near transition stages of dropout, graduation, or transfer. He considers counseling to be a part of a school's services and, in encouraging all students to participate in it, perceives his work as more closely allied to the curriculum developer than to the clinical psychologist, who professes concern about development but is more likely to work at diagnosis and remediation.[12]

The school counselor should indicate by his actions, as well as his words, that counseling is to be offered to all students. At the beginning of a year he may call in students at random or draw from an alphabetized list. In the initial interviews he will try to make clear the functions and procedures of the guidance department and invite the students to participate. The counselor recognizes that in the complicated business of coming of age in America there comes a time when a student wants to sit down with a wise friend (neither teacher, preacher, principal, nor parent, although he will want to talk to them, too) and talk about himself. He will want the student to know that he is available when that time comes.

An individual's major problems of choice and decision may probably be more surely met if he has had previous opportunities to consider some aspects of decision-making processes with a counselor. Accepting this assumption, the counselor may use noncrisis interviewing to raise questions which the student may not have thought of asking for himself, so that potential roadblocks may be considered; to relay information which the student could not obtain from any other source; to interpret information that seems likely to be helpful to a particular counselee; and even to congratu-

---

[12] Counseling is not thrust upon a student, but all students have the opportunity to participate in it after it has been explained to them.

late him for an exceptionally worthy performance in any area of endeavor. No one of these need wait till a crisis has developed, and doing them requires freedom from the constraints imposed by adherence to a particular system of counseling.

But despite the best efforts of all those who work with youth and of the youth themselves, crises do develop. On such occasions the students who have learned about counseling services in their initial interviews are more likely to come to the counselor. If they do not, and the counselor learns about the crisis from others, he may seek out the student and offer his assistance. A good counselor is aware that crises are normal phenomena, and that in working with all the students he may help in their solution.

One unfortunate consequence of a policy of selecting for counseling only those with serious problems is the lack of provision for adequate counseling of the academically talented student. It is frequently stated that school counselors tend to spend most of their time with college-bound students who least need their help, and insufficient time with those who will be seeking employment or brief periods of training immediately after completing high school. This claim is substantiated only by sample observations by those who already believe it to be true. If there were a trend in that direction it might have been accentuated by the financial support provided under the NDEA.[13]

It seems naïve to assume that academically gifted students need less counseling than those who do not perform as well in school.[14] They are equally required to make choices about personal, educational, and vocational matters. Their choices are made more difficult by their multipotentiality, which reduces their educational and vocational choices (few, for example, will be entering apprenticeships or technical schools in preparation for work in skilled trades), but makes decisions within the limited areas more vital. They recognize that their success in learning sets them off from others, and they want to learn more about themselves. They are often pressured by recruiters for educational institutions and professions and badgered by persons who expect them to perform at ever-higher levels. Their learning skills open special opportunities for enriched educational experiences (acceleration, advanced placement, early admission, special

---

[13] The following statement in Section 101 of the act indicates the purpose of the NDEA: "We must increase our efforts to identify and educate more of the talent of our nation. This requires programs that will give assurance that no student of ability will be denied an opportunity for higher education because of financial need; will correct as rapidly as possible the existing imbalances in our educational program which have led to an insufficient proportion of our population educated in science, mathematics and foreign language, and trained in technology."

[14] See J. W. M. Rothney and N. Koopman, "Guidance of the Gifted," in *Fifty-Seventh Yearbook of the National Society for the Study of Education* (Chicago: University of Chicago Press, 1958), Chap. 16, for further discussion of this matter.

seminars, and offerings beyond the usual) from which they must select the most appropriate programs.

The above circumstances indicate that the common notion that students who perform at high levels on intellectual tasks need less counseling is simply not valid. The adaptive counselor, recognizing that special talents bring special problems, and realizing the potentially great rewards to society as well as to the students' own fulfillment if their needs are met, will search out the highest-performing students and make sure that they are included among his counselees.[15] That this is not common practice is attested to by the scarcity of literature on guidance of the gifted.

When considering the general topic of choosing subjects for counseling, one must wonder why the procedures which are claimed to be so effective are offered only to selected cases. *If* counseling can help students to develop decision-making competency, self-understanding, realistic self-concepts, self-actualization, and skill in solving current and future problems more independently and effectively, why must the service be limited to those who have serious problems of adjustment? [16] Do those who do the restricting assume that, unless a person comes voluntarily with a problem, these desirable behaviors have already been developed? Or that some persons don't need them? Or that if they do need them they must go elsewhere to get help in their development? The answers to such questions are not to be found in the literature of the separate counseling systems.

Comparison of this section with the coverage of "Selection of Subjects" in Chapter 2 should make it clear that the adaptive school counselor works with subjects who are likely to differ in numbers and in behavior from those preselected by advocates of particular schools of thought. It is these differences (in addition to theoretical orientations considered elsewhere in this volume) which require the adaptive school counselor to reject the strictures which membership in one particular system imposes.

The Individual and Society

One seldom finds in the writing of advocates of particular schools of thought any doubt about their freedom to do as they choose (other than

---

[15] J. W. M. Rothney and M. P. Sanborn, "Wisconsin's Research Through Guidance Program for Superior Students," *Personnel and Guidance Journal*, XLIV (March 1966); *idem., Identifying and Educating Superior Students in Wisconsin High Schools* (Madison, Wisconsin: Research and Guidance Laboratory for Superior Students, 1967).

[16] Many such outcomes are listed in various sources. See the Proposed Statement of Policy for Secondary School Counselors by the American School Counselors Association, 1964. See also statements by several writers in W. H. Van Hoose and J. J. Pietrofesa, eds., *Counseling and Guidance in the Twentieth Century: Reflections and Reformulations* (Boston: Houghton Mifflin Company, 1970).

obviously illegal practices) with their counselees. Thus one finds them electing to condition a subject so that he will behave in what the counselor decides is a desirable manner; withholding information even though this may lead the counselee to believe he knows enough; choosing or not choosing to influence a subject's decisions; encouraging or withholding encouragement of a counselee to perform at a higher or lower level; encouraging him to reveal his inner self; stimulating him to make self-assessments; and even helping him to become more congruent. These and other activities described by various practitioners as desirable procedures suggest that counselors are free to do what they will with their subjects, based solely on their own philosophical orientations, social views, or acceptance of a particular psychological theory. Such activities are defended with such vehemence that an uncritical reader could be led to believe that society had granted counselors some incredible rights to influence persons.[17] Society has, of course, never delegated such right to the counseling profession, and unwarranted assumption of it has probably been a major factor in reducing counseling effectiveness.

It has become popular to dismiss the concerns of society about its young people by suggesting that counselees are not to be considered as "objects to be manipulated for the welfare of the state or the good of the educational institution." [18] Counselors need not engage in such manipulation, but neither can they dismiss so readily the concept that the state and its institutions must be concerned with the behavior of a person who will be a citizen for a long time, and a counselee for relatively few moments. In donning his counselor's robe, the school counselor cannot doff his citizen's role, nor can he divorce himself from his position as a member of the staff of an educational institution. He will not have done his job if his self-actualized or well-conditioned counselees become dependents on society, avoid the obligations of citizenship (including the duty to protest some of its requirements), interfere with others' rights, or break laws.[19]

Educational institutions now and in any foreseeable future will have regulations for students even when unnecessary requirements are eliminated. They are founded to reach such goals as acquisition of knowledge, participation and leadership in society, and preparation for a vocation.

---

[17] It is absolutely impossible for one person to make up the mind of another; that is an internal personal process. But all counselors must, by their very presence, influence their counselees. Regardless of their denials and rejection of manipulation as an activity, they all try to influence their subjects. The chief difference among the exponents of counseling systems is the subtlety with which they go about it.

[18] C. R. Rogers, "The Interpersonal Relationship: The Core of Guidance," *Harvard Educational Review*, XXXII, No. 4 (Fall 1962).

[19] When such statements are made, someone always points out that the breaking of laws by Gandhi or Martin Luther King were commendable acts of benefit to society. There may be need for exceptions if such persons are recognized by a counselor. But how many such persons would a counselor meet and recognize?

Educators have often indicated that their goals do not differ significantly from the ultimate aims of counselors. Goal statements such as the following appear in college bulletins:

> To help the student to develop an understanding of other people and effectiveness in his relations with them, to become socially poised, and develop leadership.

> To kindle the student's aesthetic interests and thus to enrich his life, to reinforce his moral and spiritual sensibilities, and to enlarge his understanding of himself—of his talents, his limitations, his needs, and his aspirations—so that he may make wise decisions regarding his vocation, his choice of a mate, and his way of life.[20]

Such statements are open to various interpretations, but many of them are no more nebulous than those used in counseling. Most counselors could accept them, and they do not put undue institutional constraints on staff members. If a counselor cannot accept the institution's statement of objectives, and is unable to work toward their accomplishment, he is obligated to show why they should be altered. Failing to get them changed, he has no option but to resign; otherwise he would be working at odds with his colleagues. Counseling is not an institution in itself. It is only one of the services offered in educational institutions.[21] Counselors are hired to perform a service for employers who have been delegated responsibilities by society. Their autonomy is limited when they join a school staff, but the limitations do not imply that all they do is completely controlled.

A counselor is a citizen, a faculty member, and a worker with individuals—roles that are too often neglected in academic discussions of counseling.[22] As a citizen he can work for social and educational reforms, maintenance of the status quo, or even reversion to previous conditions, depending on his beliefs. As a member of the school staff he can alert administration and faculty to particular needs of students, and he may develop and demonstrate methods of modifying student behavior when their practices conflict with counseling goals. As a counselor he can help students

[20] Many schools and educational organizations have made statements of their objectives covering most of the same areas. A sample list will be found in J. W. M. Rothney, *Evaluating and Reporting Pupil Progress*, No. 7 of the series, "What Research Says to the Teacher" (Washington, D.C.: National Education Association, 1963).

[21] As is usually the case with members of a profession, counselor educators tend to overstate the importance of counselors in a school situation. High school and college faculties are composed of specialists whose strong opinions about school and society must be given consideration.

[22] See discussion of these and related matters in L. Stewart and O. F. Warmath, *The Counselor and Society: A Cultural Approach* (Boston: Houghton Mifflin Company, 1965).

to understand themselves better so that they can see more clearly the social implications of their decisions. In so doing he will help youth to identify existing standards and to evaluate the consequences of accepting or rejecting them. But counselors are not hired to use their time with students to propagate personal ideas about the need for social reform, or the desirability of departing from institutionally acceptable behavior. The counselor should discuss such matters and make students aware of his own values when they are important to a particular counselee, but neither of these processes means that he can use the counseling session for propagandizing.

Nothing in the above suggests that the counselor is to become a flunky for the school administration. Indeed, it has been indicated that one of his important functions is to make the administration and faculty aware of changes in school atmosphere and practices which he deems essential for the growth and development of the students. He must remember that the responsibility for all his activities rests upon the administrator, who must justify it to boards of education or regents, the representatives of society.

The adaptive counselor cannot find any procedure which has demonstrated experimentally that it can serve society any more effectively than any other. In his search for evidence on this topic he usually finds little or no consideration of social issues, and only vague suggestions that those who are well counseled will be helpful to, or at least not do harm to, others. He will often find attempts to apply procedures in institutions with which the exponent is insufficiently familiar. Much too frequently he will find counselors elevated to an importance quite out of proportion with their contributions to the institutions in which they are employed. He will recognize that he must help students to cope with the requirements any institution must have, while he encourages as much individuality (but not gross incongruency) as possible. He knows that all individual problems are ultimately social problems, and that society will demand an accounting of his products, not just in terms of his own predilections, but in terms of its objectives.[23] If a counselor cannot adapt to such circumstances he can withdraw from institutional labors and enter into private practice, where his efforts will be evaluated only by his own clients. Society will not be concerned unless his practices are illegal or highly unethical.

Children and youth will probably become more effective adults if they are given more freedom than some school personnel and many par-

---

[23] One of society's objectives may be to change itself. Nothing in this discussion requires that the counselor be a "stand patter," a revolutionary, or any stage between when he is acting as a counselor. Excellent discussions of the relation of the individual to society and to its institutions will be found in D. A. Hanson, ed., *Explorations in Sociology and Counseling* (Boston: Houghton Mifflin Company, 1969).

ents have permitted in the past, but it is also likely that, as the ecologists point out, some limitation to individual freedom is required for survival. If families, schools, and even societies are to be continued, if national security is to be established, cultivation of beauty developed, conservation of talent and resources increased, and equity of opportunity raised, some restriction on doing one's own thing must be set. Counselors work for a society which has such goals and does demand some restrictions, and it has not delegated to counselors the right or privilege to change them. This does not mean that the counselor may not work as a citizen to bring about changes in society. It does suggest that he cannot use his individual contact with children to bring about his own desired changes, or to encourage his counselees to do as they please without consideration of consequences to the family, school, and society in which they function.

The above is not a plea for counselors to be supporters of the status quo. A good counselor recognizes that changes in schools, families, and society are inevitable, but he knows that the forces operating to produce such changes are far beyond his control, and that they will occur regardless of the best efforts of counselors to retard or accelerate them. He will encourage individuality of expression (but not to the point at which it becomes gross incongruity) and freedom of choice (below the level at which it becomes disintegrative). He recognizes that parents have rights and responsibilities, that schools have obligations which require regulations, and that a society which is to improve must have laws. He knows that some of these restrictions will change as new developments occur, and as current inadequacies are recognized. He will certainly be concerned about such matters as a citizen, as a member of a school staff, and as a family member, and his concerns will be reflected in his counseling, whether or not he recognizes their presence. It is essential, however, that he does not use his preferred counseling circumstances to grind personal axes.

SOME LIMITING FACTORS

All counselors of all persuasions are limited in their effectiveness by particular characteristics of individuals and their past circumstances. In the diversity of his cultural experiences, each individual has learned to adapt to other persons in many ways. Each social setting presents models which the individual, through imitation and introception, has adopted in his own life. Each has experienced norms and pressures against which he may have rebelled, has met persons to whom there have been strong attachments or repulsions, and has become familiar with individuals who have been sources of frustration or opportunity. In counseling with persons in whom such varying amounts and shades of experiences are exhibited, a high level of adaptability is essential.

Verbalization

The problems produced by such diverse experiences would be complex enough if counselees could always express their opinions, attitudes, and feelings clearly, but the complexity is increased when attempts are made to verbalize. Abstruseness, understatements, histrionics, metaphors, and hyperbole make many counselees' statements highly questionable. Inadequacy in use of language may result in misunderstanding. And deception or projection by a counselee can distort the perceptions of a counselor, and no single method can provide for such differences in counselee behavior.

For those subjects who verbalize effectively, the adaptive counselor may find that careful listening, with only occasional rephrasing of counselees' statements, may be effective. It may be necessary to help clarify the expression of those who have difficulty in verbalizing by defining words, giving explanations, providing examples, and even by using diagrams and other nonverbal approaches.

Subjects who seem to be understating their position due to lack of confidence may be helped by being given greater assurance that their opinions are worthy of consideration, while those who resort to hyperbole may be cautioned about the possible consequences of exaggeration. Explanations about the inadequacies of analogies in discussing matters of personal concern may be offered to those who depend too greatly on metaphors. It may be necessary to caution counselees who try to deceive their counselors that independent checks on statements may be made because unverified data can lead to faulty decisions. Those who tend to externalize or objectify what are essentially subjective feelings need to be warned about the possible unfortunate consequences of such practices.

At times it is desirable to ask a counselee to write out his ideas and bring the results to an interview on the following day. Some counselees can be helped by being shown how to list the pros and cons of actions they propose to take. Some may be assisted by formulating with them some of the questions they need to ask, and others may be encouraged to practice asking the questions they phrase. Some need to listen to a counselor's sometimes lengthy descriptions, explanations, and interpretations, provided that opportunities are presented to get clarification of what is not completely understood. Some counselees will profit most from talking at length and in words of their own choosing without interruption, while others need counselor reinforcement of their statements.

In the process of coming of age in America, children and youth have learned to react verbally to other individuals in many ways. The adaptive counselor seeks to find the verbal behavior that provides the best opportunity for each counselee to increase his self-understanding. Having found it for a particular counselee, he will adapt his behavior to make maximum use of it, although he will always be alert to changes that may come with new experiences and greater maturity.

Experience

Although chronological age provides a measure of the length of a counselee's exposure to his culture, it does not offer any certain indication of its quality, or of what he has learned. Youth generally tend to be impressionistic, optimistic, self-contradictory, highly unpredictable, and lacking in many experiences simply because there has not been enough time to meet them.[24] Such descriptive terms seem to characterize the total group, but they do not define the extent of differences within a particular group of counselees. They do suggest that each counselee will need some assistance in becoming more realistic and informed about himself and his environments if he is to make choices that are his own, and for which he will take full responsibility. There is little reason to believe that counselees will get enough of the assistance they need simply by talking about themselves or engaging in rather limited counseling sessions devoted to learning problem-solving skills.

The adaptive counselor recognizes that he may have to provide help by arranging for wider experiences, interpreting data, demonstrating, directing the subject to further sources of information, warning about consequences of certain behavior, and arranging for evaluation of performances by persons who are competent in particular areas. Selection of the activities will be an adaptive process governed by both counselor and counselee, analyses of personal circumstances, and culturally induced characteristics. There can probably be no really satisfactory substitutes for maturating experiences, but counselors can, if they are flexible, contribute to maturation. Encouragement of such activities does not imply intent to infringe on the counselee's right to unique self-development, the privilege of making his own decisions, and the freedom to make social adaptations to psychological needs. Indeed, the adaptive counselor will recognize that the cultivation of idiosyncrasy is vital for society, but development of gross incongruencies is to be avoided. He will adapt his procedures to that end.

---

[24] See J. W. M. Rothney, *Educational, Vocational and Social Performances of Counseled and Uncounseled Youth Ten Years After High School*, Cooperative Research Project, SAE 9231 (Washington, D.C.: U.S. Office of Education, 1963); *idem., Guidance Practices and Results* (New York: Harper & Row, Publishers, 1958).

Longitudinal Problems

Too often when persons think of counseling they think of emergency situations in which a problem has become so complex that the student comes voluntarily for help, or is sent to a counselor by someone who recognizes that an acute problem exists. Good counselors do not wait until problems reach the acute stage. They are concerned with the *development* of their counselees, and are aware that, in the process, many problems must arise. They try to anticipate them and to plan ahead so that the problems may be avoided or adroitly met.

Although counseling should be a voluntary process, it seems advisable to inform all students that counselors are available to help them to help themselves. They should also be told that they will be called in occasionally to talk about making important choices and their plans for the future. In no sense is counseling thrust upon them, and they are entitled to choose not to discuss their problems. In any case, the counselor may take advantage of the situation to raise questions that the student may not have thought of asking for himself. The continuity indicated in such practices makes it clear that counseling is not a "one-shot" affair, that all decisions do not have to be made on the spur of the moment, and that preparation for decisions might be made on the basis of previous experiences and expected developments.

The adaptive counselor considers a counselee's life as a single, connected whole, and recognizes that the events which are of concern in current interviews have developed in chronological order. This order must be understood if there is to be real understanding of current behavior and adequate consideration of the future.

When one turns to the study of a counselee over a period of time it is often found that certain current modes of behavior have been stimulated by past events. Even though the current behavior seems to be primarily related to present circumstances, it is unlikely that it can be divorced from experiences which have preceded it. Anything that has influenced a counselee's behavior previously may be important in his current counseling because its previous influence always raises the probability of its recurrence. The counselor who decides that it is not essential to get longitudinal data because a counselee's current problem behavior seems to be caused by a recent personality clash with a particular teacher overlooks the fact that he may have had conflicts with similar personalities before. What appears to be an immediate causal factor may be the product of a long developmental pattern of response to a category of individuals rather than to a particular person.

The adaptive counselor cannot ignore fluctuations in behavior which have occurred during the development of a counselee. If he has gone through a period of retardation, he may be influenced by that (regardless of current successes) because he remembers the previous consequences. Reactions to very successful experiences are not likely to be forgotten either, even in a period of failure and frustration. The influence on a counselee of self or others' comparisons of current to previous performances, and the expectations which have developed therefrom, cannot be ignored at any time. Behavior consistency (or the lack of it) may be as important to the counselor as the complete description of any current event. A pattern of cyclic behavior may predict later activity if the counselee's current location in a developmental pattern can be determined. The cycle may hold even if there is intervention in the form of counseling. If the counseling is composed of the rather brief treatments described in reports of the behavioral and client-centered schools, it may result in only minor and momentary changes in the counselee's developmental pattern.

The adaptive counselor recognizes that as his subjects increase in age their counseling needs to be changed; techniques which were suitable at one stage will be wholly inadequate at a later time. Occasionally the solution of one problem raises others to be solved. The student who, as the result of efforts by himself, his counselors, and his teachers now finds academic pursuits to be challenging is faced with the problem of financing post-high school education—something which had not concerned him until he changed. The youth who had withdrawn from other students, and subsequently responds to a counselor's efforts to help him to overcome his fear of peers, meets a new problem when his enthusiasm for group activities results in neglect of school work. Each of these situations requires much self-assessment and the learning of problem-solving skills, but the activities of the counselor vary significantly in the different situations.

Lack of longitudinal data in the reports of advocates of both the behavioral counseling and client-centered schools is particularly distressing to those who recognize that counselors are concerned with human development, and who recognize that change is characteristic of a healthy human organism. Insufficient histories of their counselees' development and lack of long-term follow-through data suggest that they consider knowledge of the previous and future development of persons as unimportant or nonessential. The adaptive counselor, in his search for patterns preceding and following his work with his subjects and his adaptation to changes as they occur, gives full consideration to his subjects' histories and futures, and recognizes that none of their pre- and post-counseling patterns are identical.

SUMMARY

It has been suggested in this chapter that adaptive school counseling is not simply an eclectic procedure. Those who practice adaptation go beyond what advocates of the various systems propose as necessary and desirable. Such counseling requires adaptation *to* individual differences, not adoption (as in eclecticism) *of* advocates' points of view. Even when an adaptive school counselor's practices are similar to those employed by members of a specialized counseling system, they may be used for different reasons, with different subjects, and with broader goals in mind.

School circumstances define the populations with whom the counselor works. The limitations (and opportunities) imposed by such definition do not permit the kind of selection of subjects available to clinicians and university experimenters. The variety of individual differences met in attempting to provide counsel for total school populations prevent the counselor from employing only one method.

Consideration has been given to restrictions imposed by society and its institutions on a counselor's freedom to act solely on his own predilections. He is a helper in an institution rather than an institution in himself, and his effectiveness will be assessed in terms of the extent to which he helps the school reach its objectives.

Limitations to a counselor's effectiveness are caused by counselees' lack of verbal facility, quantity and quality of experiences, and the changes that occur as students mature. It has been suggested that counselors can increase their effectiveness by careful assessment of such characteristics and adaptation of procedures to provide for them.

Selected References

MILLER, C. *Foundations of Guidance*. New York: Harper & Row, Publishers, 1961. One of the most scholarly books in this field. Historical and philosophical backgrounds are considered effectively.

STEWART, L. and O. F. WARMATH. *The Counselor and Society: A Cultural Approach*. Boston: Houghton Mifflin Company, 1965. An excellent view of social obligations in counseling, including challenges to counselors to consider that their work goes beyond merely fitting persons into current social patterns.

TYLER, Leona E. *The Work of the Counselor*. New York: Appleton-Century-Crofts, 1969. The writer considers this book to be the best one in the field. The discussion is well-organized and stimulating. Research reports are analyzed and presented in meaningful fashion. This is essential reading for those who plan to counsel. It is essentially adaptive in approach, although that term is not employed.

VAN HOOSE, W. H. and J. J. PIETROFESA, eds. *Counseling and Guidance in the Twentieth Century: Reflections and Reformulations.* Boston: Houghton Mifflin Company, 1970. Essays by 23 persons selected by the American Personnel and Guidance Association as widely recognized leading contributors in the field. Generally they cover major issues in counseling and guidance. Among the features of the volume are the autobiographies written by the contributors. Some of them are more revealing than the essays. A *must* book for students in counseling.

WRENN, C. G. *The Counselor in a Changing World.* Washington, D.C.: American Personnel and Guidance Association, 1962. A statement about the influence of social change on counselees and their counselors by an observer who was given an unique opportunity to look at the situation and recommend changes.

CHAPTER 4

techniques of
adaptive counseling

Since writers in the counseling area have been more concerned with techniques than with other aspects of a counselor's work, an abundance of treatises on how to counsel is available. Many of them are excellent if one accepts the assumptions on which they are based.[1] Since adaptive counseling requires modification of some techniques and consideration of others whose limitations have not been adequately presented, brief comments on them are presented below.

USE OF TECHNIQUES

Compilation of Data

Adaptive counselors try to get as much information as possible about a counselee's past. This procedure has commonly been labeled *diagnosis*, and advocates of some schools of thought often reject it as unnecessary. Others consider it undesirable because it tends to encourage the placing

[1] Jane Warters, *Techniques of Counseling* (New York: McGraw-Hill Book Company, 1964); Leona E. Tyler, *The Work of the Counselor* (New York: Appleton-Century-Crofts, 1969); A. E. Traxler, *Techniques of Guidance* (New York: Harper & Row, Publishers, 1957); R. H. Byrne, *The School Counselor* (Boston: Houghton Mifflin Company, 1963); J. W. M. Rothney, *Methods of Studying the Individual Child: The Psychological Case Study* (Waltham, Mass.: Ginn/Blaisdell, 1968).

74

of persons into categories which serve no useful function. Procuring case history material need not, however, result in categorization. It can provide evidence about individual patterns of behavior exhibited by the counselee in the past, and which may be of considerable significance in attempts to understand current acts. From separate bits of longitudinal data it is possible to derive a tentative conception of the development of a counselee as a whole. When that has been achieved, the counselor may begin to understand the parts which he observes. By making critical and orderly analyses which check undue credulousness, weigh single items, and examine their etiology, he may understand internal relationships better, which may in turn help him to recognize the unity of the individual. It would be unfortunate if such procedures resulted in the attachment of a label that signified a general categorization. They should rather result in the highlighting of a counselee's individuality, which is the only reason for making the case history.

The case history approach tends to discourage the practice of depending almost entirely on what the subject says in a counseling session. It seems unlikely that even the most skillful interviewer can expect to draw from comments made during interviews any more than questionable inferences about a subject's behavior when he is not in the counselor's presence. Some validation of such inferences may be achieved by collection of data, as illustrated in the record described below.

A counselor had worked with *Red,* who is described below, throughout his first years of high school, and had accumulated a great deal of information about him from interviews and other sources. He was quite sure that *Red* would drop in to see him early in the senior year, if for no other reason than that he liked to talk to anyone who would listen. He was also quite sure that *Red* would want to talk over his post-high school plans. To refresh his memory about the patterns of behavior *Red* had exhibited previously, the counselor drew up the following summary from his records.

I. Usual behavior

1. Described by his teachers as feeling secure in, and accepted by, groups of which he was a part.
2. Teachers reported that he was variable in his influence on activities of others, but did exercise some leadership in areas of interest to him.
3. Listed friends who he said would consider him "O.K."
4. Referred frequently to friends when discussing any topics.
5. Seemed to like everyone and suggested that they all liked him.
6. Described by former counselor as a "breezy, friendly fellow with wide grin."

7. Was chosen manager of school teams by his associates.
8. Carried on most activities with others.
9. *Only one significant variation from the above appeared.* A mathematics teacher reported that he showed some anxiety about his standing in groups.

II. Performances

A. Academic areas

1. C-minus student over past three years.
2. Teachers reported that he was persistent in completing assignments only when especially interested—otherwise needed prodding.
3. Described by one teacher as "lazy, more interested in football and hunting than in school work."
4. Test performances generally low average.

B. Cocurricular areas

1. Lineman on A football team.
2. Manager of two school teams.

C. Occupational areas

1. Held major job as assistant to athletic director.
2. Enjoyed job as helper to agricultural engineer during summer vacations.

D. Significant variations from the above

1. A grades in physical education.
2. Incomplete final mark in English because assignments were not completed. This incomplete still on his record at the end of his junior year. He cannot graduate without removing it.
3. D grade in world history last year.
4. High score on word fluency test and low score on spatial relations test.

III. Individuality

1. Unusually tall and husky.
2. Red hair.
3. Wide grin.
4. Friendly, pleasing manner.
5. Questionable realism about post-school plans. He spoke about going

to a very demanding university to undertake a difficult course in engineering.

6. Likes to sing and to hear singing.

IV. Flexibility

1. He did not improve his school performances after he had indicated many times that he would try to do so.
2. Information about low test scores did not influence his consistency in choice of career.
3. Teachers reported similar behavior in areas of responsibility, social adjustability, influence, and social concern over three-year period.
4. Similar breezy, friendly manner observed during all his school years.

V. Environmental assets

1. Comfortable home situation with only two minor and temporary sources of friction with parents (Church and scout troop attendance).
2. Enough financial support for current and post-high school education.
3. Opportunity to join father in well-established hardware business immediately after high school.
4. Sound health.

VI. Environmental limitations

1. Has not yet learned the relationship between academic performances and occupational requirements. (Wants to go into demanding college, then into engineering despite low high school performances).
2. Is encouraged by friend who is succeeding in same post-high school plans and who urges Red to follow. (Friend made brilliant academic record and high test scores).
3. Has so many friends and invitations to participate in nonschool activities which interfere with doing homework.
4. Has not learned adequate study skills.
5. Can rely on place in father's business if current goals are not reached. This provides a cushion for him because he knows that if he fails in any other activities he can always go back home and work in father's store.

Study of the record will indicate that the data were collected and summarized in an attempt to get as much information as possible on the following six questions about his behavior when he was not in the counselor's presence:

1. What has been his usual behavior with other persons?
2. How has he performed on assigned and self-chosen activities?
3. What is outstanding about him that distinguishes him from other counselees?
4. What assets in his environment must be considered in his counseling?
5. What limitations or handicaps in his environment has he met and is likely to continue to meet?
6. What do his patterns of past behavior suggest about the likelihood of change in his behavior? (Note that this is simply an inference which is subject to error.)

With the answers to such important questions in mind, the counselor need not spend his limited interview time in collecting and collating information that can be obtained by clerks or subprofessional assistants. He will want to use some interview time to find out how the subject *feels* about the data, but this is quite different from collection of them. The data may suggest the personalized adaptations which may be necessary in counseling a subject. It is always possible, of course, that previous patterns of behavior have been discarded or outgrown. In such cases the counselor will have obtained important information concerning significant variation from previous behavior. Having happened once, there is always the possibility that it may occur again.

The adaptive counselor, unlike proponents of some schools of thought, recognizes that he needs much information about other than interview behavior if he is going to serve a counselee well. He knows that self-reports offered in the interview can be highly self-deceptive, and that the possibility of conscious or unconscious misrepresentation must always be considered. Verbalizations, as noted previously, can distort, and memories may be faulty. Obtaining data from other than interview sources, whether or not it is labeled diagnosis, can reduce the excessive credulousness to which counselors of some persuasions seem to be prone.

Use of Tests in Adaptive Counseling

Just as the counselor adapts his counseling procedures to provide for individual differences, he adjusts his testing program to the same end. His first step in such adaptation is elimination of wholesale testing of all members of student bodies by massive batteries of tests which produce great quantities of data that he cannot possibly interpret meaningfully to the counselee, his parents, or his teachers.[2] He will instead use a test only

[2] Some test batteries, such as the College Entrance Examination Boards, may be required of large numbers of students, and the scores may be quite useful to a counselor in certain circumstances, but obtaining such scores may be a duty assigned

when he and his counselee decide that a score may be of some value in answering questions which have arisen in the process of trying to get better (but never complete) self-understanding. This procedure need not require individual tests such as the Binet or Wechsler, but it may entail group tests taken alone, or with a small group of subjects who have similar needs for the kinds of information which test scores may provide. No testing will be done until a counselor and his counselee see a clear and present need for the information the score provides.

The excessive use of tests and employment of instruments designed to measure inventory preferences and interests which has characterized the guidance movement has been brought about by many factors.[3] These factors include an amazing psychometric innocence on the part of test users; naïveté in considering the counseling task to be a short-term affair rather than a complex longitudinal problem; mistaken faith in statistics on the part of test and inventory producers and consumers; expediency; a desire to be like others who use them for any of the above reasons; and the hucksterism of test salesmen. It may also be due in part to the psychological support which counselors, working in a relatively new area and without assurance of their effectiveness, derive from the seeming accuracy of the numbers which the instruments provide. The results obtained from widespread use of tests and inventories have provided evidence of their inadequacy in doing what counselors had been led to think they could do, and it now seems time to use them with more discretion and selectivity. If counselors show that they have learned enough about the limited utility of tests and inventories in counseling, and therefore exercise sophistication and discrimination in purchasing them, they could be potent forces in the improvement of test construction.

There is considerable evidence that tests can be used with a limited degree of effectiveness by persons who are concerned with the selection of groups of individuals (as, for example, in choosing a freshman class for a college, or a corps of workers for some industries), but this is not a counselor's function. The differences between testing for counseling and testing for placement is indicated in Table 4–1.

---

to the vice-principal of the school. When batteries of tests are to be given for use by officials in assessing total school performances, those persons who are to use the results should be responsible for test selection, administration, and interpretation. These are not primary aspects of counseling and the counselor should not be expected to do any more than other faculty members in assisting with mass testing programs.

[3] See the critical review of the Strong Vocational Blank and the Minnesota Vocational Interest Inventory, "Review of the Strong Vocational Interest Inventory" by J. W. M. Rothney, in *Journal of Counseling Psychology*, XIV, No. 2 (1967). Reviews of many tests and inventories will also be found in O. K. Buros, *Mental Measurements Yearbooks* (Highland Park, N.J.: Gryphon Press, several years).

TABLE 4–1

Testing for Counseling or Selection

TESTING FOR COUNSELING (SCHOOLS)	TESTING FOR SELECTION (INDUSTRY, MILITARY, ADMISSION TO COLLEGE)
Concern with *all* members of a particular situation, i.e., all students in a given school regardless of range of performances and characteristics.	Concern with *limited* numbers of applicants for work or study within a specific organization.
Unique concern with one individual at a time. Counseling is an individual affair. Averages or percentages or success are of little comfort to those who are not successful.	Testing that improves over chance selection pays off in terms of the institution's primary concern.
Same obligation to all students. Individually, they are very much present and a working part of school organizations. Counselors cannot turn them away.	In a sense, no obligation to any applicant, and especially none to those not selected. Future or next steps of those rejected require no further contact, or the formulation of alternate plans.
Students are going into a future the dimensions of which are not known. Counselors work with many variables and with many unpredictables.	Selection made into a defined situation.
Concern with the individual for his own sake, his worth as an individual, *his* successes.	Not concerned with individual as such— *who* gets in not as important as getting enough in.
Many variables in persons and situations appear over a long period of time. Demands of society and differences in the definition of success by society do not permit many generally accepted definitions of success.	Selection testing can prove itself over the long run. It is effective if more successes than failures are picked.

Source: Abstracted from J. W. M. Rothney, P. J. Danielson, and R. A. Heimann, *Measurement for Guidance* (New York: Harper & Row, Publishers, 1959).

In this volume the reader has been constantly reminded that his function is to serve individuals as individuals, and that he is not employed primarily as a selector for industry or advanced educational institutions. If he does the first task well the selective processes may be improved. It will also be noted that the adaptive counselor will be working primarily with so-called "normal" cases in the setting of the American school, rather than with pathological, "clinical," or "disturbed" cases in hospitals, or with applicants for employment in an industrial setting. It is implied that his effectiveness with normals in the school situation may sometimes be improved by use of tests.

Much good counseling can be done without use of tests; there is evidence that it was done centuries before standardized tests were available. If all tests were currently eliminated from counseling it is unlikely that society would recognize the change for many years. Business would go on, schools would continue, and millions of young persons would be satisfied with their choices of training, occupation, marriage partners, and leisure-time activities. Research in education, guidance, and psychology has not conclusively demonstrated that the use of tests has increased the welfare or productivity of significant numbers of persons, despite the fact that millions of them are used annually. There is some evidence that they may be of occasional assistance in answering the questions of persons who score at the extremes of test distributions, but they do not provide final answers. They may help such persons in working out probabilities, odds, or best bets in general, on the average, on the whole, and other things being equal (which they never are). In this manner they may become valuable sources of supplementary information about students.

It seems likely that tests will be useful in counseling only insofar as they have been selected for use in answering *specific* questions of *particular* counselees. Since certain kinds of questions, such as those that refer to reading performances, are likely to be asked by many subjects, it may be desirable to administer a reading test to large groups of subjects. Except in seeking answers to commonly asked questions, however, testing is likely to be most useful when a plan of tailoring the testing program to individual cases is employed. For example, it would be a considerable waste of time and money to give a so-called mechanical aptitude test to all students in a general public high school, because only a small sample of the counselees, their parents, potential employers, or school personnel will raise questions about their mechanical performances. Some benefit may be obtained by testing those about whom such questions are raised individually or in small groups.

The above statements were designed to suggest to the reader that, with a few exceptions, testing for counseling is a *differential,* not a *mass,* procedure. Testing will be focused on particular individuals, and tests will be selected when there is a specific question to be answered and other sources do not provide the answers. "When in doubt, punt," says the football coach; "when in doubt, lead trump," says the bridge player. Though neither is an infallible rule, the counselor may take a cue from them and decide that "When in doubt, test."

It is assumed that readers of this volume are familiar with many of the tests commonly used in schools, and no attempt is made to describe them in detail here. The reader who needs a review of tests and testing procedures is referred to several books.[4] Some of the cautions to counselors

[4] J. W. M. Rothney, P. J. Danielson, and R. A. Heimann, *Measurement for Guidance* (New York: Harper & Row, Publishers, 1959); L. Goldman, *Using Tests in Counseling* (New York: Appleton-Century-Crofts, 1961); J. W. M. Rothney, *Methods of Studying the Individual Child, op. cit.;* L. J. Cronbach, *Essentials of*

which derive from the study of tests and testing procedures appear below. Counselors should not:

1. Confuse *testing* the performance of counselees with *inventorying* feelings, attitudes, interests, and what are often called personality traits. (Although inventories look like tests, they are *not* tests, and their authors do not offer sufficient evidence that they do what is claimed.)
2. Set up some mythical level of ability from a test score and expect a student to work up to that level at all times in all areas of study.
3. Compare pupils' scores with norms given for the test unless there is reason to believe that cultural circumstances are similar.
4. Give so many tests that no one has time to interpret them individually to counselees, their parents, and their teachers.
5. Be misled by test titles. Study of the items will often reveal that the christening of the instrument has concealed its true nature. The items in the test must be examined.
6. Expect too much from tests. They do not measure all of the school's objectives, and they provide only a small sample of what they do measure.
7. Use a test simply because others do so. The counselor uses only those which serve to answer particular questions raised by specific individuals.
8. Be taken in by the term "reliability." It has a special meaning in testing and measurement that is more limited than its dictionary meaning.

The golden age of testing may have passed, but perhaps a new one that will offer real assistance to students is about to emerge. Early hopes that testing instruments would be developed that could indicate precisely the occupation or educational experience for which an individual was best fitted, or those activities with which he would be most satisfied, have not been realized.[5] Disillusionment of some counselors has not, however, reduced the production of tests and inventories, and the search for quick test answers to complex questions goes on at such a pace that a high school senior may spend as many as ten days of his school year in taking tests. The adaptive counselor, recognizing the need for adapting his test procedures to suit particular counselee's needs, will not reject all testing, as proposed by proponents of some schools of counseling, nor will he join the ranks of those who urge the administration of many instruments. In test-

---

Psychological Testing (New York: Harper & Row, Publishers, 1960); R. H. Baurenfend, *Building a School Testing Program* (Boston: Houghton Mifflin Company, 1963); Buros, *Mental Measurements Yearbooks, op. cit.* Several years, including the latest in 1965. This volume contains reviews of tests and inventories.

[5] C. L. Hull, *Aptitude Testing* (Yonkers-on-Hudson, N.Y.: World Book Co., 1928). Hull wrote: "We may look forward with confidence to a day not far distant when some such system [combining of aptitude test scores by machines for predicting occupational fitness] will be operating in every large school system. Then, and not until then, will there be possible a genuine vocational guidance for the masses of the people."

ing, as in all other phases of his work, he does what his study of each counselee dictates. If this means that no tests will be used in some cases, and
many will be given in others, he behaves accordingly. But there will be no
scores in his files that have not been interpreted individually to his counselees.

It has been suggested above that an adaptive counselor may use tests
effectively if they have been chosen carefully and interpreted to counselees
who sought answers to particular questions. In making interpretations it
is essential that the counselor avoid the semantic trap produced by the
titles with which test authors christen their instruments.[6] Perhaps nothing
has caused more mischief in the testing movement than the concept that
one can measure an entity called aptitude or ability, which designates a
level of performance which a student is expected to achieve at all times.
It has become common practice to compare a student's performance on
such tests with his day-by-day achievements and, on the basis of that comparison, to label him as an under- or overachiever. If he is designated as
an underachiever, censorial terms implying character faults or moral shortcomings (lazy, irresponsible, and so on) are applied to him.

Aptitude, ability, and the so-called intelligence tests do not measure
entities that can be labeled. Tests only provide a measure of a subject's
performance on tasks set by the test maker. Going beyond the term "performance" and inferring from the score an entity such as aptitude or ability places one in a precarious area. Just why this is so commonly done is
difficult to determine, but it can probably be traced to errors by pioneers
of the testing movement and to the tactics of test publishers, who can sell
more tests if counselors believe that aptitude and achievement tests measure
quite different functions.[7] The difference in use of tests by a counselor who
uses the terms "aptitude" and "ability" and one who prefers to consider test
scores only as evidence of performance may be illustrated by consideration
of the following situation:

> Jim, an eleventh grader, tells the counselor that after he finishes
> high school he wants to go to a university to prepare for a career
> in engineering, and he asks for more information about the occu-
> pation and his fitness for it. Among other things, the counselor
> shows Jim that engineering training will require high level per-
> formances in mathematics, and he suggests that Jim might profit
> from interpretation of test scores in that field. He arranges for the

---

[6] An interesting illustration of labeling may be found in a widely used battery
of tests. One of the tests in the series contains items in arithmetic that any teacher
would recognize as a test of *achievement* in that subject. It is labeled as a test of
numerical *ability*, but it is one part of a battery labeled *aptitude* tests.

[7] For good discussions of such issues see A. G. Wesman, "Intelligent Testing,"
American Psychologist, XXIII, No. 4 (1968), and P. J. Rulon, "On the Concepts
of Growth and Ability," *Harvard Educational Review*, XVII (1947).

test to be taken and Jim returns the next day for the test interpretation.[8] His score is found to be slightly below the national average for students of his grade.

A counselor who believed in the aptitude entity concept might inform Jim that he doesn't have the mathematical aptitude or ability necessary for success in engineering. Since neither the counselor nor the counselee would really know what the words meant, the information would probably not be helpful.

The counselor who knows that tests measure performance only could draw from Jim's score the three following possible courses of action and discuss them with him.

Jim could give up his idea of entering a field in which high level performances in mathematics are required.

or

The counselor could show Jim (from his follow-up records of previous counselees) that persons who scored low on mathematics tests did not usually succeed in engineering training. (He would *not* say that Jim could not succeed because the group results could not be applied to a particular individual.)

or

Jim could be told that the test measured his performance up to that time, but that performances may change. He might then suggest specific ways in which he might go about trying to improve his performances.

The illustration shows how test information may be used to help in decision making. Information and suggestions are offered, but Jim still must make the decision. It does, however, go beyond the mere description of technique and into some basic questions about a counselor's function. If the entity approach is used, and tests are thought of as measuring some innate and unchangeable characteristic, the counselor's job simply becomes one of sorting counselees into categories—a reversion to the idea of putting the square peg in the square hole. However, if the performance concept is accepted, the counselor recognizes that he has some responsibility to help in the shaping of the peg and, hopefully, the shaping of the hole. Instead of acting merely as a sorter he becomes a professional, with the obligations and responsibilities that such status requires.

---

[8] Of course, a decision of this importance would not be based upon a score from one test.

Counselors should acknowledge that tests, regardless of the labels on them, measure only what an individual has learned, and that rates and kinds of learning may vary as circumstances are altered. When they do so they will drop from their language such terms as aptitude, ability, and intelligence, and discard the procedure of labeling students on the basis of test scores. The term "underachiever" will never be heard in their domains.

The Adaptive Counselor as a Consultant to Teachers

The term "counselor-consultant" has recently become very popular. Actually the words denote activities which adaptive counselors have performed for many years,[9] doing what is implied in the definition of counseling which appears on page 53 of this volume.

Since students spend some 20 per cent of their waking hours of each year in school, teachers must have significant influence upon their behavior. When the student leaves the counselor he returns to the classrooms or activities in which his teachers, regardless of their methods, are the dominant individuals. Their positions permit them to become supporters or denigrators of counseling, and hence potent influences on its effectiveness. A counselor who ignores or deprecates teachers loses the support of potentially effective coworkers, and risks sabotage of his own efforts.

In the past an unfortunate schism between teachers and counselors often developed because counselors tended to criticize teachers for being too subject-matter oriented, for becoming so concerned with groups that individuals were said to be neglected, and for being too autocratic in their classrooms. Much discussion of counselor activity was (and to an unfortunate extent still is) given over to descriptions of ways of helping students to develop *despite* what is said to be the negative influence of teachers. Instead of considering all school staff members as valuable coworkers in the guidance enterprise (as a good adaptive counselor does), there is a tendency for advocates of some schools of thought to ignore them, and for others to use them as pawns to be manipulated in furtherance of activities which they have decided are desirable.[10] Both of these approaches are certain pathways to ineffectiveness and consequent frustration.

All school personnel have had extensive preparation for their work. Many have advanced degrees and must be recognized as specialists in their own areas. As teacher preparation and in-service education programs improve, teachers learn more about development of persons and the learning

[9] See J. W. M. Rothney and B. A. Roens, *Guidance of American Youth* (Cambridge, Mass.: Harvard University Press, 1951). Chap. III contains descriptions of work with teachers (currently described as counselor-consultant activities) carried on from 1936 to 1941.

[10] See, for example, Verne Faust, *The Counselor-Consultant in the Elementary School* (Boston: Houghton Mifflin Company, 1968).

process and become more competent in providing for individual differences in their classrooms. In view of such developments, one must stand aghast at the self-assurance with which some counselors (at the instigation of some counselor-educators) propose to tell teachers how and what they will teach, and how they are to build "effective learning climates and whole new worlds for children." [11] Counselors with two years or less of training should not profess to be human relations experts and behavioral scientists who expect teachers to abridge their own expertise and defer to a counselor's judgment. Members of a school staff are not likely to respect the recommendations of a counselor who does not recognize their competence in the fields in which they have had preparation. They are quite aware that counselors have not been given a mandate to make over our schools. Coercion of school personnel by regulations about credit accumulation, or wooing them with meager financial awards to participate in training programs directed by counselors, are not likely to result in significant changes in their practices.

But teachers are interested in the development of their students. If counselors are willing to work with them as equals and to respect their special competencies, they can become contributing members to a guidance team. Counselors must not tell teachers how to manage their classrooms, but they may offer suggestions about work with particular students based on intensive individual study. For example, if the counselor feels that a bright student will profit from such activities as independent study or taking college courses while still in high school, he is obligated to discuss such matters with the proper teachers. It is not his responsibility or even his right to suggest to a teacher that she abandon or alter drastically her general teaching techniques. Of course, when a counselor offers suggestions about work with a particular student, he may hope that there will be transfer of concern for the one to others who might profit from individualized attention.

The suggestion that counselors begin their work with a teacher by calling attention to the needs of a particular student is based on evidence that presentation of generalizations about individual differences in student behavior is not likely to result in provision for the development of a particular student. Deluged by lectures, pamphlets, and general reports about pupils which end in exhortations to provide for individual differences, teachers may see no relation of the generalized statements to their own situations, or recognize any of their pupils in the descriptions or presentations of averages. A counselor who has spent considerable time with a counselee, has given him such tests as seemed necessary, has interviewed his parents, and has taken time to combine his data from several sources,

11 *Ibid.*

may convince the teacher that his concern is genuine and that the recommendations he brings are based upon sound knowledge. When the teacher recognizes his concern and competence, cooperation is likely to be forthcoming, and the consultant role of the counselor may be implemented.

Counseling with Parents

Observation of the practices of proponents of some schools of counseling indicates that they believe their goals can be reached by working only with the individual concerned, and see no need to counsel with his teachers and parents. Members of other schools of thought do work with parents when they think it necessary, but seem to consider them as objects of the counselor's bidding who are to be programmed to perform the tasks which he assigns. Neither the belief that an individual is totally and solely capable of making his own choices and accepting full responsibility for them, nor the employment of practices which imply that parents are to be conditioned to carry out a counselor's mandates (subtly defined as "being cooperative") seem likely to result in effective counseling.

Counseling of parents is essential when the counselor works with minors.[12] Parents are held legally and financially responsible for their children's behavior, and most of them care about their adjustments, performances, and decisions. Some parents may be ill-informed, biased, and confused by the generation gap, but others are knowledgeable, open-minded, and in tune with the times.

The welfare of all members of a family can be influenced by the behavior of any member of it, and the family situation, in turn, may affect the behavior of a minor child. In view of such interdependence, failure to counsel a student's parents would seem an unconscionable error. Consider, for example, the following situation:

> A high school student began to use drugs, became addicted, and in order to support his habit he became a pusher. He was apprehended by police and after a lengthy delay and trial he was sentenced to a long prison term. During the pre-trial period he was given intensive and expensive medical treatment. The total financial outlay for the trial and treatment was so great that the younger children in the family were deprived of funds for their post-high school education, the home mortgage had to be re-financed, and

---

12 Only three references to counseling with parents are cited among the hundreds of research reports on guidance and counseling in C. E. Thoresen, ed., Guidance and Counseling *Review of Educational Research*, XXXIX (Washington, D.C.: American Educational Research Association, 1969). Only three references on the same topic appear in W. H. Van Hoose and J. J. Pietrofesa, eds., *Counseling and Guidance in the Twentieth Century: Reflections and Formulations* (Boston: Houghton Mifflin Company, 1970) which contains chapters by 22 leaders in the field.

the family living standards were reduced significantly. But even these severe financial strains on the parents and siblings seemed minor compared to the acute mental suffering of all members of the family.

An unfortunate aspect of this case was the fact that when the boy first began to use drugs he had told his counselor about it. At that time they decided that the parents were not to be informed and that they would try to work out the problem in counseling sessions. There is, of course, no assurance that a cooperative effort which involved concurrent parental counseling would have averted the disastrous consequences, but it seems that it might have reduced the likelihood of its occurrence.

The case material above follows the perhaps unfortunate custom of resorting to unusual and highly emotionally-charged situations to illustrate counselors' activities.[13] The following brief description of developmental work with a youth indicates that counselors may work effectively with parents in noncrisis-centered circumstances:

When John was a ninth grader his counselor noted that he showed promise of high intellectual performances. Inquiries directed to his teachers revealed that they, too, had observed superior performances, and a study of records compiled in previous years indicated that, although he had not been given any special consideration, his potentiality had long been recognized.

John's parents were poor and since his father had little education and no particular vocational skills there seemed to be little possibility of change in the family's financial circumstances. The home contained few conveniences or refinements and there was no place in which the children could find a suitable spot for study. No books or magazines were available and the family did not even take a daily newspaper. Additional evidence of poverty and lack of intellectual stimulation was available.

When the counselor met with John's parents he showed them the information which he had accumulated and tried to show them his interpretation of it. He offered suggestions about how the environment might be enriched without large expenditures of additional funds, and discussed the idea that John would probably want to go on to post-high school education. Throughout the remaining school years counseling of the parents was carried on concurrently with that offered to John and his teachers. Neither of these persons was coerced, conscripted, or (unless suggestions were sought) told what he should do. Gradually the parents showed that they wanted to help by such activities as building a place for quiet study, bringing home a newspaper from the father's place of employment, giving books to the children for Christmas presents, and putting away a small sum each month to meet the expense of

[13] Unfortunate because it suggests that counselors work primarily with persons who exhibit unusual or even bizarre behavior.

future education. They found the activities to be (in the language of one school of thought) self-actualizing for themselves and they proved to be highly rewarding, as follow-up data obtained many years later revealed, for John.

In the above illustration *both* parents were counseled. Two rather conclusive studies by Hays [14] and Mueller [15] indicate that substantial disagreements among triads composed of mother, father, and student are common when characteristics of students and desirability of decisions are discussed. The link among parents, teachers, and students in a school system is the counselor, and he may play an important part when such disagreements appear. Effective student behavior in the area of human relations may depend on the extent to which the counselor can work effectively and cooperatively with members of a family. Even when parents and children are in agreement, he may serve a useful function as a stimulator of discussion of issues that must always be considered in an adolescent's planning.

Studies by Camp,[16] Jessell,[17] and Henjum [18] have demonstrated that when counselors get to know students well, share their information with both parents, and discuss possible courses of action indicated by their data, parents are likely to work out effective plans with their children. When Camp asked the 98 pairs of parents in his study about the desirability of a counselor sharing his information and suggesting several possibilities for action, all of them reported that they had found the experiences to be valuable. When the students were asked about their reaction to parent conferences (they had been informed each time they met the counselor that there would be sharing of information with parents), a large majority approved the practice. The conclusions of all those who have carried on studies in parent-counselor conferences indicate that parents want them and students generally approve of them. Conferences were most likely to result in effective action if the counselor knew the student well and had suggested trial of some procedures.

Despite all the research findings, there appears to be a commonly-held belief among counselors and counselor educators that they should

14 D. G. Hays and J. W. M. Rothney, "Educational Decision-making by Superior Secondary School Students and Their Parents," *Personnel and Guidance Journal,* XL (1961).

15 W. J. Mueller and J. W. M. Rothney, "Comparisons of Selected Descriptive and Predictive Statements of Superior Students, Their Parents, and Their Teachers," *Personnel and Guidance Journal,* XXXVIII (1960).

16 W. L. Camp and J. W. M. Rothney, "Parental Response to Counselors' Suggestions," *School Counselor,* XVII (1970).

17 J. C. Jessell and J. W. M. Rothney, "The Effectiveness of Parent-Counselor Conferences," *Personnel and Guidance Journal,* XLIV (1965).

18 R. J. Henjum and J. W. M. Rothney, "Parental Action on Counselors' Suggestions," *Vocational Guidance Quarterly,* VIII, No. 1 (1969).

not share "confidential information" about students with their parents.[19] This belief needs to be questioned. If parents discover that a counselor is not telling the whole story when he is conferring with them, two essential members of the guidance team will probably be alienated. Even if he doesn't lose them they may feel that they, too, should withhold information, and the counselor may find that he is dealing with incomplete data. An announced and implemented policy can eliminate the idea of "telling tales" on the counselee. The sharing practice may reduce a counselor's effectiveness temporarily with a few students, but it is likely to result in more desirable relationships than can be obtained when parents suspect that information is being withheld. The concept of withholding confidential information was developed when counseling in schools was devoted largely to salvage and repair. It has no place in adaptive and developmental counseling. Some discretion may be necessary in choosing the time at which information is to be shared, and parents may have to be educated in its use, but education of the parents followed by full sharing of information is likely to be more effective in achieving counseling goals than the withholding of data because of possible misuse.

An unfortunate consequence of the practice of withholding information from parents may be seen in the results of several studies of parental conceptions of counselors' roles. In general, researchers in this area find important differences between what parents and counselors think the role should be. The consequences of failure to do something about the differences may be tragic for the counseling movement. Parents are usually taxpayers, and as such they determine ultimately whether or not counseling is to be offered in schools. When counselors do not share their information and purposes, parents must get their ideas of the counselor's role from less informed sources, and erroneous conceptions are inevitable. It seems likely that these would be eliminated, or at least minimized significantly, if counselors adopted the practice of full sharing of information and ideas with parents of minor children.

The case for parental counseling must not rest merely on the fact that they are taxpayers. Parents can make contributions that no one else can provide to the information needed about a counselee. They can describe patterns of their child's development; reactions to norms and pressures he has met; frustrations and opportunities he has experienced; persons to whom he has showed strong attachment or repulsion; and the models which through imitation and introception he has adopted. Only parents can provide dependable information about financial matters when expendi-

---

[19] The mistaken idea that students do not want their parents to have conferences with school personnel probably stems from the fact that adolescents' parents have not usually been interviewed unless the student was in trouble.

ture of funds is required to further the counselee's plans. The adaptive counselor cannot afford to neglect such potentially valuable sources of information in the belief that he can discover these things solely through the counselee. He considers counseling as a team task with the parents as essential contributors.[20] In the next decades counselors can place no item higher on their agenda than parent-counselor conferences.[21]

Group Guidance [22]

Society makes many provisions for an individual's participation in groups, but nowhere except in counseling is there provision for the one-to-one "Let's talk about me" experience that all persons seem to need. In view of such circumstances, the counselor who chooses to spend a large part of his time in group work seems not to be taking advantage of the special opportunities his position offers for working with individuals. Except under the special conditions mentioned below, it seems the counselor would be well advised to let others do group work while he counsels with individuals in situations unencumbered with the presence of others.

There may be times when a counselor finds that some group sessions will supplement his individual counseling. If, for example, he has found that a small number of his subjects have exhibited a strong common interest in an area in which he thinks he can help them (choice of occupation, choice of institution for post-school education, interest in getting increased allowances from their parents), he may bring them together, discuss the problems involved, and dispense and interpret information. He may then follow the group sessions with interviews to ascertain that his counselees saw the relationship of the discussions and information to their own circumstances. The adaptive counselor uses group procedures only when he is certain that a number of individuals have common problems or needs; when he is in a position to assist them by leading a discussion on matters of common concern; and when he can follow through to see that each individual has interpreted the work of the group in a manner that

[20] P. A. Perrone, M. L. Weiking, and E. H. Nagel, "The Counseling Function as Seen by Students, Parents and Teachers," *Journal of Counseling Psychology*, XII (1965).

[21] D. S. Arbuckle, "Counselor-Parent Interactions," *Guidance Journal*, V (Winter 1967); H. B. Bergstein, "The Parent and the School Counselor: An Emerging Relationship," *Vocational Guidance Quarterly*, XIII (Summer 1965).

[22] The writer prefers to reserve the term "counseling" for one-to-one sessions with a counselor, and therefore rejects "group counseling" as a contradiction in terms. The term "guidance" may be used when the reference is to activities related to th counseling task, one of which is conducting groups on occasions such as those described in this section.

helps him in making his own choices. He will not spend time in group work under any other circumstances.[23]

Except for those who think (but never demonstrate convincingly) that group work contains some almost magical power, the chief supporters of group guidance are those with such heavy loads of counselees that they cannot provide the individual attention they know is needed. Thus group approaches are often employed to alleviate pressures after there has been a reduction in counselor staff or a large increase in the number of counselees. Resorting to the group approach is therefore an admission that it is a less than adequate procedure which has been thrust upon them, and which they would have preferred to avoid. The unfortunate result of forced acceptance of a group approach is the subjugation of the major idea of really adapting to individual differences through counseling to the lesser idea of working with a group.

Group guidance techniques may serve some useful functions. Classes in which occupations are discussed *may* assist the individual in his choice of a vocation, and may simultaneously serve the desirable social objective of teaching students about the advantages, disadvantages, problems, and conditions of employment in other fields. Even though a student has no personal intention of entering a particular occupation, he should at least be taught about the trends and conditions of employment in the major industries. Although few crucial experiments have been conducted concerning the effects upon students of teaching classes in occupations, it seems likely that gains in social understandings might be achieved as successfully in such sessions as in the more common social science courses. There is always the possibility that information obtained from such classes may stimulate the student to make a more thorough examination of an occupation which he proposes to enter. Because of their general nature, however, such classes must be supplemented by individual work with each student.

Similar statements may be made about classes in which students are shown how to make analyses of themselves based on data derived from test scores, behavior descriptions, judgments of classmates, school marks, and various other sources. Without convincing experimental evidence about the value of such group procedures, it may be assumed that they assist in the development of skills in looking for evidence before making judgments, and in making better assessments of personal strengths and weaknesses. Such procedures may have value if they avoid the common errors of attributing equal dependability to measures of greatly differing validity and reliability; of putting related measures together in a manner which sug-

---

[23] Separate consideration of confrontation and sensitivity training groups are presented at the end of this section. They are treated separately because this writer believes that they lie in the province of clinical psychology rather than that of the school counselor.

gests that they are completely independent; and of using undefined terms to describe behavior without regard to the situations in which it appears. If they remain as class exercises without personal interpretation for each individual, they may do harm to the students' confidence and cause serious errors or misinterpretations. If the exercises are discussed in conference with a counselor who is fully aware of the limitations of the data and of the risk of harm to the individual, they may be effective supplements to the counseling task.

Many justifications for group guidance are given, but they seem to boil down to these seven categories:

1. Imparting of information not available from other sources.
2. Providing opportunity to recognize and discuss common problems which are met in making educational, vocational, and personal choices.
3. Giving students an opportunity to practice the acceptance of responsibility for their own learning in group situations.
4. Learning to use democratic processes in reaching common goals.
5. Developing interpersonal relationships which will help in group situations in the future.
6. Providing students and counselors with information which may be useful in the counseling situation.
7. Establishing relationships between students and counselors which create a demand for, and facilitate, counseling services.

The list could be continued at some length, but the seven items indicate the most commonly given objectives of group guidance. Apparently many persons believe that these goals can be achieved, since group guidance remains popular. Whether or not the groups accomplish what they are designed to do, they seem to satisfy large numbers of school administrators who believe erroneously that they provide an inexpensive guidance program.

Reading about the goals of group guidance activities makes one wonder why most of them cannot be accomplished in regular day-to-day classroom activity. Such goals as imparting information, discussing common problems, accepting responsibility, learning to work together, and developing interpersonal relationships are accepted by teachers of any subject, from Latin to physical education.

What then is the difference between group guidance and good teaching? Those who promote the former suggest that the differences lie chiefly in the emphasis on topics to be discussed. The group guidance process will be centered on the student himself and matters of immediate concern to him, while the teacher is concerned with acquisition of knowledge which may have little application to the student's personal life. Its supporters say that group guidance will focus more on learnings about self which can be evaluated by the students themselves in terms of changes in their immediate behavior. Classroom instruction, they claim, is less concerned with the *process* of learning than with acquisition of knowledge which can be tested by examinations. No real distinction between group guidance and good teaching can be made in terms of methods employed, however, since discussions, pupil presentations, role playing, and sociometric procedures can be used in any class or group.

But the line between good teaching and group guidance is hard to draw. They are so close to each other that if good teaching in schools were supplemented by good counseling, there would seem little reason to label one period of instruction as group guidance. Essentially, use of group guidance suggests that teachers are using traditional rather than modern educational procedures and are not interested in their students' growth and development. Counselors should not so indict their colleagues.

Polls of high school graduates show that many have very low opinions of group guidance. Typical of how they feel when they look back at them is the following statement:

> For four years the most unpleasant part of every week was the period devoted to guidance. The books were frightful, the leaders weren't interested and the students detested every minute of it.

One observer conveyed his feelings in these words:

> The field is uncharted, the objectives nebulous, and material helps for the leaders meager. This creates a challenge in view of the fact that records and reports are getting longer, committee meetings taxing and extra-curricular activities burdensome. No wonder a good many of our brethren merely incorporate study periods, student visitation and correction of papers into group guidance and call it a day. The blame is not solely upon the leader. He often does not know what to do or what is expected of him—and no one seems to know or care much about it. There is simply not enough time, privacy, incentive, or knowledge.[24]

Perhaps such comments result only when group guidance becomes an administrative rather than a guidance device, but measures must be taken to prevent this eventuality. There is grave danger that "guidance" can be used as an excuse for the carrying out of many miscellaneous little tasks for an administrator. If group guidance is used for administrative purposes, it should be labeled as such.

Dependable evidence about the value of group guidance is scanty.[25]

---

[24] From the files of the Wisconsin Counseling Study. See J. W. M. Rothney, *Guidance Practices and Results* (New York: Harper & Row, Publishers, 1958).

[25] See the reviews in the *Review of Educational Research* by N. Kagan, XXXVI (1966), and A. R. Anderson XXXIX (1969).

In those studies which have been reported, the reader must consider the fact of novelty. Almost anything new that is undertaken by groups will produce some positive results since it breaks up routines. Experiments in industry suggest this, and it seems even more likely in school situations where one class is much like another. But novelty wears off; it is not known if the same or similar results would be obtained if group participation were a regular diet.

It is claimed by advocates of group guidance programs that some aspects of the activity will "rub off" on teachers and therefore influence all their instruction favorably. There is, however, the possibility of the opposite effect. Group guidance frequently operates on the fringe of re-spectability because it is not a *regular* part of a student's program. It meets irregularly; attendance does not appear in marks on the report card; it can be canceled in favor of other activities; and leaders who participate in it are often experts in other fields. These conditions may result in only mar-ginal effectiveness, and observers may develop little respect for it, or any-thing associated with the word "guidance."

It is possible, too, that in supporting separate group guidance activi-ties, counselors may inhibit teachers from giving students necessary help in their regular school work because "They get that stuff in group guid-ance." Provision of group guidance may encourage some teachers to con-centrate entirely on subject matter teaching and leave matters of personal concern to the guidance program. If such were the result, counselors would miss one of their most important functions—the sensitizing of all school personnel to the needs of youth.

The statements offered above suggest that the following conclusions about group guidance should be given serious consideration by the adap-tive school counselor:

1. Evidence from marks and tests make it clear that, in all group situations, large numbers of students fail to learn what is expected of them. The sub-ject matter of guidance is too important to have any student misunderstand it. Hence, such information must be considered in *individual* sessions in which counselors and counselees can, by questioning, be sure that the material is really understood. Counseling must be offered to supplement any group guidance activities.
2. It is a well-established fact that there is little use in trying to teach some-one about anything until he is ready to learn. Readiness to learn about personal, educational, and vocational opportunities varies greatly from in-dividual to individual, and the variation is probably greater in this area than it is in the regular subject fields. Group guidance is, therefore, less likely to be effective in these areas than in others.
3. Some common patterns and problems can be discussed in group situations, but these do not appear in sequences which require regularly scheduled guidance groups. It has been observed that there are vast differences in depth and stability of needs, performances, interests, and behavior. It has

also been noted previously that it is in his recognition of the timing of changes of emphasis and influence on the behavior of specific individuals that the counselor finds his justification. He does not find it in group work.

4. Counseling must *always* be an individual affair. If schools supply enough counselors there is little need for group guidance. If they don't, the substitution of a fringe activity which must be too remote, too impersonal, and too general is not likely to accomplish the goals of the counseling program.

Special Groups

The preceding discussion of group guidance omitted any mention of confrontation groups and sensitivity training sessions. The writer believes that the leadership of such groups, if they are to be offered at all, should be by specialists with more extensive training in clinical psychology than most school counselors are likely to have. He also believes that such groups are suitable only for consenting adults who volunteer to participate in them after they have been fully informed of their nature and purpose. They should not be offered in schools despite the fact that some school personnel, anxious to appear up-to-date, propose to sponsor them.

Confrontation groups usually consist of a small number of persons (10-15) who meet with a leader-facilitator who tries to develop conditions in which the members explore their own feelings. They are encouraged to drop their defenses and *really* encounter the reactions of others who have taken the risk of dropping theirs. It is suggested that such procedures will result in greater self-knowledge and more innovative and constructive behavior. Presumably such behaviors will carry over to group situations in the individual's everyday life.[26] The sessions may vary from two to three hours in length to several weeks, and so-called marathon groups may be held continuously for as many hours (12 to 72) as the members can remain awake.

The effectiveness of such groups in accomplishing their objectives is reported almost wholly in unvalidated testimony of the participators immediately after the sessions end, while the state of euphoria created by participation is still present. Critics point out that the groups tend to value sensing higher than intellectualizing; that some persons find the experiences deteriorative rather than constructive; that what was intended to be a developmental becomes a therapeutic experience; that facilitators do not accept enough responsibility for what they have undertaken; that the language employed by leaders in the movement is vague; that not enough attention is paid to definition of objectives in terms which permit evaluation; and that the seductive advertising of those who offer training insti-

---

[26] G. M. Gazda, ed., *Basic Approaches to Group Psychotherapy and Group Counseling* (Springfield, Ill.: Charles C Thomas, Publisher, 1968).

tutes raises hopes of enduring changes in personality and solution of problems which are not justified on the basis of evidence.[27]

Counselors are attracted to encounter group leadership [28] because it appears to be an easy way to work with persons who need help in getting along with others, or who appear to be depressed by the pressures of a highly mechanized society. They should consider seriously whether they are qualified to act as facilitators of groups composed of such individuals. A person who is to carry on such activities needs special preparation in the form of a degree in a recognized educative or therapeutic discipline, and an advanced degree in one of the helping professions. Solid and extensive background preparation in personality dynamics, social psychology, and sociology should be followed by an internship and extensive supervised experience in group work. Few school counselors have had such preparation, and in view of the great risk of doing harm to participants in the group, they should leave such activities to those best prepared to undertake them.[29]

However, if the school counselor refuses to participate in a movement which has become popular, he must be prepared to meet the criticism that he is old-fashioned or rigid. Many members of a community and students in a school, misled by the uninformed statements which occur on the periphery of any movement, will expect a counselor to set up sensitivity training groups; they will not be pleased if he refuses to do so. His answer to such persons should reflect his belief that the group movements may become significant factors in both development and treatment if they are led in their formative stages by those who are particularly qualified to experiment with them and to evaluate their effectiveness. Until more conclusive evidence about the efficacy of such groups is provided, it would seem desirable for a counselor to take the opportunity afforded by his unique position and training to work primarily in one-to-one counseling relationships.

Problems in Remaining Adaptive

Inherent in the emphasis on adaptability throughout this chapter is the implication that counselors are, or can become, flexible persons. Psycho-

[27] See the critique by J. Campbell and M. D. Dunnette, "Effectiveness of T Group Experiences in Managerial Training and Development," *Psychological Bulletin*, LXXIX (1968).

[28] O. H. Mowrer, *The New Group Therapy* (Princeton, N.J.: Van Nostrand Reinhold Company, 1964).

[29] Some sensitivity group training is now provided in many counselor-education curricula. Unfortunately, there has been a tendency for some students enrolled in courses intended only to familiarize them with the group movements to feel that they are prepared to undertake sensitivity group leadership. Perhaps only the good sense of school administrators in prohibiting amateurs from assuming a professional task has prevented serious repercussions for the counseling movement.

logically, the familiar is comfortable, and frequent repetition of activities highly structured by the axioms of a single learning or personality theory can be a satisfactory experience for some persons, because it is less demanding than the frequent changing of sets required by adaptive behavior.[30] The advantages of membership in a school of thought mentioned on page 50, the lasting influence of successful completion of graduate study, the pressures of numbers of counselees, and strongly-held personal beliefs tend to inhibit the flexibility which adaptive counseling demands.

Change of behavior is, however, an essential characteristic of a healthy human being (even if the change is to greater rigidity), and its direction is determined largely by the desire to seek it. Since motivation to change counseling procedures cannot possibly be derived from the inconclusive evidence about the effectiveness of any counseling method, it must arise from feelings derived through experiences. Since feelings and experiences *can* be changed, it appears that counselors can become adaptive persons if they choose.

There is a language of descriptive behavior ("Jimmie doesn't do his homework") and another of character ("Jimmie is a lazy, irresponsible student"). Both kinds are utilized frequently in discussions of students. Use of the latter by a counselor suggests that he has certain standards on the basis of which he can approve or disapprove certain behavior patterns and decide what kind of counseling he will offer a student. Use of the former suggests that the description requires investigation of the reasons for the behavior, and adaptation of counseling to what the investigation reveals. Regardless of what standards counselors espouse, social customs change, and some persons will likely disagree with them. Failure to recognize such differences and to adapt to them may make a counselor ineffective simply because he and his counselee cannot find a common ground. Unless a counselor can approach his counselees with the intent of trying to understand rather than to condemn or ridicule them because they hold to different standards, he cannot muster the flexibility of adaptive counseling.

Flexibility in practice requires recognition of the fact that professional practices change. One might conclude that evolution in counseling and guidance proceeds by leaps from one fad to another if one observed the excesses of testing performances and inventorying interests of the thirties and forties; the overemphasis on client-centered counseling in the fifties; and the surge of behavior counseling and the flight to sensitivity and confrontation groups in the late sixties. An adaptive counselor recognizes that these are periods of excessive emphasis which will pass.[31] He

---

[30] See, for example, the statement about counselor educators in A. C. Riccio, "Me Change—Are You Joking?" *The Guidepost*, XII (1970).

[31] Evolution rather than revolution best describes the process of change despite the tendency of some writers to use the latter term. See J. D. Krumboltz, ed., *Revolution in Counseling* (Boston: Houghton Mifflin Company, 1966).

will realize, however, that all of them leave a small residue of value. He will sift out from the welter of high-sounding names (*information-seeking behavior* for going to the library, *positive reinforcement* for saying, "Nice work, Joe," and *unconditional positive regard* for caring) anything in the supposedly new procedure that he may use. If he does find something, he will be pleased to add it as one of the many procedures he employs.

Such demands for adaptability on the part of counselors will require flexibility in counselor training programs. It seems likely that the graduates of such programs will be no more flexible than their instructors. Thus, a program based on a single theory in which lectures, demonstrations, and reading requirements reflect its restrictions is likely to graduate counselors who are rigid in their beliefs and practices. If this is to be avoided, counselor educators must set for themselves the goal of assuring their students that no one-best-way of counseling has yet been discovered.

It is entirely possible for students to graduate from some counselor education programs and obtain full certification without having made any substantial change in their beliefs about the nature of man, personal and social issues, and standards of morality. A bright student can recognize what he is expected to say in an examination, and know that when he has passed the test he can forget what he has learned. (This can be true even when the examination consists of submitting a tape recording to a practicum or intern supervisor.) Under such circumstances, learning the language of a school of thought does not guarantee any change in procedures. Changes in society brought about by alterations in child-rearing practices, education, the world of work, population explosions and mobility, and increased knowledge about human behavior may be recognized, but there may be no adaptation to them.[32] A counselor who holds a narrow, rigid, or antiquated concept of society is not likely to be effective with youth who, in the words of Aldridge, are "now manipulating *us* [adults], who are programming our minds to work within alternatives which *they* have invented, and forcing us to conform to their authoritarian and bureaucratic plans for the renovation of the modern world." [33] Nor is he likely to be effective with those who do not fit such patterns. Conformity to any school of thought which limits the flexibility of a counselor in dealing with the circumstances of social alterations must be avoided if the graduates of counselor education programs are to meet the challenges of change.

But there can be overemphasis on change, and retention of some basic guiding principles is not all bad. Many current social practices, despite the scorn of youth, have grown out of serious efforts to meet human needs.

---

[32] The literature on such matters is voluminous. A concise summary with some implications for counselors may be found in Van Hoose and Pietrofesa, *Counseling and Guidance in the Twentieth Century, op. cit.*

[33] John W. Aldridge, "In the Country of the Young," *Harper's Magazine*, November 1969, Part II, October 1969, Part I.

Since they are the best methods that society has yet developed, the counselor will find that he can support some of them in principle while deprecating some of the practices associated with them. He may, for example, find a particular military action abhorrent, but he cannot ignore every human being's need for security; he will be concerned about productivity of persons for the sake of their own mental health as well as for the good of society, but he cannot support every method of assuring it; equity of opportunity must be developed, but acceptance of the concept does not require support of all the practices devised to obtain it; economy of human and material resources may be accepted as a desirable goal, but some means of reaching it may be rejected; and the counselor will support the production and conservation of the beautiful, although some of its forms may be repugnant to him. In essence, the adaptive counselor will have some personal values to which he can hold while his practices vary during inevitable periods of change. Difficult as the process may be, flexibility within general holding patterns seems to be a *sine qua non* of the effective counselor.

SUMMARY

All school counseling procedures must be limited in effectiveness because counselees exhibit a wide variety of characteristics and have had vastly different experiences. It has been suggested that much may be accomplished, however, if procedures are adapted to serve individuals through careful selection of instruments, complete sharing of information, and cautious interpretation of data obtained from tests and other sources.

Group procedures have been recommended only when individual counseling has revealed strong common concerns among a counselor's subjects, but it has been indicated that leadership of special confrontation and sensitivity groups be reserved for those who have had extensive and specific preparation for it.

Work with parents and teachers, who are considered essential members of the guidance team in adaptive school counseling, has been described, and some procedures for making it more effective have been suggested. Emphasis has been placed upon full sharing of information obtained about minors by all members of the team.

Throughout the chapter stress has been placed upon the need for a high degree of flexibility on the part of anyone who would counsel in schools. Restrictions placed upon members of particular schools of thought, and on those who practice eclecticism by employing only the procedures of such schools, tend to inhibit development of the flexibility that the procedures described in this chapter demand.

Selected References

GOLDMAN, L. *Using Tests in Counseling.* New York: Appleton-Century-Crofts, 1961. This is one of the best standard presentations about tests, but takes no position on controversial issues, and has inadequate emphasis on limitations of tests and inventories. For a more critical appraisal of tests and inventories see J. W. M. Rothney, P. J. Danielson, and R. A. Heimann. *Measurement for Guidance.* New York: Harper & Row, Publishers, 1958.

OHLSEN, M. M. *Group Counseling.* New York: Holt, Rinehart and Winston, Inc., 1970. An excellent modern discussion of the state of the art in group work by an enthusiast for it.

ROTHNEY, J. W. M. *Methods of Studying the Individual Child: The Psychological Case Study.* Waltham, Mass.: Ginn/Blaisdell, 1968. The only book of its kind that is not centered on problem cases. Emphasis is on procedures for gathering information about a counselee from sources in addition to the interview, and the need to synthesize it and to interpret the product so that it will be useful in planning next steps in the education of a student.

SOROKIN, P. A. "Testomania," *Harvard Educational Review,* XXV (1955). A biting, perhaps exaggerated, critique of testing theory and practices.

TYLER, Leona E. *Tests and Measurements.* Englewood Cliffs, N.J.: Prentice-Hall Inc., 1963. A brief monograph in which strengths and limitations of testing are well presented. Probably one of the best brief considerations of this subject.

WARTERS, Jane. *Techniques of Counseling.* New York: McGraw-Hill Book Company, 1964. Thorough consideration of the methods most commonly used by school counselors. One of the few books in which the positive and limiting factors are considered.

CHAPTER 5

procedures in
adaptive counseling

Tapes, films, and typescripts are commonly used in demonstrations of counseling, and since they are produced by advocates of distinct points of view, they must be considered as examples of what their producers believe to be desirable practices. Many are excellent presentations of applications of techniques derived from a particular theoretical orientation. Unfortunately, however, such demonstrations tend to imply that the illustrated procedures should have general application, and many observers see no need to adapt the techniques to other persons in different circumstances. Few of the demonstrations deal with school counseling situations.

ADAPTATIONS OF DEMONSTRATED TECHNIQUES

Clinical Models

Demonstrations of interviews by clinical psychologists and psychiatrists tend to encourage school counselors to follow their models. They are urged to leave their desks (which are said to be barriers to communication) and to sit close to their counselees in comfortable chairs so that better rapport can be established and maintained. They are also encouraged to dispense with note-taking and rely on their memories for long periods of time.

Memories are fallible, however, and significant statements made during lengthy interviews may be forgotten. It seems unlikely that most counselors can simultaneously listen and react to a counselee's statements, assess their significance, observe their relationship to other data, and remember them well enough to use them effectively and avoid unnecessary repetition in later sessions. Interviews are likely to be improved if a counselor admits to his subjects that his memory is not perfect and he wants to jot down important statements. He can ask the counselee to sit in a position where he can read all the notes, and invite him to comment on them. Most counselees will recognize the need for reminders, will be flattered by the suggestion that their statements are worth recording, and will appreciate the fact that the counselor is concerned enough about them to keep a complete record. In such circumstances, taking notes at a desk can become a stimulating rather than an inhibiting procedure.[1]

Interview procedures employed by some clinical psychologists and psychiatrists (in which no notes are taken) seem not to be justified in most school counseling situations. An adaptive counselor recognizes, however, that for some subjects (particularly those who have been interrogated by police and welfare workers) the note-taking procedure should be eliminated. In such cases it is essential that the counselor write down what he considers important information immediately after the interview is completed. The notes will be particularly valuable when the counselor writes up his case records. From them, and from his follow-up records, he can study relationships between his counseling activities and the post-counseling behavior of his subjects.

Interpreting Records

If a counselor is to help a student in better self-understanding leading to better decisions, he should offer him an opportunity to study his complete record and to discuss the counselor's interpretation of it. Since there is no information withheld from the teachers and parents of minors (and the student has been assured that nothing is being held back), he should be encouraged to examine it fully. After that examination the counselor may go through it item by item with the student, and present and discuss his interpretations. In effect he says to the counselee, "This is you as I see you based on your own comments, those of your parents and teachers, your test and health records, and your academic and other accomplishments. Now let us consider together the next steps that you might take." Many of the separate pieces of information will not be new to the student, but consideration of their relationships and implications may be.

[1] Similar statements apply to tape-recording, but taping and typescripts are expensive procedures not commonly available for daily use by school counselors. Machines do not offer the personal touch of the pad and pencil.

The first time this procedure is used with counselees their reactions vary greatly. Influenced by previous experiences, some become defensive, many are apologetic, others are confident, and still others reject the record and interpretations completely. In any event, their reactions may add significantly to the counselor's impressions. As the process is repeated in subsequent sessions, students tend to appreciate the candor, thoroughness, and genuine interest in them as individuals. They begin to see the value of compiling data from several sources, of seeing themselves as viewed by others, and of comparing their self-concepts with the opinions of others. This process entails confrontation similar to what is presumably offered in so-called T groups, but it gives the counselee the opportunity of encountering one person who is understanding, and who has the time and skill to help him to work out next steps.

It has often been suggested that if a teacher's comments are fully disclosed to a counselee, the teacher will not be as frank as he would be if he knew that his statements would be held in confidence. This may occur if he is not informed of the purposes of the practice; or shown how the counselor will use his comments. It may be necessary to appraise all members of the faculty about such counseling procedures, and even to demonstrate them with sample interviews. When this is done, the counselor usually finds that teachers respond well, and become active participants in the process.

One caution in the practice of full disclosure of information to students, parents, and teachers must be observed. The records should contain descriptions of the students' performances rather than evaluations.[2] This procedure requires elimination of all censorial terms (lazy, careless, irresponsible, bad, maladjusted, and so on), and of evaluation of behavior in terms of the teacher's personal standards of conduct. Whenever possible, a characterization of a counselee should be by *description* of his usual behavior and significant deviations from it rather than by a word, phrase, or rating that could have widely different meanings to different persons. Name-calling will have to be replaced by descriptions which encourage discussion of the counselee's past development, his current performances, and ways in which concerned parents, teachers, counselors, and the student himself can work cooperatively toward mutually acceptable goals.

But full disclosure is not recommended solely to avoid negative con-

---

[2] This does not mean that the teacher should not appraise the quality of a student's work in his subject field. See the discussion of censorial language in J. W. M. Rothney, *Methods of Studying the Individual Child* (Waltham, Mass.: Ginn/Blaisdell, 1968), and in *idem.*, "Improving Reports to Parents," *National Elementary Principal,* XLV (1966). It may be necessary to substitute descriptions for personal evaluations for another reason. Currently, and perhaps from this time on, counselors may find themselves confronted by lawsuits brought by parents who object to censorial terms in students' records.

sequences.[3] Since pupils, parents, and teachers need complete information for better understanding and wise decision-making, there seems to be no justification for withholding anything. There comes a time in the counseling process when all cards should be on the table and all participants told what they seem to signify. The adaptive counselor will recognize when that time arrives for each of his counselees, and will act accordingly.

Judgmental Behavior

The procedures described immediately above and the sample list of adaptive counselor activities on page 54 imply that counselors do make judgments about their counselees' behavior. Such words as *commends, disagrees, warns, states his opinions,* and *interprets* suggest that the counselor makes analyses of his data, evaluates them, and conveys his evaluations to the counselee. The frequency and form of such statements will be adjusted to a counselee and his circumstances, but their use indicates an area in which adaptive counseling may differ significantly from what is proposed by advocates of some schools of thought.

The concept of the nonjudgmental counselor has been accepted for such a long time that it seems to have reached the status of an unquestioned truth. To suggest that a counselor should report appraisals of a counselee to him is almost enough to subject oneself to threats of impeachment from many members of the profession. It is said that a counselor should withhold any judgments, evaluations, or appraisals of a counselee's behavior and performances, in contrast with actions of parents and teachers, who, it is implied, are required by their evaluation responsibilities to pass judgments on youth. Adaptive counselors will recognize that the generalizations must be modified when they are working with certain individuals.

The habit of evaluating behavior of persons, developed in early childhood and reinforced repeatedly by parents, teachers, and peers in the process of coming of age, is not likely to be overcome during a relatively brief period of counselor education. In addition, few counselors are good enough actors to conceal the habit of appraising others. A raised eyebrow, an unintentional nod, shake of the head, or slip of the tongue will almost inevitably reveal to the counselee that a judgment about him has been made.

Even if judgments could be concealed, one must question the wisdom of doing so. In a world in which judgment of others is common practice a counselee may find a nonjudgmental counselor's behavior puzzling

---

[3] D. A. Goslin, Conference Chairman, *Guidelines for the Collection, Maintenance and Dissemination of Pupil Records* (New York: Russell Sage Foundation, 1969); F. J. Fitzgibbon, "The Ethical and Legal Position of the Counselor in Divulging Test Information," *Measurement and Evaluation in Guidance,* I (Spring 1968).

and disturbing. If good rapport has been established and maintained, a counselor's refusal to make appraisals may be interpreted as incompetence, uncooperative behavior, lack of courage to say what he thinks, or an indication of some other personal weakness which disqualifies him as a helper. Under such circumstances there seems to be no valid reason for withholding personal judgments about the particular behavior of a specific counselee.

The adaptive counselor recognizes that there may be great differences in counselees' readiness to receive appraisals. Some students may be ready to receive them very early in the counseling process, while others will need a lengthy process of development before he reports his judgments. In all cases, when the counselor feels that he has sufficient bases on which to make an appraisal, he is obligated to inform the counselee of the one he has made. A counselee needs this information to increase his self-understanding.

SAMPLE PROCEDURES

Complete descriptions of adaptive counseling approaches would require presentation of many longitudinal case studies involving extensive interviews. The length of each report would limit the number of descriptions of adaptations required in school counseling circumstances, and no attempt is made to present such materials in this volume. (Short samples are offered in the Appendix.) Some brief abstracts from interviews illustrating school counselors' adaptations are presented below.[4] Extensive cumulative records covering several years of school attendance had been maintained on all of the subjects. Although some of the abstracts seem to be fragmentary descriptions of crisis situations, they were significant incidents in the longitudinal picture of the students' development. (The C in the illustrations refers to counselor, the S to student.)

DIRECTION TOWARD POSITIVE ACTION

S: I've had the same teacher for two years and haven't learned a thing. It's all repetition. We had a book but it took two months to go through it and she read the whole story to us. I really got bored.

C: That's very interesting, but let's see what *you* could do about it. Here are some things you could try. You could offer to present a review of a book that you found very interesting. Or, since you draw very well,

---

[4] Examples of additional procedures have appeared in previous chapters as illustrative applications of principles. The reader might try to develop effective procedures for work with Hal, Stanley, and Rachael in the Appendix.

could you bring in some illustrations of action in the book that is being used in class? You might offer to do some of the oral reading, or ask the teacher if you and your friends could put on a skit showing some of the events in the book. If you did those things you wouldn't be bored.

S: Hmm, never thought of that. Maybe I'll try it but I don't think it will work.

C: Try them right away and let me know what happens.

S: OK, it's a deal.

The second abstract is from an interview in which the positive direction that was given proved to be so successful that the student's outlook changed significantly and her statements of appreciation for the counselor's help were profuse.

S: When I get home from school my mother is always drunk. The house is a mess. She doesn't do the dishes or clean up and she hardly ever cooks any supper. She just lies there and drinks and screams at me and I scream back. I'm so ashamed I can't ask my friends to come over and I'm so disgusted sometimes I think I'll just leave home.

C: Sounds like a tough spot but maybe you could help. Drinking like that is a sickness instead of something to be disgusted and ashamed about. I think you would want to help a sick person.

S: How? I think it's hopeless.

C: What do you generally do when you get home in the afternoon?

S: Oh, a little homework and then I just sit around—maybe watch TV or read a little, but mostly just sit around.

C: You could do the dishes and clean up and cook the supper. And you could talk nicely to your mother instead of screaming. Maybe you could read to her or tell her what you are doing in school and talk to her the way that you'd talk to a sick person.

S: That won't work. It's hopeless.

C: Ever tried it?

S: No.

C: Well, why not give it a try because what you are doing now doesn't seem to help? Try it for two days and let me know on Friday how you made out.

S: I'll try it for two days but if it doesn't work I'm leaving.

These illustrations indicate what an adaptive counselor can do in situations which occur frequently in work with adolescents. They often like to criticize adults and will do so at great length whenever they can find a listener. The counselor may listen long enough to see the direction the student is taking, and then suggest doing something positive as a substitute for nagging criticism. The idea that they might do something themselves to improve the situation often comes as a surprise, but many will follow through on recommendations. At times the suggestions may be drawn from the counselee by questioning, but in cases such as those described above it seemed desirable to state them specifically.

Presenting Alternatives

In some situations an adaptive counselor can offer challenges by indicating possible consequences of action a counselee plans to take. Sometimes this can be done very quickly, as the following succinct abstract from an interview with a high school senior illustrates:

S: I'm not going to college next year. I'm just going to bum around the country.
C: How old will you be next January?
S: Nineteen.
C: And you're healthy?
S: Yes, why?
C: Dave, within the next year you will either be in college or drafted into the Army.
S: Never thought of that. Maybe college wouldn't be so bad after all.

Dave was in college the following year. Whether or not the reader considers this a desirable outcome depends on his own feelings about college attendance, the armed forces, and bumming around. The brief abstract does illustrate, however, that a brief but pointed presentation of an alternative action may be effective in decision-making situations.

Considering Self-Concepts

The following abstract from a long interview presents a distinct contrast of counselor activities with those noted in the immediately preceding circumstance. It illustrates the adaptation of a counselor to a situation in which the counselee wanted to discuss some of his ideas about himself.

S: Well, I hadn't really observed myself—well, if you want to put it that way, "observed myself." I don't know if that's what I want to say. But I hadn't really, uh, noticed—observed how, I exactly, how I feel about this.
C: Um hm. It's hard to stand back somewhere and take a look at yourself as maybe somebody else would.

S: Um hm. That's what I tried to do. I don't know if I succeeded in doing it or not. (pause) But would you say that I, I would have a, this power hunger—this type of thing? I'm—and if I do have it, is it something I should try to avoid, or try to control or limit?

C: I gather that somebody said this to you. Somebody implied it.

S: We were discussing this the other day, or not, not that, but we were discussing, ah, Tennyson's *Idylls of the King*.

C: Yes.

S: And—I've forgotten. (pause) You know, he always writes in these allegories—

C: Yes, um hm.

S: —in this allegoric fashion, and everything comes out—you know, and you can, you try to apply it to, you know, situations that you come across in your, ah, your daily life. This type of thing. And we discussed this other person who, whose name was not given, but who said in the discussion of ah "power hunger," and, ah, put it this way—material symbols, or popularity or something like that—. It was in connection—. Now I remember—with the Holy Grail and how some of the knights of the Round Table had this compulsion to see it, and others did, it didn't make any difference whether they did or they didn't.

C: Um hm. Some of them had a real hunger for this and others could get along tolerably well without it.

S: Um hm. They, they didn't think it was important. Because all it really was was a symbol—of the, you know, of strength of their faith.

C: Yes. For those who needed a symbol, it had meaning.

S: And some—just knowing, just having the faith to start out with—that was enough, but for other people, they needed it.

C: Some people could live with—that is, some people could accept the idea and just believe in it, and others had to keep searching for the symbol —to try to prove it—to try to figure out some concrete proof for whatever this idea was.

S: Um hm. And well—and anyway, that's how we got into it. And someone—joke—I don't know if he meant it jokingly or not—I hope he didn't. I don't know. But, ah, he said, he, they, he pointed at me and I just laughed at the time, but I've been thinking about it. I don't know, what do you think about it, about that? Do you think that—

C: You laughed at the time, but you're not sure it was funny.

S: No. I'm not sure. Well, ah, ah, ah, what do you do when someone—you know? You've gotta respond somehow, and didn't know what to say.

C: You couldn't bust him in the nose.

S: (laughs) No. So I didn't know what to do.

C: But you sort of hoped he wasn't completely in earnest.

S: He, he was, he—no I don't—I didn't know if he was or if he wasn't.

C: But you suspect he was, I gather, or you wouldn't have been so concerned about it since.

S: I don't know. I don't, I really don't. He, he could have been—I don't know. But I just don't want to let or give people the idea that I, that I want this type of thing for, purely for the sake of having it.

C: That is—you recognize that you've done some things that might lead some to conclude that—

S: Um hm.

C: —but not—

S: Well, I would hope—

C: —for that sake alone—

S: I would hope that this was not my motive.

C: It's a better purpose that you have in mind than just—just to have just to have power.

S: The point is—well, I was trying to examine my motive in doing some of the things that I do. I don't know why I do them. I, it seems—I, I forgot to write this down, but I—I can be very impulsive at times. Some nights, for instance, I'll come home and I'll see a book on the shelf, and I'll read the book, you know, the whole book in one night.

C: Um hm.

S: And this is not any great feat or anything, but it's just—I just get an idea, you know, and well—

C: This wouldn't relate to this power business too much?

S: No. Well, yes. It's just that I see something and I want it—this type of thing.

C: Then you go after it.

S: —go after it—

C: Um hm. Once you get the idea that it might be nice to do something, then you go ahead and work at it.

S: Um hm.

This interview continued for an hour, and further self-examination sessions were held later. It seemed essential in this case that the counselor listen much and make comments only when they were requested, or when the counselee seemed to need assistance in phrasing his ideas.

Providing Sources of Information

The time comes in many interviews when further discussion of a decision-making situation is less than helpful until further information is obtained. In the following excerpt the counselor took the initiative because he felt quite sure that the counselee would not. It was hoped that, in addition to helping her in this particular instance, it might start her on a series of explorations which she could carry on without assistance.

C: At each time we have discussed your future you have said you were going to become a medical doctor. I know you have read a lot about the field but have you ever talked to a woman doctor about it?

S: No, but I'd sure like to.

C: Well, I'll arrange for you to talk to one.

Following the above exchange, arrangements were made and a time for a conference set. When the counselee returned from it she made the following statement:

> I was extremely satisfied with my interview with Dr. Mary Brown. She was very obliging during the interview and answered my questions quite thoroughly.
>
> Dr. Brown strengthened my determination to be a doctor. She emphasized the fact that a doctor does not always help people, but is always improving the condition of society.
>
> Dr. Brown felt that I would not have any trouble getting into medical school. As long as the grades are high, the applicant usually gets in. It was mentioned that attending this university would probably increase my chances of getting into medical school there.
>
> I think the most outstanding comment made during the entire interview was, "People in a minority must be a little better than the majority of their colleagues." Dr. Brown thought that women entering the medical professions were, in most cases, more intelligent than a majority of the men.
>
> I would recommend sending someone else to Dr. Brown.

Response to Requests for Assistance

One student wrote the following statement to a counselor and then repeated essentially the same thoughts during an interview:

> I have felt that the counselors are afraid of having an influence on my decisions. This, I feel, is wrong. I have a great deal of respect for the counselors and I would like to be able to turn to someone with a good knowledge of my problems. If the counselors refuse to influence my decisions, then they will probably be influenced by someone not as experienced in the field my problem lies. As of now they lie in education—where to get it—how to get it—and what kind to get.
>
> If I could make one request of counselors, it would be to ask them to help me to a greater degree in deciding on these questions. I wish they would make an effort to influence my decisions. I have virtually nowhere else to turn at this time.

The student who made the statement did *not* want the counselor to make up his mind for him, but he did want an opinion from the person he thought best qualified to give one. His last sentence seemed to state exactly how he felt when he sought the counselor's help.

The counselor's response was not recorded in this case, but his notes indicate that, in essence, he would accept the challenge. Since the counselor had known the student for four years and had accumulated voluminous data about him, his school, and his circumstances, he recommended enrollment in a specific university, in a program which seemed particularly suited to his desire to have a broad exploratory experience. He suggested a way in which the student could earn the financial support he needed.

Longitudinal follow-up records over a period of seven years indicated that the plan had been followed. The student found what he wanted, earned almost all his university expenses, contributed greatly to the university community, completed graduate school with two degrees, and reported great satisfaction with his first full-time job.

It should be noted that the procedure was effective *for this particular individual.* It might not have been suitable for any of his classmates. His case is simply an example of how this counselor adapted his procedures to meet the needs of one person under special circumstances.

Informing

A school counselor is often required to report and interpret information to counselees who seek it, and also to some who, without being aware of it, need to have it. The information-giving process requires careful adaptation of language levels, and checking to see that the subject grasps what is being said. At times the process, as in the abstract below, can lead to fruitful discussion that was not anticipated.

S: I sure can't do any good on them tests. I always run out of time and then I get all nervous.

C: Well I can see that you had trouble with some of them but you did pretty well on the arithmetic test.

S: Oh, I hate that stuff. I'd never take a job where I had to make change and things like that.

C: Let's look at this arithmetic test. (shows her a copy of the test) You scored at the 45th percentile and that means you did as well as or better than 45 per cent of eighth graders in the state. What percent scored better than you?

S: Gee, I don't know. I can't figure that one out.

C: Let's try it again. (repeats previous statement)

S: I can add and subtract and things like that but I can't do the thinking problems.

C: I take it you just don't like numbers and you don't want to work in any place where you'd have to use them. That right?

S: Sure is. You know there is one thing I really like—taking care of kids. Are there any kinda jobs where you can do that and you don't have to do school work and don't have any figuring to do?

From this point the discussion turned to consideration of the counselee's strengths, including her pleasing manner, good grooming, and interest in children. Further interviews, visits for observation, and a tryout as a volunteer helper in a summer playground program were arranged. Two years after graduation she found a satisfying job as an attendant in a children's hospital.

Enrichment

Occasionally, it seems desirable that a student who can perform at a higher level than most of his classmates be stimulated to go beyond the usual requirements. The following abstract shows how a counselor may initiate such activity. (The procedure should not be undertaken unless the teachers are involved in guidance as a cooperative venture, and the faculty has approved the general idea of independent study for selected students. In such circumstances the counselor is not interfering with the teachers' prerogatives.)

C: You say you can get most of the class material out of the book without going to class?

S: Yeh, usually I can.

C: What do you mean by usually?

S: Well, sometimes I don't get it but most of the time I get the idea. If not I ask somebody.

C: Maybe then we could talk to your math teacher about working on your own, going to some place like the math center to work on your own ideas in math instead of going to class every day. They call it independent study.

S: Would I have to write a paper or something?

C: The teacher would decide, but it probably wouldn't be a lot of *extra* work and it wouldn't be a big thesis. Maybe you would just talk over with her what you learned.

S: Well, I don't like to do busy work all the time doing the same problems.

C: This way you could work at your own speed.

S: But I'd be missing classes. Would I get credit for the class that would be good for getting into technical school?

C: You'd likely have to take some examinations but these wouldn't be anything to worry about there. (further explanations were added)

S: Sounds good. I'll talk to my teacher and come back and tell you how it worked.

This interview situation is simple and direct. Behind it there had been much study of the counselee and the school situation. At times it may be wise to discuss such suggestions with a concerned teacher and have him introduce the idea to the student.

Confrontation

Some counselees have been so successful at avoiding issues that they find it difficult to change patterns of behavior which seem destined to produce unfortunate consequences. In such cases the adaptive counselor may decide that a confrontation is most likely to be effective. That procedure is illustrated in the following statement:

C: John, you know now what your test scores and school marks are, and you have told me about your educational plans. Now let's consider these things in relation to each other and see where they lead us. As I see it you can do one of these three things: you can change the level of your performances; you can change your plans; or you can expect to have lots of trouble ahead. Your past performances just don't jibe with your plans.

S: How do you know I'll have trouble?

C: Our follow-up of students in past years who hadn't done well on the tests and had low marks showed that most of them didn't succeed.

S: Does that mean I won't?

C: Not for sure, but it doesn't look good.

S: Well, I don't want to change my plans. What would you suggest?

C: You have knocked out one of the choices—changing plans—and I take it you don't want trouble so I guess you've knocked out another one. That leaves only the first one—to improve your performances.

S: What do I have to do to change?

The next steps in this conference, too lengthy to report here, required reduction of activities, working out of a study schedule, conferences with teachers about completing late assignments, and some suggestions about excessive guessing on multiple-choice tests.

Encouraging Exploration

The subject in the following abstract had not responded to previous attempts to get him to consider his post-school plans. He said that he had not given any thought to the matter other than deciding that he did not want to go on to post-high school training. It seemed to the counselor that the time had come when some planning was essential.

S: I have no idea of what I want to do when I finish high school. I've never even thought about it.
C: You see policemen every day. Would you want to be a policeman?
S: No thanks. I wouldn't want that kind of a job.
C: And you see a lot of teachers. How about that?
S: I don't want to go to school that long.
C: And you've worked some with your dad. How would you like to do what he does?
S: No, that's one kind of work I wouldn't want to do.
C: Then you have thought about different kinds of work.
S: Yeah, guess I have, but I haven't seen anything I'd like.

From this point self-analysis processes and study of occupations were begun.

Examining Values

Occasionally a counselor suspects from long observation of a counselee that verbal statements are not valid indications of his values. Sometimes socially desirable values are voiced to conceal personal motives that the subject thinks may not be acceptable. The following abstract illustrates how one counselor adapted to that circumstance:

S: I really want to be a doctor.
C: Why are you so set on that career?
S: I want to help people. I feel sorry for people who are sick and I think I would be doing a service to people.
C: That's really what you want to do—to help people?
S: Yes.
C: Suppose that something happened so that doctors couldn't make as much money as they do now. Would you still want to be a doctor?
S: Well, then, I might think about something else.
C: Should I gather from that answer that you really want to find a career where you can make a lot of money?
S: I sure do. I want to make a million and enjoy the things that money can buy.

Six years after high school, the subject who made the statements above, is engaged in a very lucrative enterprise and seems well on his way to that first million.

Selection of an Activity

As the subject indicates in his statement, he was much under the usual height and weight for his age. He was a sports enthusiast and really wanted to participate, but thought his physical development prevented it. The situation described below is an illustration of how a counselor can get students to ask questions that they had not thought about asking for themselves.

S: I'm too small to get into sports. I weigh only 109 pounds and I'm so short I can't go out for basketball or football. No one wants me on a team.

C: There is one sport in high school where people of the same size are matched up. You could go and talk to the wrestling coach.

S: I never thought of that. I think I'll do it.

C: Maybe you should do more than think about it. You could do it tonight after school. Let me know tomorrow what happened.

The illustration seems so simple that an adult is inclined to doubt that such an obvious answer to a student's dilemma could have been overlooked by the student himself. The counselor who works with a broad segment of school populations finds that he must often help some counselees to find answers that others can get without assistance.

Presentation of samples of counseling techniques tends to encourage the reader, despite warnings that they are just samples, to consider them as descriptive of the total process. Nothing short of a longitudinal case study of each counselee, including complete typescripts of interviews, could demonstrate how a truly adaptive counselor meets the needs represented in the gamut of individual differences among students. Presentation of such materials is impractical, but substitution of samples entails the risk of encouraging overgeneralization and stereotyping. The reader will recognize that full descriptions of the techniques of truly adaptive counselors presently defy meaningful and restrictive classification. When one looks at techniques for meeting individual needs, all generalization must be modified.

SUMMARY

It has been suggested that, except in special cases, school counselors eschew the interviewing techniques commonly employed by clinical therapists and psychiatrists and use techniques more suitable for school populations. It has also been suggested that counselors encourage students to study their own complete records (including appraisals by counselors) and to participate in discussion of their implication.

Abstracts from interviews have been presented to illustrate techniques in giving direction, presenting alternatives, informing and providing sources of information, considering self-concepts, confronting, enriching, encouraging exploration, examining values, responding to requests for assistance, and selecting activities. They have been presented only as samples of techniques which may be employed to meet the needs of particular counselees, and the reader is warned of the risk of overgeneralization from the samples.

Selected References

BENJAMIN, A. *The Helping Interview.* Boston: Houghton Mifflin Company, 1969. Specific illustration of techniques in recording, note-taking, phrasing of questions, responses, and leads in attempts to make the interview a helping relationship.

COTTLE, W. C. and E. M. DOWNIE. *Preparation for Counseling.* Englewood Cliffs, N.J.: Prentice-Hall, Inc., 1970. Presents a good overview of procedures for organizing information about a counselee in preparation for individual counseling.

KAHN, R. L. and C. F. CANNELL. *The Dynamics of Interviewing.* New York: John Wiley & Sons, Inc., 1964. Good discussion of theory and techniques of interviewing with illustrative materials.

KATZ, M. *Decisions and Values.* College Entrance Examination Board, 1963. A meaty discussion of the importance of knowing about values. The "asides" are interesting.

MEEHL, P. *Clinical versus Statistical Prediction.* Minneapolis: University of Minnesota Press, 1964. A good inhibitor if you tend to be quite sure that you can predict what persons will do in the future.

ROEBER, E. C., G. WALZ, and G. E. SMITH. *A Strategy for Guidance.* New York: The Macmillan Company, 1969. Excellent discussion of some procedures for providing effective guidance in schools. More down-to-earth than many books in this field.

ROTHNEY, J. W. M. "Some Not-So-Sacred Cows," *Personnel and Guidance Journal,* XLVIII (June 1970). Questions the validity and usefulness of some commonly-stated concepts in counseling and guidance.

CHAPTER 6

evaluation
of counseling

If one were to estimate the importance of evaluation in counseling by the words of those who write about counseling most frequently and at greatest length, one would be forced to conclude that evaluation is an essential part of it. Judged by their actions, however, evaluation appears to be more honored in discussion than in practice. Counselors, and even counselor-educators with few exceptions, do not state their objectives in terms that permit evaluation, nor do they follow through by evaluating their work in terms of the stated objectives. As a consequence, counselors would find it difficult to justify their existence on the basis of evidence rather than on faith.

PROBLEMS AND ISSUES

Lack of Evaluative Studies

There are few sound evaluative studies of counseling. The reasons for this scarcity may be that many persons feel that their faith requires no data; that the outcomes of counseling are too intangible to be appraised; that so many variables influence the behavior of persons that change cannot be attributed to the work of the counselor; and that counselors are so busy with their counseling that they have no time to spend on evaluation. None of these reasons, perhaps better described as excuses, justify the fact that evaluation of counseling is seldom done.

Reasons for the lack of soundness of such evaluation studies as do exist may be found in such matters as these:

1. The complexity of human beings.
2. Difficulties in devising suitable instruments.
3. The mobility of persons in a free society.
4. Inadequate self-reports.
5. Inaccuracies in reports of observers.
6. Insufficient numbers of subjects.
7. Brevity of periods between treatment and appraisal of outcomes.
8. Difficulty in getting suitable criteria.
9. Differences between individual and societal values.

The lack of comprehensive long-term follow-up evaluation studies means that much counseling is based on boldness and faith—boldness to offer it and faith that it is effective. One reviewer of the literature on evaluation of counseling came to this conclusion: "Our faith in counseling may be highly desirable, but we should keep in mind that it is essentially a faith and that there are good arguments for becoming unfaithful. Stated bluntly we have more faith in counseling than is warranted either by research findings or by empirical observation." [1] The most recent review of research in the evaluation of counseling [2] is limited by its authors' lack of experience and their adherence to one school of thought, as revealed by such statements as, "Most of our progress has been attenuated by the failure to *design treatments* to *promote specific outcomes* [italics added]." [3] It begins with the statement that "Research resulting in definitive knowledge of counseling outcomes is still wanting." In selecting evaluation studies for review, the authors defined counseling as "*Any* ethical procedure used by the counselor to help promote change in the client [italics added]." Although this latest (1969) review of the literature is not as free from bias as those which have been prepared every third year for the American Educational Research Association, its gist is similar to previous reviews. All the authors have suggested that there is much to be done in the evaluation of counseling by organizations which can conduct large-scale studies and by the counselor on the job.

Despite the limitations of all reviews and summaries of evaluation, the counselor should become familiar with them because they indicate the

[1] F. C. Young, "The Ineffectiveness of Counseling" (Unpublished seminar paper, 1967).
[2] C. E. Thoresen, ed., "Guidance and Counseling," *Review of Educational Research*, XXXIX, No. 2 (1969). Chap. 5 is entitled "Changes Through Counseling."
[3] See pages 39–40 for what is meant by specific outcomes. One can only conclude that counseling is considered to be a salvage and repair process.

place of evaluation in the profession as a whole, and because they may offer suggestions for improvement of his own attempts at evaluation. No summary of evaluation studies in counseling will be presented here, but some of the major problems and criticisms considered in them are presented below.

Insufficient Description of Counseling Sessions

One of the most common criticisms is aimed at researchers who are said to provide insufficient descriptions of what actually took place during counseling. This criticism is applied most frequently to adaptive counselors who are not confined by *a system* to the use of *a method*, and who believe that procedures which seem suitable for one counselee might be undesirable for another. Behavioral counselors particularly decry the lack of description of a method and the failure to link a procedure to a particular theory. The concept that there is no single learning or personality theory adequate for the justification of selected counseling practices seems too difficult for them to grasp.

There is also the practical problem brought about by the length of reports required to illustrate adaptive procedures. The researcher who has attempted to adapt his procedures to many individuals over long periods of time would require so many volumes to describe his adaptations that they would not be accepted for publication, and would probably not be read in detail even if printed. If he describes only a few of his cases and procedures, there is a risk (particularly if interviews are presented) that he will encourage readers to generalize beyond the specifics presented. Generalization to many from one is a step that the adaptive counselor would like to discourage. Those who have not conducted longitudinal follow-up evaluative studies of adaptive counseling cannot appreciate the difficulties entailed in their reportage, and hence criticisms of those who have done so seem naïve.

Nonspecificity of Outcomes

It is common practice to decry the lack in evaluation studies of statements of specific individual outcomes of counseling. The desire for preciseness in relating particular outcomes to specific counseling techniques seems to be a product of a period in which idolatry of automation has blinded many persons to the individuality of counselors and counselees. The search for specificity often leads to presentation of short-term behavioral outcomes in specific situations without any evidence of transfer to life situations over a protracted period.

Dependence on Counselor Testimony

Some evaluation studies are criticized because they depend too greatly on the testimony of the counselor himself. Statements by therapists that they saw at the end of the treatment "rather considerable reorganization of the client's personality," or uncorroborated statements by others that undesirable behavior has been eliminated, are said to be too vague and too subject to bias. When the evaluator employs more highly structured methods by using as evaluative criteria the responses of subjects to so-called personality tests or Q-sorts,[4] it is suggested that such instruments have been insufficiently validated. Rating scales have always been considered a dubious procedure, and recent attempts to use them have indicated that questions raised about their validity have not been answered.[5] Doubts about all such procedures and the lack of longitudinal data result in the casting of considerable doubt on claims of counseling effectiveness.

Disagreements Among Schools of Thought

Criticisms of members of one school of thought by proponents of other schools suggest that there is not likely to be substantial agreement about how counseling efforts are to be evaluated. Those who want statements of specific outcomes for each counselee, and who limit their counseling to those subjects who exhibit specific shortcomings, are not likely to accept general statements about self-actualization or reorganization of personality. On the other hand, those who claim that counselors should have more comprehensive goals are disturbed by the emphasis on specificity of what seem to them almost trivial outcomes.

In the eyes of adaptive school counselors, most evaluation studies seem to show a lack of concern for the goals of society and its institutions. They recognize that a counselor must give due consideration to the goals of the school in which he is employed, and that it will demand an accounting of his contributions to the attainment of these goals. They are aware that reports of simple, uncorroborated short-term changes in the behavior of a few highly selected counselees will not be sufficient evidence of a counselor's contributions to justify his presence in the school.

Some of the problems met by adaptive school counselors when they

[4] C. R. Rogers and R. Dymond, *Psychotherapy and Personality Change* (Chicago: University of Chicago Press, 1954).
[5] J. W. M. Rothney, *Methods of Studying the Individual Child* (Waltham, Mass.: Ginn/Blaisdell, 1968), pp. 45–46; C. B. Truax and R. R. Carkhuff, *Recent Advances in the Study of Behavior Change* (Montreal: McGill University Press, 1963).

attempt to evaluate their work, and some suggestions for their solution, appear in the following pages.

Those who conduct long-term evaluation studies soon recognize the influence of social circumstances on their results. The writer's first follow-up was conducted when the country was in a deep depression,[6] the second when World War II had just begun.[7] The first phases of a ten-year follow-up had to be done during the Korean conflict,[8] and recent efforts in following up counseled superior students were confounded by the Vietnam situation and an era of increased protest.[9] None of these social conditions existed at the time of the counseling, and they could not have been forecasted with enough assurance to justify their consideration during the counseling sessions. Lack of funds for education and employment opportunities during the depression, the demands of military service during the wars, and even the economic booms in a post-war period served to set educational and vocational plans awry, and required personal adjustments that could not have been anticipated at the time of the counseling. Since the counselor cannot change such social circumstances, he must recognize that his evaluation will be a function of the characteristics of his former counselees as well as of the society in which they live.

The reader should note before he reads about evaluation by adaptive counselors that there is a common but unfortunate tendency to confuse evaluation of counseling with descriptions of it. There are many so-called evaluation reports in which rating scales have been used to describe the behavior of counselors during their interviews.[10] The makers of the scales have decided that certain counselor behaviors are more desirable than others, so they construct scales in which the behaviors they approve get high ratings and those they disapprove get low ratings.[11] This widely touted and apparently highly regarded procedure provides descriptions, but not evaluation, of counseling. *The outcomes of counseling can be determined only by study of the behavior of counselees following the sessions and when they are not being directly influenced by the counselor.* That

[6] W. F. Dearborn and J. W. M. Rothney, *Scholastic, Economic and Social Background of Unemployed Youth* (Cambridge, Mass.: Harvard University Press, 1938).

[7] J. W. M. Rothney and B. A. Roens, *Guidance of American Youth* (Cambridge, Mass.: Harvard University Press, 1951). (Publication was delayed by the war conditions.)

[8] J. W. M. Rothney, *Guidance Practices and Results* (New York: Harper & Row, Publishers, 1958).

[9] J. W. M. Rothney and C. W. Lewis, "Use of Control Groups in Studies of Guidance," *Personnel and Guidance Journal*, XLVII, No. 5 (January 1969).

[10] J. D. Linden, S. C. Stone, and B. Shertzer, "Development and Evaluation of an Inventory for Rating Counseling," *Personnel and Guidance Journal*, XXXVIII (September 1965).

[11] C. B. Truax and R. R. Carkhuff, "Experimental Manipulation of Therapeutic Conditions," *Journal of Counseling Psychology*, XXIX (1955); *idem.*, *Toward Effective Counseling and Psychotherapy* (Chicago: The Aldine Press, 1967).

point of view is maintained throughout this volume, and it is stressed be-cause it has been underemphasized in the literature of counseling and guidance. Counselors cannot expect the respect of their publics and the opportunities they need to help counselees if, in response to questions about their effectiveness, they respond only with descriptions of their ac-tivities. The only justification for the existence of counseling, regardless of the techniques employed, is some change in a counselee's behavior. If there is no change, there is no justification. Evaluation of counseling, then, must be in terms of counselees' behavior. It will not be enough to describe the counselor's activities, facilities, or intentions.

Summary of Problems in Evaluation of Counseling

It has been suggested that evaluation of counseling has been infrequent and ineffective. The reasons may lie in the difficulty of making appraisals and lack of incentive for doing so, the expense involved, and lack of recog-nition of the value of evaluation in revising current practices and develop-ing good programs for informing others about counseling practices and results.

1. *It is difficult to obtain valid measures of the results of counseling.* The aims of counselors are frequently expressed in such generalizations as "the assistance of youth in making satisfactory educational, vocational, and social adjustments." Accomplishment of objectives stated so broadly and vaguely is extremely difficult to measure. What appears to be a satisfactory educational adjustment for someone may simply mean that he has decided that conformity in all phases of a school or college program results in fewer conflicts with teachers or administrators, and that further attempts on his part to tread beyond the beaten paths are likely to be futile. Job satisfac-tion, which has not yet been measured satisfactorily, may be expressed when the individual is at less than potential achievement levels; it may mean resignation to circumstances, a statement of compensatory feelings, or simply the result of a rationalization process. Data about wages do not allow for the fact that people may be willing to work at low levels because job satisfaction is high, or because a low beginning wage promises a high ceiling.

Social adjustments must vary with individuals and with circum-stances. Who can determine with certainty in any particular case that divorce, legal separation, or other breaking of family ties is undesirable? Does evidence of treatment by a psychiatrist always mean that there is lack of adjustment, or simply that the individual has made a good adjust-ment? Could the fact that an individual does not participate in social affairs indicate only that he is making a good temporary adjustment to more personal matters?

These are samples of the problems that inhibit counselors who have recognized the need for appraisal of their work. When the counselors have accepted the fact of individuality and the wide range of behavior which may be satisfactory for any person, the complexity of the problems which they must solve in appraising their clients' behavior appears insurmountable. Inhibited by this complexity, they are prone to overlook the fact that measurable criteria can be set up for large groups. Appraisal of counselees' performances with respect to these criteria can produce evidence about the *general* value of counseling, even though many individuals within counseled groups may not meet the general criteria. For example, *most* counselees will probably profit from continuing in some post-school training, although *many* may not. Even the crude measures of job satisfaction that are available may provide valuable data about the success of groups in general, on the average, and on the whole. If a counselor finds that his counselees are generally more satisfied than students who have not been counseled, he has taken one step forward in the justification of his position. Since he cannot ignore the fact that our society measures success in part by financial gain, evidence that his counselees receive higher average wages than others may be presented as partial justification of counseling.

2. *The optimum time for application of measures of effectivenss of counseling is difficult to determine.* Even if adequate measures are devised, despite the difficulties mentioned above, there arc always differences of opinion concerning the time or times at which they should be used. Counselors speak about "preparation for life" and "preparation for life careers," but one may ask if they really mean what these words imply. If these terms arc taken literally, measures of success must be applied continually, and nothing short of evidence of success throughout life could be adequate. If they mean less than a whole lifetime, what fraction must be considered? Shall we assume that success in a boy's first position in the year after he leaves school indicates successful counseling? What can be said if four years later he does not meet even the minimum levels that have been established? Should not the counseling, in addition to the other experiences offered by the school, have prepared the counselee to cope successfully with new problems during those four years? Can successful placement in a first position be the end of counseling process?

It appears likely that the difficulties posed by questions such as these have inhibited persons who might otherwise have attempted to make studies of the effectiveness of their work. If, despite these difficulties, counselors are to make such studies, the implication is clear. They must define their objectives, at least in part, in terms of the time intervals at which they expect to apply the measures of effectiveness agreed upon when the counseling process was begun. (This obligation is one that all educators might consider with profit.) If schools and colleges are going to take credit for the success of their graduates half a century after graduation, they should also accept the responsibility for those who have failed. If they set time limits within which they are absolved of blame for failures, the same limits should be applied to those who succeed.

3. *Appraisal of counseling is an expensive procedure.* Follow-up procedures require time and financial support. Working under the pressures of large numbers of students and short school days and school years, counselors frequently think that they will accomplish more if they devote their efforts to current counselees rather than work with those whose cards have been filed and whose absence makes their study seem less urgent. Postponing the day of reckoning, which must come as more demands are made for appraisal of procedures, they fail to appreciate that time spent upon appraisal studies may provide valuable hints for more efficient use of time with those currently being counseled.

4. *Sufficient incentive for appraisal of counseling has not been provided.* Too often, after new personnel have been added to an educational institution, they are permitted to remain because they establish tenure, seem to do no particular harm (no one checks the graduates to see whether any harm has been done), lighten the loads of others by accepting their obligations (counselors may, for example, be given odious discipline and attendance chores), and after a position is established it becomes traditional to employ such personnel. Since it has not yet become the practice in education to demand evidence of effectiveness (other than certain minimum compliances), the counselor may drift along without disturbing routine by undertaking what seems to be a formidable task. As time passes on, familiar procedures become comfortable and the conscience easier. The administrator who appoints a counselor may prevent such developments by demanding that appraisals be made, and by seeing that the ratio of counselees to counselor is not so high that it precludes consideration of postschool performances.

5. *Many persons fail to appreciate the need for appraisal of counseling.* The basic theory of counseling goes far back into history. Its value has been so generally conceded that there is a common tendency to believe that it *must* be good. Many counselors imply that if the theory is good, its practice must produce good results, and such persons see no reason to question its value. If required to make appraisals of their counseling, they report only in terms of what they have offered. They appraise counseling programs in terms of numbers of classes provided, career conferences held, and interviews arranged. One of the strangest phenomena in an era in which great progress has been made in appraisal of the worth of educational offerings is the common practice of setting up counseling programs in colleges, the Veterans Administration, high schools, and private agencies without any provision for the study of the effects of counseling upon the

subjects. The counselor and the student must learn to distrust all agencies that do not accept the responsibility of follow-up as an essential part of their work.

This condition appears due in part to the traditions that have developed about the whole guidance movement. Since there has been steady growth in the practice of counseling without adequate appraisal, it has now become acceptable (even, at this early period, almost traditional) to omit provisions for appraisal in the planning of counseling programs. If counselors are to avoid criticism concerning the lack of convincing evidence of their worth, there must be a significant increase in the number and quality of evaluative studies.

6. *Many counselors have not learned the value of follow-up data in furthering their programs of public relations.* The success of counseling must always depend in large measure upon the degree of cooperation among school faculties and members of the community. Persons of both categories are often unimpressed by mass statistics, but may become enthusiastic about case reports in which the counselor recounts the success of individuals. A series of such personalized reports, used as supplements to statistical procedure, is invaluable when the counselor is called upon to justify his presence to parents, school personnel, and school committees.

Samples of procedures employed in evaluation of counseling, and some results of their application, are described in the following pages. Use has been made of actual follow-up reports from persons who had been counseled by an adaptive counselor while they were in high school. These are followed by statistical summaries. In presenting both case and statistical reports, the writer hopes to emphasize that evaluation of counseling does not require simply counting, tabulation, and computing. Those processes will be needed, but the counselor must recognize that statistical data may obscure interesting development of individuals.

The following reports of *Bob, Pete,* and *Jane* indicate that evaluators of counseling must be concerned with such matters as choice of training and careers, attitudes toward the social scene, self-confidence, changing self-concepts, social responsibility, and satisfaction with counseling. As he studies the reports about these individuals, the reader may find it interesting to see if he can categorize their responses into such classifications, and others that he may devise.

EVALUATION BY THE ADAPTIVE COUNSELOR

Follow-up Results

The letter below was written to a counselor by *Bob,* a young man in his seventh post-high school year:

Dear former counselor,

Despite the perils of the last seven years, I have endured and barring the unforeseeable, shall be rewarded with a Ph.D. in philosophy from _____ University this spring or summer. As your files will show my unswerving intention has been to become a college or university teacher. At present I am being considered at a wide variety of schools. However, as you are aware the academic unit of currency (the Ph.D.) is suffering from inflation and often will not secure an academic position, even though one is anxious to buy into the business.

In view of all this I would ask you, "What if any, other jobs seem to be of special interest to people of the sort you keep track of?" I realize that this is terribly broad, but perhaps you know what frustrated "lovers of wisdom" seem to do well at outside a college teaching position.

I understand that you cannot resurrect my file and attempt to re-counsel me, taking my idiosyncrasies into account. Nonetheless, both my wife and I would be happy to hear any advice you may have.

Thank you for your time.

Sincerely yours,

Bob

During Bob's high school years, the counselor had worked with him, his parents, and his teachers for the purposes indicated in the definition of counseling on page 55. He had tried to help him with several adjustment and choice problems, and Bob had managed, not without financial difficulty, to get through seven years of post-high school education. He had chosen to work for a Ph.D. in philosophy after considering many other options, and he had reported his progress orally or in writing in each of the six years after high school graduation.

Bob's letter illustrates the following interesting aspects of evaluation in counseling: [12]

1. He believed that the counselor was still interested in him long after counseling was finished.
2. He had been willing to make six annual reports about his progress. The reports seemed to indicate that he had become "a self-actualizing individual" (client-centered definition) who had learned to "solve current and future problems more effectively and independently" (behavioral counseling language).
3. He knows that a cumulative record was maintained and that it contains

---

[12] A succinct statement about problems in the evaluation of counseling and an excellent appraisal of evaluation studies appears in Leona E. Tyler, *The Work of the Counselor* (New York: Appleton-Century-Crofts, 1969).

significant information about him ("taking my idiosyncrasies into account")
which may be valuable many years after it was obtained.
4. He may now have reverted to dependence on the counselor.
5. He realizes that he is an irreversible human being and that the past cannot
be changed. ("I understand that you cannot resurrect my file and attempt
to re-counsel me. . . .")
6. He has not differentiated counsel and advice clearly. In the quotation immediately above he uses the word counsel, but in the next line he says that
he and his wife will be happy "to hear any advice you may have."
7. Social conditions (as Bob puts it, "the academic unit of currency [the
Ph.D.] is suffering from inflation") now reduce his freedom of choice, even
though for the past six years he seemed to have chosen well.

The following excerpts were drawn from a taped interview with *Pete*
five years after he had graduated from high school. A coworker of a counselor who had counseled Pete during his high school years conducted the
session at his home. An attempt has been made to select pertinent samples
from the complete interview. The I indicates the interviewer and the S
responses are by the subject, Pete. Preliminary comments have been eliminated and the first questions relate to his employment status because he
seemed to want to talk about that subject.

I. Your status right now is working; you're employed?
S: That's right.
I: Would you tell me how you like it by naming one of these four cate-
gories? I really like it; my likes just balance my dislikes; I don't like it
but I'll put up with it; and I hate it.
S: Well, I'd have to say that I really like it.
I: Why do you name the one you do?
S: I really like it because I believe that I've been given an opportunity,
not only with this particular job that I'm doing now, but throughout
the time I've been working for the company to learn things that would
help me not only in the field of foundry work but also in any other field
I might go into. In other words they've let me do almost, it's a fact, it's
hard to believe that they've let me do almost any thing I've wanted to
do. I have had very little supervision. They don't tell me every morning, "now you go to such and such a time and do this," and then two
or three hours later come and ask me why I didn't do it. They've really
treated me good.
I: You've mentioned that this will lead into other things. What training
have you had that would carry over into other areas and what other
areas could you go into?
S: Well, engineering, I think I would have a practical background, work
experience with problems that might crop up again sometime. Such as
I worked in a quality control lab for awhile, testing sand and things

like that and you become familiar with control methods and you can apply them to other operations.

I: What is there about you that makes you successful in what you are doing?

S: Well, if I'm successful I believe it is because I like what I'm doing. I recognize now that I have been given an opportunity and I'll try to take advantage of it. When you try to take advantage of an opportunity, things usually work out pretty well.

I: What is there about you that handicaps you in what you are doing?

S: Well, I believe that at the present time, if I had say a metallurgical degree there's a lot of things that I've wanted to try in the foundry business that I would hesitate to try now without the title so to speak. Right now, if someone were to stop me on the street and ask "What do you do?" why I'd be up against it so to speak. I'd have to say, "Well, I work for a foundry and I'm a core rigger," they would say, "What's a core rigger?" You see that's what I'm classified as now, and before that a layout man. I'd have to say well, "I'm a casting layout man." "Well, what's a casting layout man?" Whereas if I had a job title or something "Well, I'm a metallurgist." Not only the title but I'd be able to try the various things and have more of a free rein.

I: You feel then that the lack of a degree and a title handicap you most in what you are doing?

S: Lack of the recognition that comes with having a degree, I would say, or having the education.

I: What would you like to be doing five years from now?

S: I would like to be in engineering, in the engineering field. I could be happy doing that. I've never been unhappy at work. That's a fact. I've been fortunate. I think that I'd like to be testing in the automotive field. Testing possibly in the foundry end of the automotive field.

I: And ten years from now?

S: Progressing in the field.

(Pete then described his experiences in the armed forces during the past two and one half years. He reported favorably on them.)

I: If you could live over again the last five years since you left high school, would you do the same things as you have done?

S: I think I would have. With very few exceptions I think I would have done the same things as I have done.

I: Why?

S: Well, when I left high school I had no idea of what I wanted to do. And I of course knew that sooner or later I'd be drafted. I didn't want to hurry up things. At the time I didn't believe it was good policy to hurry up things, get in and get it over with because at the time the war was on. And I didn't try to dodge them but I waited until they wanted me. And so I really would have waited anyway until I completed my military obligation. And possibly I might have started school right after getting out of the army. In other words that following September I could have started you know.

I: Had you any thoughts of going on to school at the time? Was it in your mind at all?

S: Yes, it was. I think the only thing that stopped me was we were contemplating going into business. My father and I as a family, and I thought that I had to devote full time to it. And there was a lot of other things too. We had property over in another town. We had tenants in there and we had a little trouble with them because my parents were in Florida and you can imagine how it is, renting a house when you're in Florida and the house is up here. We got rather undesirable people in there. We had quite a bit of trouble that way. And then we decided not to go into business, fortunately. Up here anyway.

I: Looking toward the future, do you think things are going to work out well, for you?

S: I think if the work holds together they will, yes.

I: Why?

S: Well, I'm going to do everything in my power to make them. I'm going to do the best I can in everything and everything that I attempt.

I: What do you actually do on the job now? You told me before we had the tape on, but could you sum it up for me?

S: Well, at the present time I'm modifying this machine. It's owned by the company. And I'm modifying some of our older core boxes, in other words, the core boxes that were used to make cores the old way and modifying them so that we can make them with a shell core method. At times I do run the machine, in other words make cores. That's about what I do.

I: Apparently there's more of a challenge in modifying the machine than it would be to grinding on a machine, do I gather correctly?

S: There is no challenge to running the machine at all. That's the object of the whole thing . . . to set up a department to make cores using unskilled labor. We have an overabundance of unskilled labor that want to work in the foundry. It costs quite a bit to teach core makers you know, old time core makers. They don't have any formal education, but they do have considerable skill in making cores. And it costs quite a bit to have them make a core. So it will benefit the company to use the shell core maker.

I: Why did you choose the job you have now?

S: The shell core job or the company? Working for the company?

I: Well, let's take that one first, why did you take that one?

S: Possibly you will remember Mr. P——— from our high school. He's dead now, but at the time he worked summers for the company as a personnel man. I had a class by Mr. P——— and just before we graduated he asked me if I had a job for the summer, and I said no. I had a job, but actually it wasn't too good and I had thought about looking around for another job. He asked me if I'd like a job. He didn't mention it or what it was or anything and I said sure. And he gave me the address of the company and they were evidently expecting me. They interviewed me and offered me a job as a shipping clerk. And I accepted it. And when I came back, I think it was five or six days later, they had changed their mind. They had put me down on loading ovens that come in with red hot cores on them and I'd have to take these cores off. Well, I really wasn't prepared for that. I wouldn't have gone after that job, you know ordinarily. So a few days later, three days later when I was going to quit they put me in the laboratory testing metals and testing sand. Then I was put on layout.

I: Why did you choose this particular job you have now?

S: Well, mainly it was that they offered me the job and it meant a little more money. That's always a good item I think and I thought it would give me a little more experience which would be very valuable to me. Because the layouts, once you've done layouts for a year or two for the same company, unless they're changing constantly, changing their methods and types of castings it gets to be pretty general, pretty habit forming. You don't really learn anything. Oh, you learn things every day, actually in life, but you don't seem to progress. It doesn't get boring but it approaches on the boring, you know. So that was the main reason I thought I might pick up some information. And then of course I'll have to be truthful. There were a couple of people in this pattern shop where I was doing the layout work and I felt it might be better for those people and myself if we were separated.

(Pete then reported that he had obtained several raises in pay.)

I: What if anything would make you change jobs?

S: Well, if the work was as pleasant and held the opportunities that the work holds now that I'm doing and if it offered me more money, I would go and take the job.

I: Do you plan to change jobs?

S: No, I don't.

I: What is the difference between the work you did when you began and the work you are doing now?

S: I would say it is the difference between doing a job that was a laborer's job and doing something now that is actually working with the development of new methods in our shop.

I: Have you had any training since high school: college, apprentice, short courses, or anything like that?

S: Technical courses, academic courses? Well, let's see, I took a welding course. Would that be what you are talking about?

I: Well, yes, that might be a self-improvement course. Was it at night school?

S: Night school. I took it just so I could weld on my own car. I like to work on cars and I intend to build cars someday as a hobby and that's why I took welding. Then I took a blue print reading course. That really helped. Anyway I took that before I went into the Army. Since then I attempted a short story course from the University Extension. That didn't pan out too well, because I really didn't agree too well with the way things were running. In other words, I didn't know how to write a story and he wanted a story and possibly I'm not a writer, or don't have the ability, so I thought it would be a little more interesting than it turned out for me. Possibly it helped most of the people there. Then I'm taking drafting and mechanical drafting at the vocational school.

I: Looking back at your high school experience tell me how it helped you most.

S: Well, I have to say that I wasted four years that I shouldn't have wasted. It was no one's fault. I can't blame it on to teachers or my parents and I can't even blame it on to myself, when you come right down to it, psychologically that is. But how it's helped me? I think I might have picked up a little English usage in high school and in world history I certainly learned a little bit about world history. But actually I didn't let high school help me too much.

I: Could you tell me how high school failed to help you?

S: If it failed I don't believe that it was the high school's fault. But I do believe that they should have, evidently I had the ability, at least average ability to learn. I believe they should have used more discipline than they did use to make me learn. Do you know what I mean? I believe someone should have gotten to me in the ninth grade or so, or whenever I tended to become lax in my studies. I believe someone should have said to me, "All right boy," you know, "let's get with it!" Possibly they were so overcrowded that they just didn't have the people to do that sort of thing. Possibly they can't do that sort of thing, I don't know. So I do believe that they should have pushed me, not only me, but people like me. When I went into high school I didn't know what I would need to get in to college, in other words, what courses to take and a lot of those courses like algebra and geometry are electives. They are not required and if I would have known. Well, actually I can't say that I didn't know that you'd need mathematics, but as a high school kid I didn't think I'd have to get an A in algebra because I'm going to go to college in five years. I just didn't think like that and I should have been trained to think like that. They train the mind to think, don't they? That's what they're supposed to do and I don't believe that they did train my mind to think along those lines.

I: Looking back at the *counseling* you had in high school, could you tell us how it helped you?

S: Counseling by who? By the counselor or somebody else? I think that I had some, if you can call it counseling. I think you could call it counseling by the vice-principal of the school. He tried to straighten me out, but I knew just what he was trying to do, and I wasn't about to shape up. I think I did a little bit better after I talked to him, but only because I *had* to talk to him and I didn't like to talk to him. . . . I wanted to stay away from him. But as far as counseling with counselors I believe that they were the ones. If I ever became educationally minded why I think it was because of them. And I think that I started to think about them not so much when I was in high school but more so when I was in the Army. Isn't that funny? I thought about it then. When you are in the Army you have a lot of time to think, on guard duty or one thing and another, and I thought about their counseling and wondered about it. I really did wonder about it. I wondered about things like their tests. I believe they gave an aptitude test. I believe it was given through the counselors and I began to wonder about things like that you know. When you wonder then you began to think about finding answers to the things that you wonder about.

I: How did counseling fail to help you?

S: I don't believe you can say that it actually failed. Actually if anything done to help you, fails, it's because you don't let it help you. I believe that I just floated through it. Whatever they tried to do I just didn't take it too seriously.

I: Your comments about that delayed effectiveness are very interesting.

S: About what?

I: The delayed effects of counseling . . . coming back to you while you were in the service. It stimulated your thinking.

S: Another thing, off the record, if that's all right?

I: Sure, and if you want the tape recorder off?

S: Oh, no, no. Another thing that strikes me, and I think people should know this and I think it should be installed in the minds of people in high school. A person, a man particularly, should become aware of his responsibilities to himself and to society. He's not just for himself. Guys like me that are capable, I believe that I'm capable of becoming, not anything, but a few things anyway. I believe it's guys like me that should be coaxed into this thing and they should become aware of their responsibilities to society. It's that responsibility that I've become aware of that's another factor in my contemplating going back to school.

I: Would you give me the names of any political organizations, clubs, social, recreational or church groups you have attended regularly during the past three years?

S: I don't belong to any clubs or anything of that sort.

I: What sort of interest or hobbies do you have? I gather that cars are one.

S: Interest with me is a thing that is not a matter of subject. I don't believe that a man should say, "I'm interested in physics and I'm not interested in baseball." I believe that any interest is a matter of his whole life. He's interested in life and life includes baseball and physics. So actually I'm interested in anything that people can do or, in the line of a hobby, in anything. I could be interested in just about anything. I don't claim to know everything, or know anything about everything but I can be interested. I can work up quite an interest in anything if it's presented properly or uniquely, you might say.

I: Do you have any specific hobbies?

S: I can't say that I have a specific hobby.

I: Have you voted in any political elections?

S: Yes, the last election I voted and that was the only one I voted in. No, I voted on an absentee ballot once in the Army too.

I: Why have you voted?

S: Why did I vote? I had been brought up by my father who is a firm believer that if the man is a citizen he has an obligation to vote, and do various other things by becoming at least partly familiar with current events and things of that sort. Although, I think I fall down on it a little bit, because I don't like to read about Egypt and Israel. Things of that sort, I don't like to read about things like that actually. I should but I don't like to.

I: We mentioned self-improvement activities. The short stories, the blueprint, the drafting, and the welding course. Any others?

S: No, I can't think of anything else I've got. Oh wait. I took a rapid reading course when I was in the Army. And I really think that was something. I suppose you have something like that in college.

I: No. I've often felt a need for it, but I'm aware that these courses of training exist. Since people spend the hours that they do in reading it might be a wise thing for everybody to do.

S: Although when you're reading Hemingway, I happen to like to read Hemingway, I don't believe that you should read 400 to 500 words a minute. In fact I take a paragraph a day and actually *feel* what he writes. A wonderful writer, prose writer.

I: Do you find time to do a lot of reading?

S: I do, at times. I do find a lot of time to read. And at other times I don't find any time to read. But I don't think there's a week goes by, but what I don't read something, you know. But mostly, in the wintertime I read practically every night and every day. You know that's one time when I do read. The summer, well I like to get out in my car and sort of run around a little bit.

I: Do you have confidence in the actions you take when you have to make decisions?

S: I have to. I really haven't made too many grave decisions. But I haven't had any trouble along those lines, making decisions.

I: If you needed help in the last five years in making decisions, to whom did you go?

S: Well, mostly my parents or my employer.

I: Any interesting plans for the future?

S: Well, I think that the future can only be interesting, but interesting to what extent?

I: In your own mind.

S: In my own mind, I think it would be mighty interesting if I go to school and if I complete the training, you know, and get a nice job somewhere. I think that'll be very interesting.

I: Well, two more questions. First, if you could give one bit of advice to a high school student on the basis of your experiences, what would it be?

S: Well, I would say that I would advise him to think more seriously of what he's doing in high school and what he will do. Think more about the future, but especially about what he's doing in high school and so that he will be prepared in case that he decides to go to school. Go on to school, or whatever he decides.

I: And the last one. What things in life give you the greatest satisfaction and happiness?

S: Well. I think we all like to have a job well done. Complete a day and really have accomplished something. I really don't think that gives complete satisfaction.

I: What gives you the greatest happiness or satisfaction?

S: Well, I'd really say that having completed a job very well would give me possibly the greatest satisfaction. Or if I have been of some use or value to society.

Pete's responses, like Bob's, illustrate some of the situations and problems encountered by an adaptive school counselor when he undertakes longitudinal evaluation studies. As in Bob's statements, the influence of social conditions (in this case war and the draft) may be seen. It seems clear that both have solved many of their problems independently; have not differentiated clearly between counsel and advice; know that a record of their performances was kept; and believe that the counselor is still interested in them long after counseling is finished.[13]

Although there are some common elements in the reports (and more might have been found if Bob had been interviewed), Pete's reports contain some of the following differences and additions:

1. Pete does not seek assistance. He is quite sure that he can manage his own affairs and make his own decisions, and he is optimistic about the future.
2. He seems to imply that the counselor had some goals for him in mind during the counseling.
3. He did not enter formal post-high school education (Bob had been in such training for seven years), but he has carried on informal self-improvement activities.
4. Choice of occupation seems to have been a very casual matter despite the fact that the counselor had done his best to provide what is said to be good vocational guidance.
5. Despite the random nature of the choice, Pete's job satisfaction appears to be high.
6. He seems to be quite vague about what counselors do. He does, however, differentiate between being coerced by a vice-principal to "shape up" and the counselor's activities. He also seems to have forgotten many of such activities reported in the counselor's records. He appears to remember only that the counselor gave him an aptitude test (actually he took several) and urged him to continue into post-high school education.
7. He seems to be self-confident in decision-making.
8. He shows some evidence of creativity.
9. He says that he has recognized his responsibilities to society.

---

[13] Although Pete had no formal training beyond high school, he was described by the interviewer as "quite a philosopher and a deep thinker." The interviewer also reported that he seemed to do more thinking about himself and analyzing questions about himself than most, and there seemed to be a good deal of introspection in his answers. He was described as giving the impression of "an easy sort of confidence and assurance," and had the interviewer not known otherwise he would have thought he was a college graduate. None of these attributes appeared in his cumulative high school record.

10. He seems to have done considerable self-analysis.
11. In general he appears to reveal a positive view of himself.[14]

The reports from Bob and Pete have been offered in an attempt to put some flesh on the dry bones of statistics and statements which commonly appear in discussions of counseling evaluation. Among the issues revealed by these reports are questions concerning times at which evaluation should be done, techniques to be employed, and appraisal of the data obtained.

Counselors need to consider seriously the question of when evaluation should be done. If, for example, they consider counseling as a process designed to produce immediate and specific results, and are not concerned with transfer and carry-over effects, their goals will be more easily attained and evaluation seemingly easier to accomplish. However, if they are concerned with broader goals that imply a carry-over to new situations and continue for long periods of time, the counseling task becomes more complex and evaluation more difficult.[15]

If counselors are concerned about the broader and longer picture, for how long should they follow their subjects? Does a counselor who gets annual reports from former counselees over a ten-year period go to the well too often? Should he stop evaluation at the end of one year because factors over which he has no control will intervene, or should he continue for many years in the belief that good counseling will be demonstrated by the manner in which his subjects handle the interventions? The answers to such questions must depend on a counselor's statement of objectives, since the evaluation should be made in their terms. Unfortunately, most definitions set no time limits. One finds statements to the effect that "The purpose of counseling is to help people to become self-sufficient and effective problem solvers," [16] or that the goal of client-centered therapy is "the

[14] Since so little follow-up work has been done, there are no guides, other than one's own judgment, for conducting interviews. Obviously some questions need to be structured to be sure that certain areas are given consideration, but beyond that point our subjects were free to talk about their own concerns in words of their own choosing. Pete wanted to discuss his employment at length and was encouraged to do so. It did not seem proper to divert him, and it can be seen that he did reveal a good deal about himself. No two of all the follow-up interviews conducted were alike.

[15] There has been much debate about whether counselors are concerned with making of current decisions or with the development of decision-making skills. In actual practice both are important. The time comes when a counselee must decide whether or not to take a job or enter a program of training. It is desirable that he be helped in the process of making that decision at the time, and *also* that he be given assistance in developing skills which will be useful in the future. The two processes are not antithetical, and the debate seems futile.

[16] J. D. Krumboltz and C. E. Thoresen, *Behavioral Counseling: Cases and Techniques* (New York: Holt, Rinehart and Winston, Inc., 1969), p. 290.

development of a reasonable independence in a client who takes responsibility for himself, his behavior, his choices and decisions, and his values and goals," [17] but there is no indication of how long these characteristics of self-sufficiency and reasonable independence are to last.[18] Has counseling failed if these behaviors are not found in counselees at some later, unspecified time? There is probably no consensus on this issue, and much consideration of it is needed. Discussion might result in more realistic statements of goals for, and much more thorough evaluation of, the counseling process.

Discussion of techniques for evaluation are considered in other sections of this volume and need not be repeated here, but the difficulties in interpretation of the large amounts of complex data obtained in longitudinal follow-up studies need much consideration. An evaluation of counseling must be prepared, for example, to grapple with problems caused by differences in personal and group definitions of such terms as success, self-sufficiency, adjustment, independence, and good decision-making. Some of these problems are revealed in the short reports on Bob and Pete, but they are highlighted in the description of *Jane:*

> Jane scored at superior level on tests and made top grades during all her years of attendance at a high school with a graduating class of 200. During her first years in school she had difficulty in relating to her peers, but she became well accepted and a small group of friends sought her as a companion in many activities. After much consideration of occupations and choice of an institution for post-high school education she indicated a preference for social work and was admitted with a scholarship to a large university with high academic standards. She had been counseled regularly during her school years.
>
> During her first three years at the university she made high grades and she said that she was well satisfied with her choice of career and place for training. She participated in many of the usual university-sponsored activities and reported that her social life was highly satisfactory. At the end of her third year she, her parents, her teacher, and her counselors believed that she had made good decisions and was making excellent progress.
>
> In her response to a follow-up questionnaire near the end of her fourth year at the university Jane described several changes in her values, and investigations showed that her behavior reflected the

[17] C. H. Patterson et al., "A Current View of Client-Centered or Relationship Therapy," *Journal of Counseling Psychology,* I, No. 2 (Summer 1969), p. 13.

[18] The definition of counseling used in this volume unfortunately suffers from the same lack of limitation of time. Evidence that the author takes the long-term view may be found in his follow-up studies and the fact that at the time of this writing he was conducting his 20-year after high school follow-up of students counseled during the years 1948–1951.

changes. She was asked, for example, to tell about her activities with respect to items commonly reported by superior students by checking a list of 29 conventional statements which included the six listed below.

Published your work in the college paper

Took a role in college dramatics

Represented a college department at a
special event

Appeared on a television or radio program

Participated in a symposium.

Jane noted that she had done the first and last of the items above, and then went on to ask why the former counselor had not asked her if she had done the following activities.

Gone to jail

Argued endlessly with liberal professors
(especially behaviorists)

Sold drugs

Got her head cracked by cops

Co-opted young liberals into the radical
movement.

She indicated that she had done these things and then she added that, "I went to jail after a demonstration. I learned a lot and became more active. Class orientation is hard to see objectively. . . . Jail helps you in this as you keep your class privileges while others are oppressed in front of your nose."

She indicated further that she would not graduate with her class because she had accumulated too many incompletes while carrying on political activities; that she considered her fellow students as too uptight and unimaginative; that the best minds are in the radical movement; and that she would not advise others to go to the same university or similar "high class places, as there is a direct inverse ratio of class and educational relevance." She said that she expected to be in a detention camp for radicals five years later.

Four years after Jane's counseling there were indications of dissatisfaction with self (including a reference to suicidal tendencies), unsatisfactory educational performances, social behavior which included breaking laws, uncertainty about a career, and pessimism about the future. Her parents were heartbroken and her teachers disappointed. All of the above suggest that Jane had not done well according to conventional standards. On the other hand, she had made independent decisions, showed considerable social concern that went beyond mere verbalization, was self-actualizing in what she considered to be a responsible manner, and believed herself to be a self-sufficient and effective problem solver. Is there evidence in Jane's behavior of effective counseling? Ineffective counseling? No residue of counseling? No relationship to counseling? Changes in social circumstances for which there was inadequate preparation by parents, teachers, and the counselor? Can counselors expect to have any influence on a subject four years after counseling is completed? Should evaluation have been discontinued when there seemed to be specific and precise (and seemingly desirable) outcomes immediately following the counseling? Is it possible that the ancient (but also current) belief that "As the twig is bent so grows the tree" is no longer credible?

Study of the vignettes of Bob, Pete, and Jane, and comments concerning them, suggest that evaluation of counseling is not an easy task. However, it must be undertaken by counselors to assist them in clarifying their objectives, grasping the complexity of work they undertake, recognizing the need for cooperation with others, realizing that there are requirements of accountability, and adapting their procedures as evaluation data suggest may be necessary. Some suggestions for performing evaluation that may assist in such processes are presented in the following pages.

If a school counselor has urged his colleagues to join him in some evaluative follow-up studies of former students, and they have accepted the challenge, the first step would require them to state their objectives in terms that permitted evaluation. Many lists of school objectives have been offered, and while they differ in words used, they have much in common. None is all-inclusive or universally acceptable, but in some cases, as in the following list, there is enough specificity within the general categories to give direction to a faculty's evaluative efforts.

CRITERIA FOR EVALUATION OF A SCHOOL IN TERMS OF THE
CURRENT AND FUTURE BEHAVIORS OF ITS STUDENTS

1. *Intellectual Competence:* Scholarship, intellectual curiosity and drive, use of scientific methods, study skills and habits
2. *Cultural Development:* Arts, sports, student activities, social service, hobbies
3. *Practical Competence:* Common sense and judgment, ordinary manual skills, environmental adjustability
4. *Philosophy of Life:* Ethical standards, respect for others' points of view, vocational objectives
5. *Character Traits:* Integrity, responsibility, initiative, and similar behavior
6. *Emotional Balance:* Worry, self-control, confidence, sense of humor, sense of security, sensitivity, independence
7. *Social Fitness:* Making and keeping friends, voice, courtesy, social accomplishments
8. *Sensitivity to Social Problems:* Concern for local and general contemporary social, economic, and political problems; assumption of responsibilities of citizenship
9. *Physical Fitness:* Health habits, activities

To apply the criteria in a follow-up study in a cooperative endeavor, it seems likely that various faculty members, although they might profess concern for developments in all the areas, would indicate *primary* responsibilities in selected categories. Thus the physical education staff would elect to accept accountability for the ninth, the social studies staff for the eighth, and the school psychologist for the sixth items on the list. Unless the counselor has stated his objectives with evaluation in mind, he will be faced with a difficult problem. When staff members ask him to state the area in which his chief responsibilities lie, it will not be enough for him to say that he, too, is concerned about all the areas.

If the counselor employs the definition of counseling given on page 55, he may find some assistance in naming his areas of accountability. He can indicate that he has attempted to help his counselees toward better undertsanding of self, which should result in better decision-making than might have been achieved if there had been no counseling. He may point out that accomplishment of other goals might be futile if they did not result in the making of effective choices in important personal matters. Thus he could propose as his prime responsibility the securing of information about the choices which former students made at decisive points. (The reader is reminded that this will be a follow-up study. Evaluations of performances of current students may require similar, but not identical, procedures.)

If there has been proper planning for the follow-up work during the period of counseling in school, the counselor can obtain valid information about a former counselee's post-high school activities which have resulted from the decisions he has made.[19] Questionnaires can provide dependable data about counselee's post-high school educational, vocational, avocational, and social activities, and although the data are less likely to be dependable, useful information about personal development can be procured by supplementing the questionnaire data with sampling interviews.[20]

The results obtained by application of such instruments may be of considerable interest and value to the faculty and to citizens in the community, but the difficult problem of appraisal remains. Since society and its educational institutions have not delegated the evaluation of human behavior to the counseling profession, the counselor's interpretation of the results may be considered as only one small voice. Even if persons do not have any right to judge one another's behavior, they will certainly continue to do so. Former counselees themselves, parents, colleagues on school faculties, members of school boards, representatives of the press, staff members of law enforcement agencies, and sundry others will appraise the col-

---

[19] See suggestions for doing so with 100 per cent results in J. W. M. Rothney, *Guidance Practices and Results, op. cit.; idem., Educational, Vocational and Social Performances of Counseled and Uncounseled Youth Ten Years After High School,* Cooperative Research Project Report No. SAE 9231 (Washington, D.C.: U.S. Office of Education, 1963).

[20] R. M. Jackson and J. W. M. Rothney "A Comparative Study of the Mailed Questionnaire and the Interview in Follow-up Studies," *Personnel and Guidance Journal,* XXXIX (1961).

lected facts. No counselor can ignore their voices; [21] the audacity with which this has been done by proponents of certain counseling systems has not enhanced the reputation of the counseling profession.

Grinding of personal axes in interpretation of follow-up data is no more proper in evaluation than it is in counseling situations, but this should not inhibit the counselor from stating his interpretations. He just needs to remind himself that he is speaking as a member of a school staff, and to remind others that he has had the opportunity to know the counselees well through depth interviews over a considerable period of time, that he has kept cumulative records of their activities, and that the counselees' plans had been discussed with him.

Some problems in evaluation may be seen by consideration of the following data actually obtained in a follow-up study. The counseled students whose post-high school training performances are reported in Table 6–1 had been counseled by adaptive counselors during their high school years. The comparison students, whose test scores, home backgrounds, and previous academic performances were similar to the counseled students', had not had any contact with a professional counselor.

TABLE 6–1

Percentages of Subjects
Ten Years After High School Graduation
Who Had Completed or Were Enrolled
in Post-High School Training [a]

STATUS	COUNSELED STUDENTS (N=343)	COMPARISON STUDENTS (N=341)
Hold bachelor or advanced degree	23	15
Current college undergraduate	4	3
Post-college graduate study	1	1
Hold certificate (includes RN)	10	9
Completed apprenticeship	2	4
Took no post-high school training	49	57
Dropped out of training	11	11

[a] For details of the study see Rothney, *Educational, Vocational and Social Performances, op. cit.*

The only major difference indicated in the table is that 8 per cent more of the counseled subjects held bachelor or advanced degrees, and 8 per cent fewer members of the comparison group entered post-high school

[21] This point of view does not require that the counselor be a defender of the status quo. Despite statements that persons in established positions do not want change, the extent of change in society indicates that there are many who do not resist it.

training. These differences might be accepted as socially significant by those who consider the financial outlay necessary if 8 per cent more of our high school graduates entered and remained to graduate from colleges. Others might consider the differences socially insignificant and, further, might suggest that they indicate the ineffectiveness of educational guidance. Another group might quibble about statistical procedures, note the absence of any significant (statistical) difference, and reject the data completely.

But perhaps the data do indicate social significance. Education is the largest industry in the country, and the increasing extent to which it is supported financially indicates that society wants its young people to get all the education from which they can profit. Those who accept the latter statement might decide that, since the data indicate that counseling is supportive of society's desire, educational counseling, at least, is worthy of support.

Another observer, thinking of each of the 684 persons whose group status is presented in the table, might decide that, in view of the individual differences which must be represented in the groups, the data do not indicate that each person was well served. It might have been better for some of the college graduates to have dropped out; some who took apprenticeships might have profited more from college attendance; and some who undertook no post-high school education may have made wise decisions.

At this point the school counselor may well point out that an attempt had been made to help the counseled students in important decision-making, and choice of post-high school education requires the making of an important decision. He will also point out that, since furtherance of education seems to be in the direction that the school and society desire, and since he is a citizen and a helping member of a school staff, the results permit him to say that adding a counselor to the faculty of a public high school makes it more likely that the school will accomplish the objectives (in this case with respect to post-high school education) it set out to achieve.

The illustration above suggests the manner in which the adaptive counselor will go about one phase of his evaluation efforts. Note that the goals were derived from his assumption of accountability to school and society as well as to particular counselees with respect to a decision (educational choice) important to both institutions and individuals. The period of follow-up was long enough to determine whether there had been any lasting residue from attempts to help the counselees, and the data were verified by records which could not be slanted by wishful thinking on the part of the counselor, his coworkers, or the subjects themselves. The information is based on records of accomplishment rather than impressions of raters or responses to questionable instruments which attempt to measure attitudes toward post-high school education.

Readers will probably point out that the illustration represents an area in which definite verifiable evidence about former counselees can be obtained. It is more difficult to get dependable data about the subjects' personal-social adjustments, feelings of adequacy, assessments of his personal worth, and many other items commonly under the headings of character and citizenship in lists of school objectives, and under such terms as self-actualization and congruency used by psychologists. The counselor would be well advised to admit to critics that no sound answers are available to questions about the validity of self-assessment techniques. He can only use the best techniques he can find, point out their limitations and strengths, report what he has found, indicate his own interpretations of findings, and encourage his coworkers to draw their own conclusions.

As strengths of his evaluation techniques, he may note that his questionnaire data were supplemented by sample interviews; his subjects were not forced to make choices among undefined self-descriptive terms, but were permitted to report in their own words and at the length of their own choosing; all census-type data (marriages and divorces, for example) were verified; and observation of patterns of usual behavior and significant deviations from them were obtained over a period of time.

Among the several limitations of his techniques, he should indicate that social circumstances often influence results; there is great variability in the extent to which persons can and are willing to report accurately about themselves; it is difficult to appraise evidence of development of persons who started counseling at widely different levels; and there is a problem in assessing a former counselee's behavior in view of the variety of individuals' personal philosophies and the goals of society.

Counselors should make it clear that attempts to get satisfactory data about counselees' feelings about themselves and about their satisfaction with counseling have revealed so many shortcomings in the techniques employed that all reports of such studies are suspect. A critical appraisal of these techniques must lead to the conclusion that the difficulties of getting completely valid data are so great that they are currently unsurmountable. In view of these circumstances, the counselor should be exceedingly cautious about basing much of his evaluation on counselees' self-appraisals or reports.

Analysis of reports of former counselees' self-appraisals leads into a semantic jungle. It was pointed out previously (page 69) that verbal behavior during counseling may be influenced by abstruseness, understatements, histrionics, metaphors, and hyperbole. All of these can appear in combination with attempts at self-aggrandizement, alibis, and projections in follow-up reports. There is always the possibility of unintentional or deliberate deception and highly personal interpretations of word meanings. Thus when Tom reports that he "feels like a new man" (page 39) without some point of reference or definition of his terms, one must question the significance of his statement. When a teacher reports without elaboration that a student "has shown significant improvement in being socially responsible to many of his peers" (page 39), the listener is left to decide for himself what is meant by "significant," "improvement," "socially responsible," and "many." When a former counselee of the writer reported that counseling had helped him, "By getting me on the right path in life and giving me a broader outlook," one month after he had been sentenced to a long prison term for absconding with his employer's funds, there was reason to doubt the validity of the statement. The counselor who recognizes the problems in use of uncorroborated self-assessment and counselee satisfaction data will consider them of lesser value than verifiable census data in his evaluative reports. He will not deny their importance, but will simply indicate that techniques for procuring them are unsatisfactory. He may experiment with methods that he devises for his own purposes in the hope of increasing their effectiveness.

Reference up to this point has been to the responses of individuals, but there are times when a counselor and other interested persons may want to get information about the general reaction of a group of former counselees to what they had experienced. One counselor asked a group of 300 persons who had been counseled during their high school years [22] to respond to the question, "Looking back at the counseling you had in high school, tell how it helped you." The question was posed to the same group when they had been out of school two and one-half, five, and ten years. Their freely-written responses were then placed into the categories in Table 6–2.

Even with all the limitations of such data, it is possible to interpret these as indicating that a majority of the subjects looked back favorably upon the counseling they had received, although there was a decrease in satisfaction as the years passed.[23] (Did this counselor extend his study too long?) The counselor could also find in the figures some suggestions for revision of his practices. For example, he might decide that in future counseling it would be desirable to make it clear to his subjects that the counseling sessions provided opportunities to talk things over. In addition, the data might make him more cautious about claiming that counseling reduces the school dropout rate. Thus the *group* data do offer general information about counselee satisfaction, indicate possible improvements in practices,

---

[22] The numbers varied slightly over the period of the study due to death and the failure of a few subjects to respond to the question.

[23] The ten-year data are from Rothney, *Educational, Vocational and Social Performances, op. cit.*

TABLE 6–2

Responses of Former Counselees

RESPONSES [a]	YEARS AFTER HIGH SCHOOL		
	% 2½ YEARS	% 5 YEARS	% 10 YEARS
It helped my personal development (provided help in self-analysis, built self-confidence, helped with adjustment problems, made me aware of assets and limitations)	22	25	15
It helped in planning for the future (made me aware of opportunities, made me think of the future, etc.)	20	12	16
It helped vocationally (helped to choose the right vocation, channeled thinking on vocation, established vocational goals, etc.)	18	14	16
It helped educationally (helped to choose right courses, get better grades, stimulated educational planning beyond high school, etc.)	12	13	13
It gave me a chance to talk things over (provided someone to talk to, someone interested in me, someone who cared about me, etc.)	7	5	5
It kept me in school (It kept me in school when I was going to leave)	0	0	1
I received no counseling	0	1	3
It did not help	8	17	19
Sub-totals	87	87	88

a Approximately 12 per cent each year gave irrelevant responses which could not be placed in the categories.

and suggest cautions to be heeded in claiming effectiveness. Regardless of the interpretations that he and his colleagues make of reports of counselee satisfaction, the counselor will make it clear that, because no valid instruments for measuring it have yet been devised, the reports in themselves do not provide evidence of counseling effectiveness.

These samples of evaluation attempts have been drawn from studies of the post-high school performances of counseled adolescents, but there is reason to believe that the basic concepts are applicable in the evaluation of counseling at all levels. Elementary school counselors can study the performances of their subjects when they move into high schools, and college counselors can determine whether there has been any carry-over as their subjects enter graduate or professional schools and employment. Both elementary and college counselors, since they are comparative latecomers to the field, are subject to considerable questioning of their contributions by those who are asked to support them, and they need evidence to justify their endorsement. Practitioners at those levels can profit from observation of difficulties caused by the failure of high school and college counselors to evaluate their efforts. By making evaluation an intrinsic part of their work, they may forestall the criticism which has been leveled at counseling and, what may be more important, they may find in their evaluations some suggestions for improvement of their performances.

Comparison Groups in Evaluation Studies

Only one reference has thus far been made to the use of control or comparison groups in evaluation studies. For many years the writer has maintained that lack of a control group in an evaluation study vitiated any conclusions that researchers presented. After conducting many counseling evaluation studies in which control groups were used in the manner commonly employed by social scientists, he is now forced to the conclusion that their use cannot be justified.

When a researcher sets up a control group, he finds subjects who are comparable to his experimental subjects *at only one point in time.* The subjects may seem to be alike in terms of averages and variances of relatively few of the thousands of factors which may be operating to influence their behavior, but their histories up to that time are not known. Similarity of level of performance at one point of development does not assure that individuals in both groups arrived at those levels at similar paces, that the subjects are not at quite dissimilar levels in their own developmental patterns, and that the future development of members of the control and experimental groups would remain parallel if no intervention occurred.[24] Such considerations are dismissed by some researchers who assume that differences will be equally common to the members of both groups. This assumption must be considered less tenable for complex human beings living in complicated environments than it is in experiments with lower animals, plants, and inanimate objects. Another usual assumption is that if large populations are used there is more chance that differences will cancel out, but the accretion of subjects serves only to *increase* the number of individual differences. Such considerations prompted the writer and a colleague to make the following statement:

> In view of the complexity of persons, and the various ways in which persons reach any state of complexity, the common procedure

[24] For illustrations of how individuals who are at similar levels at one age differ at earlier and later ages, see W. F. Dearborn and J. W. M. Rothney, *Predicting the Child's Development*, rev. ed. (Cambridge, Mass.: Sci-Art Publishers, 1963). Discussion of some implications of such differences appear in Chap. I of this volume.

of using control groups in experiments in which a few currently obtainable variables are controlled, and in which assumptions are made that others of the countless uncontrolled factors will cancel out, is highly questionable. *Concluding that differences between experimental and comparison groups are necessarily related to an experimental treatment rather than to the extension of patterns of individual development that may have preceded, continued through, and persisted after an experiment should be done very cautiously, if at all.* Few controlled experiments in the guidance field have provided enough longitudinal data on the subjects. Those authors who heed the caution about possible interpretation of results as development rather than as effects of treatment are few. We seem to need either studies in which the cautions noted above are heeded, or the relegation of control group studies to that oblivion to which matched pair experiments have been assigned.[25]

A decision to eschew use of a control group raises another problem. Without comparison group data an evaluator will be hard put to give a satisfactory response to any skeptic who asks the counselor for evidence that change in a counseled individual would not have occurred without counseling. There is simply no good answer to that question. The counselor can only show that he and the counselee worked together with particular objectives in mind, and that they were accomplished. If his records have been kept well and his follow-up data are validated, he may *infer* a relationship between the counseling procedures and later performances of his counselees. If he writes out a few well-documented case studies each year and accumulates longitudinal records of their subjects, the results of his work may be more readily demonstrated. In following such procedures he recognizes that control group studies can be used effectively in many kinds of psychological and educational research, but that their usefulness for evaluation of counseling has not yet been demonstrated.

SUMMARY AND A SUGGESTION

A friendly visitor from a foreign country recently spent a year in study of counseling and guidance as it is practiced in schools and taught in American universities. In writing about his observations he commented as follows: "Counseling and guidance struck me as a hybrid mélange of watered-down child psychology, mental health, tests and measurements, and non-practical clinical psychology. The subject never struck me as having any academic significance and its existence pre-supposed that the teacher was a fool. The less distinguished the institution the greater was

[25] Rothney and Lewis, "Use of Control Groups in Studies of Guidance," *op. cit.*

its proliferation of courses in counseling and guidance." Perhaps the critic was too harsh, but his comments do reflect some of the skeptical attitudes of many persons who have looked at the field.[26] Like many others, he was mistaken in his belief that he could evaluate the movement by observing its processes, but, as indicated on previous pages, it seems likely that study of the results of attempts at evaluation would still have produced the negative feelings prompted by his observations.

There can be no doubt that the counseling movement, which has existed and even grown for more than half a century on the basis of boldness and faith, is under fire, and there must be some doubt that it can long continue with any semblance to what it has been in the past. It must define its objectives more adequately, indicate more clearly the nature of a counselor's specialty in a community of specialists, and provide sound evidence that it can accomplish its stated intentions. The time has passed when counselors can refuse to accept responsibility for their activities. There is no reason to believe that they have arrived at a point where mere description of the processes they employ will be accepted as evidence of their efficacy.

Counselors are not usually in a position to conduct *large-scale* longitudinal studies of their counselees, and they would be well advised to leave such work to the universities and state or federal offices of education which have the necessary resources. They may find some value in them, but it appears likely that they will obtain better evidence of counselor effectiveness by conducting *local* studies using the procedures described below.

1. Get a statement of the major objectives of the school in which you work. If you can't find one suggest that some be formulated and help in their formulation.
2. Take *one* of the objectives and reword it in terms which permit evaluation. (Try to break down the generalities into specifics of student behavior upon which you can get valid information.)
3. Ask yourself how you think you can contribute to the development of the specific behaviors you have named.
4. Work with a sample of students, their teachers and their parents this year on the development of at least one of the behaviors.
5. See if you have made any difference without getting involved in the exotic statistical procedures that are currently popular. (You may lose your public if you use them.)

[26] H. Rosen, "Vocational Guidance: Room for Improvement," *Guidepost*, XII (1969), R. Barry and B. Wolf, *Epitaph for Vocational Guidance* (New York: Teachers College, Columbia University, 1962); E. Ginzberg, "Guidance—Limited or Unlimited?" *Personnel and Guidance Journal*, XXXVIII (1960); A. V. Acourel and J. I. Kitsuse, *The Education Decision Makers* (New York: The Bobbs-Merrill Co., Inc., 1963).

6. In your procedures and in your working toward major objectives don't sacrifice consideration of individual differences in desires, performances and particular needs of your counselees.[27]

In doing a local study of this kind the counselor would be expected to observe the cautions given in this chapter about interpretation of data, particularly of self-reports, counselee satisfaction statements, and unverified observations. Hopefully, he would follow up the sample of students with whom he worked to see if his influence had any carry-over effect beyond the year in which his study was done. His results should be reported to members of the school staff and citizens in the community in terms which they can understand, and it should be well illustrated by case reports about students with whom they are familiar. Examination of the results may be a very humbling experience, but the counselor may find in these results some suggestions for modification of previously employed procedures.[28] If, on the other hand, the results show that something of value has accrued, the counselor may assuage his critics, find personal satisfaction in the feeling of a job well done, and decide to make efforts toward further improvements which he will also evaluate.

It has been suggested that many persons get very unfavorable impressions of the nature of counseling. Unfortunately, there is considerable evidence that their conceptions are fully warranted. Before generally unfavorable judgments are passed, however, consideration should be given to the fact that many school counselors carry a load which would be comparable to that of a teacher who had 60 or more students in each of her classes.[29] If appraisal of a teacher's work under such circumstances were attempted, unfavorable impressions would probably be at least as common as those about counselors. Evaluation, of all processes in education, requires consideration of circumstances in which a person works as well as his performances.[30] Despite one's impressions about the ineffectiveness and uncertainties of the counseling movement in school situations, there are many individuals in it who can demonstrate that they contribute signifi-

[27] J. W. M. Rothney, "School Counselors: Do They Make a Difference?" *Guidelines,* Madison, Wisconsin: State Department of Public Instruction, IV (1966).
[28] K. B. Hoyt, "What the School Has a Right to Expect of Its Counselor," *Personnel and Guidance Journal,* XL (1961).
[29] *Review of Progress, Title V-A, National Defense Education Act* (Washington, D.C.: U.S. Office of Education, 1969). Data presented in this pamphlet show the 1967 counselor-student ratio in secondary schools to be one to 450, and in elementary schools one to 6,485. The latter figure is misleading, since most elementary schools do not have counselors.
[30] It is probably true that when educational systems have serious flaws, the counselors' efforts will be less effective. Social circumstances, too, may be limiting. Widespread poverty, unemployment, and war can make many counseling efforts futile.

cantly to accomplishment of the objectives of the educational institutions in which they are employed.

Selected References

ROTHNEY, J. W. M. *Guidance Practices and Results*. New York: Harper & Row, Publishers, 1958; *Educational, Vocational and Social Performances of Counseled and Uncounseled Youth Ten Years After High School*, Cooperative Research Project Report No. SAE 9231. Washington, D.C.: U.S. office of Education, 1963. Mimeo copies available. The only long-term longitudinal evaluation of guidance in public schools. The first entry describes the setting and procedures and describes the follow-up through the first five years of post-high school performances. The second reference carries the subjects through ten years after high school. A 20-year follow-up was completed in 1971.

——— and C. W. LEWIS. "Use of Control Groups in Studies of Guidance," *Personnel and Guidance Journal*, XLVII, No. 5 (January 1969). Questions the use of the control groups about which one hears so much in research.

——— and B. A. ROENS. *Guidance of American Youth*. Cambridge, Mass.: Harvard University Press, 1950. The first attempt at evaluation of guidance by study of differences between counseled and uncounseled high school students.

SHOBEN, E. J., JR. "Some Problems in Establishing Criteria of Effectiveness," *Personnel and Guidance Journal*, XXXI (1953). An older but still pertinent statement of the problems met in setting up procedures for evaluation.

TAMMINEN, A. W. and G. D. MILLER. *Guidance Programs and Their Impact on Students*. St. Paul, Minn.: Minnesota Department of Education, 1968. A detailed report of findings in a study of the outcomes of guidance offered in Minnesota high schools. Suggests, despite rather negative results, that counselors can play "an exciting, broad, and effective role in facilitating the total educational endeavor."

TERMAN, L. M. and M. H. ODEN. *The Gifted Group at Mid-Life: Thirty-Five Year Follow-up of the Superior Child*. Palo Alto, Calif.: Stanford University Press, 1959. Instruments and techniques of follow-up are worth examining, and the results are enlightening.

THORESEN, C. E., ed. "Guidance and Counseling," *Review of Educational Research*, XXXIX, No. 2 (1965). Chapter 5 is entitled "Changes Through Counseling," but the interpretations represent largely the orientations of the behavioral counseling school. It presents a review of current efforts at evaluation.

VOLSKY, T., *et al. The Outcomes of Counseling and Psychotherapy*. Minneapolis: University of Minnesota Press, 1965. Interesting consideration of criterion variables for assessing counseling effectiveness.

CHAPTER 7

synthesis
for adaptability

In this final chapter some of the major issues discussed previously are summarized and synthesized. Particular attention is given to problems in the selection of subjects, counseling and therapy relationships, demands of society, and evaluation of counseling. The need for adaptability in reaching at least partial solutions to such problems is emphasized throughout.

ADAPTATION

Students of the field of human development must have become acutely aware of the extent of individual differences in all kinds of behavior among all groups; of the amount of change which is characteristic of healthy human organisms, and their irreversibility to previous states; of the complexity of each individual; and of the worth of each one to himself and to others. When a person attempts to counsel individuals who are unique, complex, changeable, and precious, he undertakes such a formidable task that variable and flexible procedures must be employed. In short, he must become an adaptive counselor.

The need for adaptability seems to follow so directly from recognition of the characteristics noted above and elaborated in Chapter 1 that one must stand aghast at the naïveté or boldness with which some persons propose and promote single approaches to the counseling task. It seems just as absurd to suggest that all counselors employ procedures derived from a single learning or personality theory with all their counselees as it

152

would be to exhort all teachers to use the same methods at all times in their classrooms, or to recommend that all physicians employ identical procedures for all patients in their clinics. Just as good teachers sense from observation that the time has come to change from lecturing to leading a discussion, or to turn from the use of audiovisual equipment to encouragement of independent study, the adaptive counselor perceives that he may help most by adjusting his activities to the circumstances that develop as he works with a counselee. In the same way that a teacher may sense that it is now time to direct his students' activities, the counselor may lead his counselee in what he feels is a desirable direction.

The damage that advocates of single approaches do to the counseling movement may be compensated for in part by the discussion, thought, and criticism stimulated by the presentations of all counseling procedures. As pointed out previously, the promoters collect a coterie of followers (some of whom go far beyond what their leaders advise) who bask in the reflected glory of the sponsors of a movement, and their statements and activities get considerable attention. As the movement ascends in popularity it becomes attractive to be "with it," and there is much activity unaccompanied by critical self-appraisal. By that time, however, the activities, pronouncements, and studies have been examined by those who have not joined the movement, and they begin to expose the shortcomings of all single theories about human behavior. It is at this juncture that the contribution of single-theory advocates is greatest, not because their theory is defensible, but simply because it stimulates others to think about their own beliefs and procedures and to consider what limitations in previously-held theories brought about presentation of a new one. The next step, hopefully, is the recognition that counselors have been offered another way among many of adapting procedures to serve the widely different individuals they meet.

After their period of ascendancy, all of the schools of thought leave some residue of value. Although client-centered counseling advocates seem to make too much of the need for empathic understanding, nonpossessive warmth, genuineness, and specificity (conditions which have been known for centuries to be important in helping persons), their emphasis on these characteristics has probably served to remind many counselors that they are desirable behaviors. Those counselors who had talked too much and listened too little, who had not really tried to understand their counselees' feelings, who had developed bossiness, and who tended to provide too many answers to questions may have profited from the cautions offered by advocates of client-centered counseling. It is unfortunate that such advocates have implied that what appeared to be desirable were also sufficient conditions for effective counseling; the implication of universality of application is particularly regrettable.

Behavioral counseling seems to appeal primarily to those who think of counseling as a salvage and repair process. Using pretentious names for timeworn remedial techniques (reinforcement, systematic exclusion, behavior modification, task-oriented behavior, systematic desensitization) appeals to those who try to impress others with ostentatious language. There seems to be considerable merit in the behavioral counselors' insistence that specific goals be named by each counselee, but the short duration of their concerns and the emphasis on working toward only the personal (perhaps even selfish) objectives of the subject lessen their effectiveness. As in the case of the client-centered advocates, however, some benefits will likely ensue after the behavioral counseling emphasis has reached its peak of popularity and becomes just one of many procedures employed by counselors.

Those counselors who have used vague language in describing their purposes, who have ignored specifics in pursuit of major personality changes, who have depended solely on verbal activities, and who have expected to accomplish too much simply by providing for good communication during interviews may profit from considering the emphasis of behavioral counselors. The residue as this school of thought wanes and a new school takes it place will, hopefully, be recognition that adaptation to individual differences may be furthered by use of *some* behavioral procedures for *some* persons at *some* time and under *some* circumstances.

SELECTION OF SUBJECTS

It has been observed that private counseling clinicians can select their counselees to suit their own purposes or methods, and university experimenters in counseling can choose to work with subjects who meet the criteria they impose. School counselors who must serve the total population of their schools do not have such freedom. Even if they believe themselves to be behavioral counselors, they do not have the same opportunties as their university laboratory counterparts to choose only those subjects with problems which are most likely to respond to conditioning. Neither can they, if they are of the client-centered persuasion, choose to work only with students who come to them voluntarily, "for special help because they are emotionally disturbed, unhappy, in conflict with themselves or others, dissatisfied with themselves, lacking in self-respect or self-esteem—in short unable, or impeded in their efforts, to be self-actualizing persons." [1]

All students must make crucial decisions about careers and courses; information about jobs and training opportunities and scholarships, which only a counselor will have available, must be provided; tests need to be

---

[1] C. H. Patterson et al., "A Current View of Client-Centered or Relationship Therapy," *Journal of Counseling Psychology*, I, No. 2 (Summer 1969).

interpreted; interviews about personal problems must be held; and conferences with parents and teachers need to be arranged. These are samples of demands made on school counselors, and they cannot be ignored simply because the persons involved are not the types of subjects preferred as counselees by practitioners of a particular school of thought.

Counseling has been variously defined to serve the purpose of advocates of specialized techniques. Some exclude from their definition any reference to education, reeducation, skill training, or any conditioning techniques; others suggest that such exclusion is simply an attempt to evade a counselor's responsibilities. The writer tends to hold the latter view, but whether or not it is a sound one, the school counselor is faced with the task of trying to assist in better self-understanding, and consequent better decision-making, all of the students who come to him voluntarily, are referred to him, and are invited by him. This obligation does not require him to set up special groups for development of skills, the offering of information and test interpretation, or remedial training in school subjects. He is obligated to provide *individualized* assistance in such areas only when he sees that a particular counselee needs special information, distinct short-term skill training, or a personalized interpretation of data.[2] If a school counselor finds a considerable number of students who require extended periods of special training, he will make arrangements with teachers, remedial specialists, or others who can provide such services for groups.

Even though some individuals refuse to include such activities in their definitions of counseling, the counselor cannot exclude some teaching, information giving, and limited skill training when it is of particular importance to one of his counselees. A student cannot be rejected simply because he doesn't fit the counselor's concept of what a suitable counselee should be. Any decision by a school counselor to reject a student must be based solely on the criterion of his competence in the area in which the student seeks assistance.

Few school counselors are prepared to work with seriously disturbed persons, and those who have attempted to do so have done much harm to the public impression of school counseling. Well beyond their depth, but misled by the simplistic and sentimental language of therapists who have made brief visits to counselor workshops and guidance conferences, coupled with concern about the welfare of others, they attempt to achieve

2 It is possible, for example, to help a student who lowers his test scores, and thereby restricts his opportunity to enter the kind of training he wants, by wild guessing at test items. Brief explanations of how multiple-choice tests are scored and the penalties assessed for incorrect answers may help him to improve his test performances and expand his opportunities. Unfortunate as the practice of using test scores for some kinds of selective admission may be, it is a fact of life that young persons must currently face, and a counselor may assist them to do so.

what their lack of competence makes impossible. The good school counselor recognizes that certain students need help from a clinical psychologist. He also recognizes that he is not a specialist in health or an expert in the teaching of particular subjects, and will refer students who need help in those areas to the proper specialists.

All the evidence about individual differences suggests that a school counselor's preselected population will contain a wide array of challenges. The samples given in Chapter 1 indicate some common patterns of behavior for which counselors can be of assistance, but it is in the recognition of their depth and stability and in their differences in emphasis and influence on the behavior of specific individuals that the counselor will find clues for dealing effectively with them. Knowing these challenges, he will adapt his counseling procedures to serve them.

COUNSELING AND THERAPY

This volume has emphasized the need to adapt counseling procedures to meet individual differences, but the stress does not embody the concept of school counselor as therapist. There has been much pedantic debate about where counseling ends and therapy begins, and some writers have suggested that no clear distinction can be made. It has been indicated directly and by inference throughout this volume that there are real differences between counselors and therapists in the basic concepts of tasks, selection of the subjects, training, and obligations.

Most of the work reported by behavioral counselors lies in realms usually reserved for school or clinical psychologists, family welfare workers, and remedial specialists. The subjects most commonly described by client-centered advocates are those who are usually seen in various kinds of mental hygiene and psychological clinics. For the subjects of both schools there is something that needs to be *re*paired, *re*adjusted, *re*conditioned, *re*inforced, or *re*modeled. All of the *re*s suggest that the individual has broken down, is failing to function adequately, or that something has gone awry. There are persons in such conditions in all schools who need help, but they need the help of specialists in giving corrective treatment. The counselor is not such a specialist, and need not become one. He has his own tasks and should not try to perform psychological remediation when there is no specialist available, any more than he should undertake medical treatments because no physician is present.

Counseling for better self-understanding and better decision-making, if well done, could be so valuable that no student should miss it in the process of coming of age. It certainly shouldn't be restricted to those whose behavior is so unusual that they require immediate remedial treatment. The school counselor does not wait until a student is in academic difficulty, has an adjustment problem, or is near the transition stage of graduation, dropout, or transfer before he offers his services. Neither does he wait until a student seeks him out before counseling is initiated. He considers counseling as an essential part of a school's services. In seeing that all may participate in it, he perceives his work as more closely allied to that of the curriculum specialist who is developing desirable experiences for all students than to that of the school or clinical psychologist, who, while professing concern about development for all students, is more likely to work at diagnosis and remediation of special cases.

THE INDIVIDUAL AND SOCIETY

The reader of this volume must have observed the writer's insistence that school counselors assume some responsibility to society as well as to individual counselees. Frequently repeated assertions in the literature that the counseling task is one of helping persons to get precisely what they want, and to behave as they choose, have come primarily from those who work with college students and adults, or from professors in universities who are not familiar with school situations. They do not always realize that the freedoms which derive from attainment of legal adulthood, living away from home (and often providing for a large measure of personal financial needs), and enrollment in institutions not governed by compulsory attendance laws are of a different order from the commitments of dependent minors living with their parents and siblings, required to attend schools, and residing in communities which enforce regulations (such as curfews) for minors. Failure to recognize such differences has caused some writers in the field of counseling to extrapolate their beliefs about freedoms of college students and adults to children who have practically no control over their environment.

Counselors of minors will certainly try to help them to develop individuality, and try to reduce unwise restrictions on them, but they cannot escape the fact that they must serve the larger public as well as particular counselees. They cannot, for example, even consider with a healthy underage youth the pros and cons of dropping out of school because the law will not permit the student to do so, but with a college student this may be a highly desirable activity. Even in areas in which there are no specific regulations or laws, the school counselor must consider whether he is serving the society which employs him when he meets needs of his counselees. In such matters as conservation of talent and resources, cultivation of beauty, and equity of opportunity society offers restrictions, demands, and opportunities for youth which an adaptive counselor cannot ignore.

The above statements must not be interpreted as implying that school counselors must always be defenders of the status quo. They recognize that society changes as time passes as inevitably as people change as they grow older, and they should be quick to point out necessary revisions of regulations to their colleagues. However, society has not delegated the function of changing it to the counseling profession, and it expects that those who counsel children in schools will help in accomplishment of the objectives it has commissioned the schools to achieve.

EVALUATION

Much consideration was given to the subject of evaluation in Chapter 6 because it seems likely that there will be little progress in the field until counselors make assessment of their effectiveness an ongoing part of their jobs, and are willing to revise their practices on the basis of their determinations. In a period where there is considerable doubt about the value of counseling, provision of evidence about effectiveness may simply be a matter of survival. The coach displays his value on the playing fields and courts, the results of efforts of members of the music faculty may be seen in marches, recitals, and concerts, the English, art, and industrial arts teachers provide evidence of their instruction in creative publications or displays, and scholarship awards attest to performances of students in academic areas, but the counselor may be hard put to show what he has accomplished. (Whether or not one agrees with the worth of such practices, they are, and seem likely to be for the foreseeable future, the facts of school life.) Although effectiveness of counseling is more difficult to appraise, methods and techniques can be found if counselors accept the challenge and get on with the job.

Large-scale long-term evaluation studies may well be left to universities and state or national agencies which have the necessary resources. The counselor can only be expected to contribute support to such studies by providing data and making suggestions for procedures in areas in which he is most concerned. He can, however, encourage school staff members to join with him in efforts to determine the extent to which the school is meeting its stated objectives. He may consider, as his part of the cooperative effort, the securing of information about the educational, vocational, and social decisions made by his counselees while they were students and for a designated period after they were graduated. He will emphasize the helping and cooperative role of the counselor, recognize the strengths and limitations of his own procedures, and, perhaps, justify his job.

It has been suggested that the counselor's evaluation will be best performed by compilation of statistical data in a form which permits comprehension by his public of students, teachers, and parents, and by offering case reports of counselees which illustrate the adaptive procedures he employs in his counseling and follow-up studies. It has been indicated that a substitute for the control group studies, which can no longer be recommended for use in evaluation of counseling, may be found in simple tabulations of decisions made by his counselees, and in carefully accumulated evidence of the counseling offered during the period of a counselee's development. Writing case reports from the accumulated evidence can provide continuous reminders that counseling is an adaptive and highly personalized process.

SUMMARY

The concept of adaptive counseling as a means of providing for the needs of students who vary so greatly in all their characteristics seems to be so sound that it should be continued and expanded. It is difficult to find fault with the idea that there should be an adequate supply of adaptable persons in schools who are available when a student wants to sit down with a concerned and informed adult who is neither teacher, preacher, principal, nor parent (although he will talk with them, too), and talk about himself and his place in current and future society. This opportunity should be just as available as his chance to learn to read, write, and compute. The student need not have met setbacks in his development to receive such attention, since the provision of such opportunities to all students is the school counselor's job. If the counselor recognizes that his challenge lies there, and realizes that it requires a high level of adaptability to serve the vast array of differences in school populations, then the essentially sound practice of adding adaptable counselors to their faculties will assist schools in reaching the objectives for which they strive.

Selected References

ALLPORT, G. "Psychological Models for Guidance," *Harvard Educational Review*, XXXII (1962). Provides some good advice for those who would counsel, based upon the author's extensive work on individuality.

BENTLEY, J. C., ed. *The Counselor's Role*. Boston: Houghton Mifflin Company, 1968. A collection of essays and statements about what and who determines the role that the counselor plays with only indirect references to the counseling process. One of the better books of readings.

CARLE, R., C. KEHAS, and R. MOSHER. "Guidance—An Examination," *Harvard Educational Review*, XXXIV (1962). A thorough consideration of some of the basic issues involved in the offering of guidance services. Raises some fundamental questions.

HANSEN, D. A., ed. *Explorations in Sociology and Counseling*. Boston: Houghton Mifflin Company, 1969. Essays written by sociologists who have looked at counseling as a social phenomenon. A good book because it presents views of this field by persons who are not members of it.

LANDY, E. and A. M. KROLL, eds. *Guidance in American Education: Current Issues and Suggested Action.* Cambridge, Mass.: Harvard University Press, 1965. An excellent statement of issues, with specific recommendations for action that should result in improved practices.

LLOYD-JONES, ESTHER M. and NORAH ROSENAU, eds. *Social and Cultural Foundations of Guidance.* New York: Holt, Rinehart and Winston, Inc., 1968. Provides a number of points of view on the place of counseling and guidance by non-practitioners in the field. Not a how-to-do-it book but one that goes back to basic principles in the social environment.

APPENDIX

use of case studies

The following case materials are offered for study of adaptation of counseling to meet individual needs. In the cases of *Hal*, *Stanley*, and *Rachael* the reader should try to decide what counseling is necessary and the manner in which it could best be done. The report on *Paula* contains descriptions of a counselor's work with her. It would be an interesting exercise to criticize (with reasons) the counselor's actions of which the reader disapproves, and to justify those to which approval is given. In all cases it would be desirable for the reader to decide just what he might have done if he had been the counselor.

Most students who attempt such exercises indicate that they would have liked more information about the subjects. Such statements simply reinforce the author's belief that counselors must learn much more than they commonly do about their counselees if they are to be effective.

Instructions for work to be done are presented as each case is introduced. Additional suggestions are offered below.

In the cases of Hal and Stanley the student might diagram his reports in this manner:

ACTIONS A COUNSELOR SHOULD TAKE	SANCTION FOR ACTION	EVALUATION OF ACTION	
		METHOD	WHEN EMPLOYED?
e.g., Try to convince Hal's parents to provide funds for his university education	Hal said he wanted an education	Interview Hal and his parents about actions they took	Autumn after high school graduation

161

The adaptations required of the counselor by *Paula's* particular characteristics and circumstances may be highlighted if the student attempts to summarize them under the following headings:

ACTION OF THE COUNSELOR	APPROVE OR DISAPPROVE	REASONS
e.g., Pointed out to her the difficulties suggested by her language handicap	Approve	Essential to increase her self-understanding when decisions about course selection and dropping out of school were considered

Rachael's development in lower and middle school years is described in some detail. There was no counselor in the school she attended. The student will find it a challenging exercise to suggest what actions an adaptable counselor might have taken, and to speculate on what differences they might have made in her development.

HAL

Assume that Hal, who is described on the following pages, comes in to see you during January of his senior year in high school. He is very much concerned about making a decision about his post-high school plans, and he describes his problems as they appear in the third paragraph on this page and next to the last paragraph of this case study.

Tell what actions you as a counselor would take, why you think you would have the right to do what you would do, and how and when you would determine whether you had done your job effectively.

Writing a report about him at the end of his senior year in high school, Hal's English teacher said:

> He stood out among a great number of boys in my world literature class. At the beginning of the semester I noticed him because he was the largest boy in the class and because he regularly entered quietly into the class discussions, revealing his independent reactions to what was being discussed. As the weeks went on, my first impressions of Hal were strengthened. Here was a boy who participated in class not as a show-off, not as a monopolizer of the class, but because he had something he wanted to contribute. He seemed to be an individual who not only read the assigned material but who thought about what he read—who questioned the truth of what he read. I had no other boy who challenged him. My problem was to stimulate him to further thinking—to help him grow. I began to make special assignments for him.

If this teacher had added that Hal was a serious person and one whose feelings of uncertainty and insecurity at the time of high school graduation were many, she would have completed a good description of him.

Hal's insecurities were compounded by worry about getting drafted into the armed forces, the problem of choice between making a career on his own or staying with his parents on the family farm and, further, by the difficulty of talking this out with parents whom he respected and, to some extent, feared. He would also like to get married within the next year.

With respect to entry into the armed forces, Hal expressed himself frequently in these words:

> Things are so uncertain and mixed up that I don't know where I will be next with the war going the way it is.
>
> It bothers me to feel uncertain because I do not have a feeling of security.
>
> The war has made me uncertain of my future. I may be drafted for Service.
>
> I don't know whether to stay on the farm in hope that I will be deferred, to start college in September, or enlist and get it over with.
>
> I'm not anxious to get into Service.

Much of Hal's behavior can be attributed to the situation in his home. He was brought up on a farm where, as the eldest of six children, he was required to put in many hours of labor. Both parents had come from Germany and had attended six years of elementary school. They had strong feelings about the need for harsh discipline and they tolerated neither "nonsense" nor disobedience from their children. Hal had learned to disapprove of young people's lack of respect for authority and, discussing the German system of demanding obedience to parents he exclaimed, "Oh boy, that is something we need here!" He was glad, he said, that he lived in the country so that there were chores to do and he didn't have to hang around the city's youth center, pool halls, movies, and taverns. He spoke frequently of his appreciation of all that his parents had done for him—of their love and affection for him and of his realization now that they were building him a foundation for moral success. He criticized the materialism of other boys and wondered what kind of parents they had. Yet, when the final choice was to be made, among enrolling in college, entering the armed forces, or remaining on the farm, Hal was too timid to raise the issues with his parents. He was waiting for his father to tell him what to do.

The question about college attendance arose when Hal's test performances were noted, and when a counselor thought that his occupational choices of farming and engineering might be combined in training for agricultural engineering. The test scores in Table A–1 represented Hal's best efforts and seemed to verify generally the performances that he and his teachers expected. The low scores on all five sections of the Primary Mental Abilities Tests, which require the student to work very rapidly, may not be representative of what Hal could really have done had he not been a thorough, methodical person who stopped to check his work. As he became more test-wise and learned that speed was important (as indicated, for example, by the subtitles on the cover of the Cooperative Reading Test), he performed at a higher level. He found the space and mechanical tests to be so easy that he was amazed when told that many students were unable to grasp the directions for the test. He had guessed that his num-

TABLE A–1

Hal's Test Scores

TESTS	PERCENTILE GRADE 10	PERCENTILE GRADE 11
Henmon-Nelson Test of Mental Ability	81	85
Reading Tests		
Cooperative reading vocabulary	83	92
Cooperative reading comprehension	79	98
Cooperative speed of reading	81	98
Primary Mental Abilities		
Verbal	50	
Space	92	
Reasoning	42	
Number	29	
Word Fluency	40	
Differential Aptitude Tests		
Number		50
Mechanical reasoning		95
Space		95

ber scores would be low because of inadequate preparation in arithmetic in a rural school, but he was obviously pleased at the general level of his test performances.

Largely because he was not challenged by some of his teachers, who had not recognized his potentialities and considered him just another big "hick" who would return to the farm, Hal achieved only the mediocre academic record presented in Table A–2. It resulted in the attainment of a rank of only 182 in a graduating class of 250 by a student who might have reached much higher levels. The tendency to get lower marks in the second semester of each school year than in the first was due partly to the fact that

TABLE A–2

Hal's Academic Record

SUBJECT	9		10		11		12	
English	B	C	C	D	C	D	C	C
Latin	C	C	D	D				
American History							C	D
Civics								
Social Science	B	B						
Geography					C	D		
Algebra	B	B	C	D				
Geometry								
Biology								
General Science	B	B						
Physics					C	D		
Physical Education	B	A	B	B	B	B	C	B
Band			C	D	C	B	A	A

he commonly lost more than two weeks of school when spring planting required his presence at home on the farm. Hal said that he liked all but one of his subjects, and he ranked physics, band, and mathematics in that order as best-liked subjects. English, until his senior year, was not a favorite subject, and he dismissed geography as a waste of time and the one course that he would not have elected had he known more about it.

During his senior year, Hal, in commenting about his courses, wrote:

> In the past semester I feel that I have learned something more than just English. I have acquired a new method of thinking which differs from my original in that now instead of taking certain things for granted, I now unconsciously question them. As far as good books are concerned I have an idea of what is considered good reading.
>
> I feel that in the last semester I did not learn all that was required in sentence structure. It's hard to say what I didn't learn if I don't know what I didn't learn.

Notable for a farm boy was the fact that Hal elected none of the agriculture, machine shop, auto mechanics, mechanical drawing, or woodworking classes offered at the school. When asked about it, he said that he learned enough about those things on the farm and that school was a place to learn the kinds of things he couldn't learn at home. His parents had encouraged him to choose the academic courses.

Band membership as a cornet player was Hal's only school activity. Although the coaches in the school would have liked to have this rugged and husky boy on their squads, he did not participate because farm chores limited his time for practice and because he had frequent, unexpected, and unexplained nosebleeds. Group activities with other youths took place only in occasional sand-lot baseball games and through membership in a 4-H Club, which he thoroughly enjoyed. The reading that he did voluntarily was described by him as adventure "psychological" stories and he said that he enjoyed such books as *The Return of the Native, Kim,* and *I Chose Freedom* when they were assigned in senior English. He said that such books gave him "intelligent opinions and ideas."

At the time of graduation, Hal's uncertainty about the future was reflected in the statements noted earlier in this report. Satisfied, when he first started high school, with the idea of returning to the farm, he became less sure of that career. Occasionally he commented that farming required a lot of money—the family farm would have to be expanded if he were to work with his father—and "There are lots of easier ways to make a living." He did feel, however, that he had had the benefit of practical experience which "I would never lose and which I can always turn to," and he could not keep some aspect of agriculture out of his planning. Agricultural engineering seemed a likely choice and, near the end of his senior year, it seemed that he would enroll in that course at the state university. Then came the possibility of being drafted into the armed forces and the difficulty of telling his parents that he might want to leave the farm. At the time he graduated he was in a dilemma, with all the feelings of uncertainty and insecurity noted above. Hal was not a happy person when commencement seemed to require that a choice must be made.

"Regardless of what Hal does after graduation," one of his teachers wrote, "I think he will make an excellent citizen. He has high principles and is not easily influenced by the popular trend. He is not aggressive; he finds satisfaction with his life as it now is. He is a thinker. His comments on certain phases of school life reflect penetration and understanding worthy of a mature person."

STANLEY

Actions of the counselor in working with Stanley over his four years in high school have been omitted from the following report. Assume that you had been Stanley's counselor in grades 9 to 12. What kind of counseling would you have offered? Be specific about purposes and procedures.

Probably the characteristic people notice most about me is my general sloppiness. Practically everything I do has an element of this in it, my writing, dress, thoughts.

The above was Stanley's response when asked to describe the kind of person he was. His counselor agreed with the self-description, saying: "He has succeeded in convincing me that he is 'messy.' He produced some of the messiest pages I have ever seen." Stanley realized that his messiness would be a handicap in whatever occupation he chose but he did not seem bothered by it enough to do anything about it. He said that his father had told him that he ought to attempt to become less messy because his messiness somehow influenced his thought organization. He cited as a major factor in his messiness his "identification with the absent-minded professor stereotype." He explained that "I unconsciously act like the stereotype in certain manners to get proof that I might also possess other and more significant characteristics of absent-minded professors." Apparently, he thought that sloppiness was a characteristic trait of brilliant scientists.

Stanley's father was a renowned leader in science who wanted very much to have his eldest son follow in his footsteps. His mother, who held a Master's degree, shared her husband's aspirations for his future. He recalled that his parents tried to get him interested in science as early as first grade by stimulating him to do simple experiments and encouraging him to read simple books on science or technology. The subtle pressure to achieve exerted on Stanley apparently succeeded because, as early as he could remember, he had always wanted to become a scientist like his father whose "strong opinions and ideas" he admired because "most of these seem to be quite sound and well thought over." Stanley often had nagging self-doubts, however, and he repeatedly turned the question of his academic adequacy over in his mind. He said he was unsure as to whether he was intelligent enough to become a scientist like his father, and he recalled that he had "attempted unsuccessfully to build motors, prisms, electrical devices, and similar stuff." He reported that he was on the constant lookout for signs of creativity in himself but also that he usually tried his best to argue against any evidence of creativity he discerned in himself.

Stanley's self-doubts were not totally unfounded. On the School and College Ability Test (SCAT), Henmon-Nelson Test of Mental Ability (HN), and Terman Concept Mastery Test (TCM), Stanley's scores were far above national norms. On the Abstract Reasoning section of the Differential Aptitude Test (DAT), however, he scored only at the seventieth percentile (national norm for ninth grade). It seemed likely that Stanley's high scores on the other "tests" were largely the result of the vast amount of reading he had done. Examination of items in the SCAT, HN, and TCM seemed to bear this out in that high scores on such tests reflect an excellent vocabulary, and familiarity with words not usually encountered in regular class reading assignments. He reported spending as many as 20 hours per week in leisure reading and, according to his counselor, he had already read more books commonly recommended for college-going students than most boys of his age and grade. It seemed reasonable, therefore, to expect that he would be more familiar with many of the difficult words and thus score very well on the verbal tests.

In academic work Stanley performed consistently at a high level and he graduated with a cumulative grade-point of 3.78. Some of his lower grades might have been affected by his poor penmanship and by the fact that he often did things that pleased him rather than things he was asked to do. When he disliked any assignment intensely, he did not hestitate to make known his feelings. Such behavior was interpreted by some teachers as uncooperative.

The amount of time Stanley spent on leisure reading was certainly atypical of the average teenage boy. Also atypical was his choice of reading materials, since he read much more nonfiction and books about mechanical development than most of his classmates. He was not only selective but consistent in his reading habits. Throughout his four years in high school he regularly read such magazines as *Scientific American, Saturday Review, Science Newsletter,* and *The New York Times* sunday magazine. These were available in his home.

It appears that Stanley's unusually strong interest in books may have been partly a result of his being unsuccessful in gaining acceptance as a member of his peer group. He was not active in any extracurricular activities except band, and he held no elective or appointive offices in any student organizations. He said he would have liked to participate in sports but said he could not because he was overweight. He hated physical education classes and would have liked to drop the course. Since he was unable to compete effectively with his peers in sports, and other noncurricular activities, Stanley turned to scholarship. Here he had little difficulty surpassing most of his peers and this achievement was satisfying. At the same time, his academic superiority probably led him to show contempt for some of his less successful peers and thereby removed him further from their company. The leisure activities he reported engaging in almost daily were those which did not involve other people, namely, reading, swimming, daydreaming, playing a musical instrument, just sitting around, doodling, and making things at home.

Stanley was a loner and he made no attempt to win new friends or keep the five close friends he listed in the ninth grade. Not only had the number of his friends been reduced over the years but the degree of his intimacy with those who remained friendly also decreased. He reported that his close friends in the ninth and tenth grades would describe him as "messy," "somewhat nonconformist," "unsocial," "slightly impractical," and "quite intelligent," but he said he had no idea how his two closest friends in the eleventh grade would describe him.

Stanley admitted that he was not getting along with people as well as he would like to. Throughout his high school years, he had not attended parties and had never engaged in social dancing. He had never dated in high school and he felt awkward in the vicinity of the opposite sex or even in mixed company. He explained that he lived in the outskirts of the city and so it was very inconvenient for him and his friends to get together after school. The fact that the family did not own a television set and that he had rarely seen movies suggests that Stanley and his few friends would have had very little of mutual interest to talk about even if they had gotten together.

Stanley was isolated from his peers and largely ignored by his teachers. None of his teachers encouraged him to do creative work or to develop further in those areas in which he had performed at a high level. This seemed unfortunate because, according to Stanley, he worked more effectively when he had much to do than when he had little. His teachers apparently took him for granted since none had ever commended him for doing excellent work. Although Stanley took more courses than were required, he did not elect any honors level courses. It appeared that no teacher had ever talked to him at length outside of the classrooms. He did not seem to be bothered by their actions because he spoke favorably of his high school experience.

In commenting on Stanley's intellecutal make-up, his counselor wrote: "If one overlooks the mess and can finally decipher his handwriting one finds evidence that he has some ideas that are worth expressing." Witness, for example, the insightful remarks in the following portion of the junior essay he had written in response to the general topic, "Do you think you should be permitted to make more decisions?"

> I am already permitted to make many more decisions than I make. I probably ought to make more decisions. But many opportunities for decisions are artificially constructed by other people, not chiefly to be decided, but to test the individual who is deciding. In most cases, I intensely dislike making a decision, it is like being tested for a Pavlovian Reaction. I most dislike this sort of decision when I have no personal preference. . . .

The above excerpt suggests that Stanley was a thinker. Indeed, his counselor reported that his written ideas were at a higher mental level than he usually found among students. Stanley seemed, however, to have great difficulty communicating his thoughts on paper. Much of this had to do with his handwriting, with frequently crossed-out words and phrases, inserted words, and lengthy sentences. Such performances could be traced partly to his identification with his faulty stereotype of the "absent-minded professor." Stanley seemed to think that a complex response was, in and of itself, more desirable and more communicative than a simple answer. He not only had difficulty communicating his thoughts on paper but, according to his counselor, he had difficulty expressing them orally. His hesitancy in speech led the counselor to recommend to the speech specialist that he be given some help, a recommendation which was repeatedly ignored.

During counseling sessions Stanley seemed to be crying out for opportunities to make decisions instead of having his parents make them for him. His ambivalence towards his parents was evident. He felt deeply grateful to them but, at the same time, he seemed to resent their interference in his life. He cited "parental direction" as his reason for not making long-range educational and vocational decisions. He seemed to be saying that "My parents always have the last word anyway, so why bother making a decision now?" That he had resigned himself to accepting the status quo (as he perceived it) was evident in the fact that although he had planned to attend college following his graduation, he had, at the middle of the senior year in high school, taken no steps to implement that plan. He was apparently relying on his parents to take the appropriate steps for him. And they did not fail. Stanley's mother told the counselor of her efforts to get her son to sign up on time to take the Scholastic Aptitude Test. Her comments raised the question of which college would be most desirable for him. She mentioned that she and her husband had suggested making applications to two state universities in cities in which relatives of the family lived.

One Year After High School Graduation

Stanley enrolled at a state university following his graduation from high school. On a follow-up report, he checked "good reputation" and "away from home" as his reasons for choosing the university. He admitted, however, that he had not done much investigating of colleges prior to deciding to enroll there, and he was uncertain that he would go to the same place if he were to do it over again. It appeared that his parents had chosen the college for him. Academically, he did quite well. His 3.38 first semester grade-point average was well within the range predicted by the counselor. He obtained two A's and three B's. One of the two A's was in freshman English, despite his almost illegible handwriting. His follow-up report did not indicate any improvement in his "messy" habits, but apparently they had not worked against him in impromptu quizzes. He said that he overcame the problem with his handwriting by enrolling in the honors section where there were a minimum of impromptu written class quizzes and where he was permitted to type his papers.

Stanley continued to be a prolific reader in college but he remained inactive in extracurricular activities. He reported no difference between his social life in college and high school by saying that in both settings his social activity was "virtually none." Even so, he felt "reasonably satisfied" with his success. He rated himself as being better prepared academically and more familiar with college classes and procedures than most freshmen. He also rated himself as one who knew his strengths and limitations better than most of his classmates. Another plus for him was the fact that he read more good books than most freshmen. Also the fact that he found college competition "definitely encouraging and stimulating" might have contributed to his academic success. Perhaps he had been faced finally with the challenge which had been lacking in high school.

Stanley had not chosen a career and had not selected his major although he was leaning towards the physical sciences. He explained that he was "waiting to see if anything conclusive emerges, and getting a liberal aducation meanwhile, and pretending (sic) to go into science."

PAULA

In the following case report the actions of the counselor appear in italics. Indicate whether you approve or disapprove of each of his actions. Don't generalize from other cases. Consider Paula only.

A tall, thin girl with a drawn expression, Paula struggled to achieve her ambition of completing high school, despite the fact that she could not understand much of what took place in her classes. When first seen she was in junior high school and was already much overage for her grade. She was required to spend most of her out-of-school hours at menial jobs in order to pay her own way.

School Record

Paula never hestitated to question matters she could not understand and was good-natured when the class was amused by her strange questions, or when she made obvious blunders. She was persistent in keeping at a task as long as she had time. Her written work was neat and carefully prepared though there were frequent errors in spelling and many confused ideas.

The following comments and statements about her work in various subjects reveal the nature of her difficulties:

ENGLISH—GRADE 7   She found grammar and spelling "hard." The teacher stated, "She seemed just visiting in class until she had failed two terms; but once she started coming back for extra drill, she really worked hard, showing childish glee as each new point became clear to her."

GRADE 8   She was considered weak in reading and language usage.

GRADE 9   Reported reading some western and detective stories, movie magazines, and *True Confessions* every night. Her teacher reported erratic work but occasional excellence, a peppy and enthusiastic manner, and a language handicap which was partly due to use of a foreign language at home. In oral English, Paula said she failed occasionally because "I just can't give speeches." The teacher of this class reported slight effort and constant giggling.

Interpretation of Test Record

Paula tried hard on all tests. On the New Stanford Achievement Test administered by the school in grade 8 at the age of 13 years 10 months, she showed retardation of two years and two grades. The only two sections of the test on which her grade equivalents were up to her school status were Geography (grade 8.0) and Arithmetic Computation (grade 7.6). In grades 8 to 12 she ranked in the lowest third of her group on most tests of general mental ability, reading, language, and mathematics.

Family Data

Paula was the older of two daughters of foreign-born parents. Her sister, three years younger, was in a special class for backward children until she left school to be married. Eventually, the sister returned home to live with her parents, working occasionally at a domestic job. Paula's father, employed occasionally as a casual laborer for building contractors, was a market-gardener who frequently peddled his own vegetables. Neither parent had attended high school. They spoke a foreign language at home much of the time. When English was attempted, it was broken and ungrammatical. They were proud of Paula for staying in school, and they were ambitious for her to secure "a good job," though they could not provide her even with minimum clothes and spending money while she was in high school. The home had few books or magazines and those that were available were of the sensational, pulp, movie, or "confession" variety.

Health

Paula was thin, of a rather wiry build, and usually pale. She often appeared to have a drawn and tired expression, but she reported that her health was good. Routine school examinations indicated that there were no defects. In grade 12, she gained weight and looked stronger and more rested than ever before because, she said, "My boss [on a part-time job] makes me eat two good meals a day with lots more milk than I ever had, and then my boyfriend has been drafted so I don't stay up late on dates."

Leisure Time Activities

Paula did not participate in extracurricular activities, because she was too engrossed in job responsibilities. Her sole recreation was obtained in her own home and with relatives. In junior high school, she rarely read or did anything of an academic nature. The distance of her home from school and her lack of pocket money made it difficult for her to do things with school acqaintances or go to movies. She helped with sewing and cooking in the home, and peddled vegetables with her father until her school homework became too heavy. She found employment away from home that was more remunerative and less time-consuming. Later, part-time employment enabled her to afford an occasional movie or pulp magazine and time to listen to the radio. Almost all her activities were still shared with her immediate family or other relatives. In grade 11 she admitted an ambition to work on the school paper, but considered herself "too dumb" to dare to try out. She had made friends with a crowd that went roller-skating, dancing, and to the movies together, until halfway through her senior year the boys were called into active service by the National Guard.

Work Experience

While in junior high school, Paula had a vegetable route on which she sold the vegetables that her father raised. She was successful and enjoyed the work. Later, she began to secure evening jobs as a baby-sitter. One employer's introduction got her a summer job finishing pocketbooks, and she earned up to $20 a week at piece work. She thoroughly enjoyed this work and was very proud of her earnings. In grade 11 she had an after-school domestic job four or more afternoons a week. This was a hard job that included washing and heavy cleaning. Paula needed the money so badly that she refused to jeopardize her wages by asking for shorter hours or investigating other jobs, even when there was danger of her failing to graduate because of lack of time to study.

Occupational Choice

Grade 8 Stenographer: "Looks like a nice job."
Grade 9 Stenographer: "A friend of my father's says he can get me a job."
Grade 10 Stenographer: Family pressure to have one member get through school trained for a "good job."
Grade 11 (1) Office work: No reason given
          (2) Factory piece work: "I liked my job and made good money."

(3) Power stitching: Learned from counselor that training was available and said, "I want to get training on something I can really do."

Grade 12 (1) Dressmaking: Considered this occupation because she was doing well in sewing and failing in business subjects.

(2) Light assembly work: Liked working with her hands and was interested in jobs described by the counselor.

Progress of Counseling

In grade 8, at the age of 14 years 10 months, Paula was considerably older than most students in her class. She was failing in Business Practice, and her other grades for the first marking period were below what might have been expected from her seventh-grade performance. Her rating on a test of general ability, previously administered in the school, placed her on the lower fringe of the normal group, and this rating was verified by her poor performance on the *language and mathematics tests administered by the counselor.* The test scores suggested that her good marks in the past had been partially due to conscientiousness and good conduct rather than to actual achievement.

The counselor's first impression of energetic, quick-moving, and tense Paula was that she was taller and more mature than most girls in her grade. She was thin, dark-complexioned, and she had somewhat prognathic facial features. Her bizarre combinations of clothes made her outstanding in any group. She was friendly and responsive, and *she was so anxious to tell her story that only an occasional question was required to keep up her rapid flow of language.* She welcomed a listener and told details of her family life without reserve. She was obviously closely bound with her home, parents, and other relatives, for she quoted her parents continually to back up her statements. She displayed a keen interest in her job of selling vegetables with her father, which suggested that her very enthusiasm must account in part for her success in selling. *The counselor observed that she did not participate in clubs and athletic activities,* either in school or in her neighborhood, but that she did attend a number of community dances. She complained that she never had money for movies or other activities because all her earnings were turned over to her family.

Paula displayed little enthusiasm about school. She was much concerned with home interests and responsibilities, felt that the school had little to offer her, and was resigned to the fact that she was not a good student. Her work was, however, done very conscientiously, and she was pleased to have avoided assignment to the special class for dull students which her sister and cousin had attended. She wanted to leave school to help at home as soon as she was sixteen, and *the counselor saw no reason*

to encourage her to continue. She was needed at home, and it seemed unlikely that she would succeed in further academic work or profit enough
by commercial training to justify the time involved.

In her selection of subjects for grade 9, Paula was *less influenced by
the counselor's comments* than by a visitor at home who promised to find
work for her if she was trained for stenography. There was no relationship
in her mind between failure in Business Practice and chance of success in
stenography. *The counselor pointed out difficulties suggested by her language handicap,* but since he was convinced she would drop out of school
within the year, *he did little to discourage her in this choice.*

On tests administered to her in grade 9, Paula's general mental-abil-
ity rating was below the normal group. She was three years below her
grade level in reading. Her vocabulary was very limited, but she could
read the simple magazines, and newspapers in which she was interested.
She was doing well in the household arts and her marks in other subjects
—all C's—seemed to reflect conscientious effort rather than real accomplishment. *The counselor discussed with her the advantages of electing* the
household arts curriculum for the duration of her schooling, but Paula, influenced by family ambitions and the interest of friends, started senior
high school in the stenographic curriculum.

The counselor's analysis of her study habits showed that she had to
spend several extra hours a week at typing to produce the required "perfect copies" and that home study in other subjects took all of her free time.
In view of her marks, *the counselor was obliged to admit* that her diligence
and her strong desire for success had been rewarded. These and the fact
that she was overage for her grade should have been given more weight in
earlier predictions, the counselor suspected, so that when Paula insisted
on continuing in the stenographic curriculum, *the counselor advised, but
did not insist, that she avoid shorthand.*

By the time she was interviewed in grade 11, Paula was now among
the shorter members of her class, still thin and wiry, all elbows and enthusiasms. Occasionally, however, she showed bitterness toward school
work and teachers, as her difficulties in typing and shorthand increased.
Her diction was not clear and her speech occasionally ungrammatical, but
she had no difficulty or reticence in expressing opinions. She reported inability to keep up with assignments. "Even if I do every bit of the homework, when I get to class it's marked wrong, or the teacher asks different
questions." Her painstaking memorizing no longer carried her through
classes where the required reasoning was frequently beyond her, and her
weakness in language was an insurmountable obstacle in stenography. And
now she did not have time for extra study or extra afternoons in the typing
room because she worked four afternoons a week as a domestic.

The counselor's suggestion that she give up this job temporarily did not prove feasible, for it was Paula's only source of funds for clothes, recreation, and the contribution which she thought she was obligated to make to her family. She was even unwilling to jeopardize her job by asking her employer to shift her free afternoon to the one day a week that her typing teacher could take students for make-up work. *The counselor concentrated on developing study skills to enable her to make her points toward graduation.* Meanwhile, *he pointed out the necessity of shifting to an easier curriculum during her senior year* if she intended to keep up her outside work and still do enough of the school work to graduate. *During a discussion of Paula's successful summer experience* in the pocketbook factory, the *counselor pointed out possible openings in other industrial plants* where she might do assembly work, certain finishing jobs, and power-machine stitching. She was willing to consider any job which would offer her as high wages as she had earned during the summer, but she would not leave school until she had secured the high school diploma that she and her family desired. The teachers of commercial subjects reported that Paula was frequently discouraged in class, but she did not seem seriously disturbed by her failures. She continued to be pleasant and friendly with her teachers and associates and often "kept the girls laughing." She confided to her favorite teacher that her real ambition was to follow her sister's example and get married soon. Save for the morale value of fulfilling a strong ambition, she seemed likely to gain little from another year of the type of study in which she had been engaged, so *the counselor's main concern was to see that she selected courses that she could pass.*

The counselor recommended further consideration of a transfer to the household arts curriculum, *suggested summer training* in power-machine stitching at the Opportunity School (which would allow job-hunting during half the day) until she found summer work, and *worked out with her a comprehensive program* of job-hunting in fields related to her experience. Paula showed considerable common sense in planning this program, and quickly grasped the gist of *the counselor's suggestions of simple readings* in magazines. She had several interviews for jobs but did not find an opening so she continued her part-time domestic work. During the summer, she twice raised the question of continuing the clerical course, *and twice was told that her mark in Office Practice was not high enough, according to school regulations, to permit further study in that field.*

She started out in grade 12 well-pleased with all her household arts program. She was doing the work of a full-time maid for her employer in order to double her weekly income, because, she said, "This last year I just have to have some new clothes and enough to pay for my yearbook and all the extras. Of course, Mother needs extra money at home, too." She began to get failing marks in English and Economics because she did not have enough time to study. *The counselor urged her to arrange with her employer for time off* on afternoons when the teacher could give her help, but Paula refused either to do so or to let the counselor consult the employer, until it became certain that she was going to fail to make enough points for graduation. When she *threatened to leave school the counselor supplemented her mother's urging to give up the job* and finish her year at school, and she finally did arrange time for regular make-up sessions which *the counselor arranged with teachers* who were beginning to lose patience. The vigor and persistence which she put into these sessions convinced teachers that she was doing her best, so they cooperated with the counselor in giving her simple assignments in Commercial Law and in English for the last half of the year.

Looking forward to employment after graduation, *she discussed with the counselor light assembly jobs* with local radio and soap manufacturers, printing, and printing supply concerns. She *was introduced to personnel managers in these industries.* To check her manual skill, she *was given a rate of manipulation test,* on which her score was average for the general population, and then *referred to the Y.W.C.A.* for further dexterity tests. Her performance on the tests was reported as adequate for light assembly work. The day after graduation, she was one of a group of girls who *accompanied the counselor on a visit to laundries and manufacturing concerns* to observe the work being done and to apply for a job. She stuck it out among dozens of applicants at a manufacturing company where, *upon the counselor's recommendation,* she was employed as a stem-winder in the radio tube department. *Her success in securing employment appeared to be due to the counselor's sponsorship,* for the employer had previously decided that he would not employ any more girls of foreign descent in the particular department in which the vacancies had existed. *The counselor helped Paula to obtain the necessary working papers* and recommendations in time to start work the next day.

It was expected that she would want to make a change in employment before the year was over, due to unpleasant working conditions, the possibility of eyestrain, and danger of burns from working with hot metals. When *interviewed by the counselor during the spring following graduation,* she had many complaints about these factors, about criticism from her new supervisor, and her new work. She had been transferred when her original department was reduced in size. She liked her associates, however, was interested in all the different types of work available, and was stimulated by the challenge of "keeping ahead of the other girls" in a single repetitive process. These and her satisfaction in a raise in pay *made her unwilling to accept easier work suggested by the counselor.* She was proud of her pay, enjoyed social activities at the plant, and looked forward to doing similar work until she could get married, saying, "I'd like office work because it would be cleaner, but I could not make as much as I am making

I'm sure. Guess I'd better stay where I am." Her family was proud of her earning power and worried only because the long hours tired her and strained her eyes.

Eleven Years After Initial Counseling

Paula worked at the factory for two years and then married the "boy-friend" of high school days. At the time of her marriage he was in the Army and Paula followed him throughout his training periods and later assignments. She supplemented the family income by working as a waitress, factory worker, and restaurant checker. She disliked the inconvenience of travel but felt that it was her duty to be with her husband.

After he was discharged they returned to their home town. She secured a job as a checker in a chain grocery store while her husband worked as a mechanic. They live in a modest home which is furnished in good taste, and she appears to be an excellent housekeeper. At the present time Paula is expecting a child. She has a good deal of confidence in herself and is very proud of her accomplishments so far.

RACHAEL

Assume that Rachael is a pupil in a school in which you have recently been appointed a counselor. The following descriptions have been accumulated over the period of her first six years in school.[1] What kind of counseling would you offer Rachael? Give reasons for all of your activities.

I. Rachael as a First Grader

Rachael was a healthy, clean, neat-appearing child. Because of a change in schools she started first grade for the second time and she did not think it was justified. Her aloofness extended to the teacher, and she was reluctant about her work, but her good training in manners prevented overt disobedience. When she did work, she was very capable. At times she was lethargic, as shown by the low volume of her voice and disregard of classroom responsibilities. She was receptive to a challenge, and when it was provided she worked independently and efficiently. She used her splendid vocabulary occasionally.

Rachael was a shy child whose feelings could be hurt easily. She was affectionate and friendly with those whom she knew.

---

[1] Abstracted from C. V. Millard and J. W. M. Rothney, *The Elementary School Child* (New York: Holt, Rinehart and Winston, Inc., 1957).

She was absolutely truthful and did not resort to protective or wish-fulfillment distortions. She quarreled only under real provocation, but she generally responded pliably with most children. She showed only occasional lustiness or spontaneous gaiety. At times she was moody, withdrawn, and generally passive in the classroom.

II. *Background and Development*

1. Rachael was the youngest of three children. The oldest, a daughter, died at the age of six when Rachael was eleven months old.

2. Rachael received no special attention as the youngest child. She showed affection easily, freely, and warmly. Relations among all were supporting and satisfying. She and her parents enjoyed each other, had fun together, and respected one another.

3. Rachael had many real satisfactions with her brother. They took pride in each other and played together. They quarreled occasionally but neither of the two assumed a dominant position.

4. In reference to home life Rachael had the following to say during an interview at age eleven: "They usually let me have my own way but I don't ask for anything unreasonable. Maybe I'm a little spoiled, both of us kids are in a way. My dad is a little roly-poly, quite heavy, not tall. My brother said when he first saw him he looked funny, like he didn't have any neck. He's got black hair and brown eyes, and Mother has too. My father was always jealous if she ever looked at anyone else. Seems like they never showed any real affection before us kids. My dad likes fishing and hunting. He belongs to the Masons and the Eagles but is not very active. The only thing my mother does is church circle, but neither Dad nor Mother attend church regularly."

5. "It seems that my brother and I have always been close to my mother. We can take our problems to her and she will listen and try to understand and help. I guess it's because my father might get mad. My brother was always afraid of Dad. I was the only one to sass him back. My mother always makes the final decision. Everything is left to my mother to do. She takes care of the family budget too."

6. The family seemed to be characterized by a good give-and-take attitude with common goals and interests. The parents took pride in the achievements of their children.

7. Rachael began school in another district at midyear. When she transferred to this school she had the opportunity to begin the second grade, after completing only one half year of the first, or to repeat the first grade. The latter alternative was taken. Consequently Rachael went through elementary school slightly advanced chronologically for her grade placement. As a first grade pupil she often appeared somewhat lax in her efforts, as if the work were boring and "old stuff."

8. As measured by the standardized tests, Rachael's performances were mediocre. Her average educational age came close to matching her grade placement. Since she was at least five months older than most for her grade, her educational average was below norms.

9. At no time throughout elementary school did Rachael receive less than a B grade. Her record in grades five and six was outstanding. She was given grades of A with the only exception of a B in reading while she was in the sixth grade. Rachael impressed all her teachers consistently in the same way.

III. *Teachers' Ratings*

In the following teachers' description of Rachael, movement toward freedom of expression is rated as "Desirable," and change in ratings from freedom to a more restricted, anxious type of category is labeled as "Undesirable." Where the ratings are the same they are placed under the "No Change" category.

A. DESIRABLE CHANGE

From Kindergarten	*To Sixth Grade*
1. Shares under pressure.	1. Shares normally with those who share with her.
2. Excessive care and protection of objects; can't enjoy or let others enjoy toys or possessions.	2. Very careful of toys, furniture, and dishes. Cares for them and puts them away, but not so fussy she can't enjoy them.
3. Happier when being waited on than when doing things for self. Expects help on things she can easily do for herself.	3. Normally dependent in appropriate situations, independent in others. Seeks attention and service if available, but functions easily without it.
4. Extremely reserved, practically never expresses feelings. Extremely inhibited emotionally.	4. Reserved with some people but not with others.
5. Extreme fearfulness or apprehension in new situations.	5. Watches others first before participating; always tense, so that efficiency is lowered.
6. Extremely uncomfortable if things are not just so.	6. Likes things neat and orderly.
7. Unsuccessful in social relationships; not popular but with no intense reactions about it.	7. Not outstanding. Some playmates may not like her, but has approving supporters.
8. Extreme, active withdrawing.	8. Some mild withdrawal; retiring passive participant. Avoids center of stage.
9. Extremely passive and submissive. Lets anyone dominate her.	9. More submissive than many others; takes orders readily.

B. UNDESIRABLE CHANGE

1. Accepts her achievement as a matter of course.	1. Considerable tension and very sensitive about her standing and approval or disapproval.

C. NO CHANGE

1. Hardly ever reprimanded or spoken to regarding behavior.
2. Takes teacher for granted; little expression one way or the other.
3. Prefers quiet games and quiet companions, although occasionally enjoys playing active games.
4. Refuses to quarrel either by withdrawal or excessive yielding to opponent.
5. Extreme gentleness; strong protective drive; avoidance of any statements or actions which might hurt feelings of another child.
6. More susceptible to hurt feelings than most children her age.
7. Seldom free from mild tension.
8. Characteristically serious-minded.
9. Follows routine as a matter of course. Accepts suggestions easily.
10. No real competitive relationship; enjoys games for the fun of playing them, but relatively unimportant to her who wins.
11. Considerable (not extreme) lack of confidence.
12. Feels she is not liked as well as other children. Insecure but not extremely so.

IV. *Overall Impressions*

The overall picture gained by observers who studied this child throughout all grades was of similarity throughout. It appeared that her patterns of behavior were well formed by the time she entered school.

The ratings of behavior tend to give Rachael the picture of a quite somber, serious, and anxiety-centered child.

Rachael did, however, have a gay side. She smiled easily and often. She liked to be active, to have fun. Observers felt that these occasional bright spots were the real Rachael rather than the frequently described phases of depression and anxieties.

references

ACOUREL, A. V., and J. I. KITSUSE. *The Education Decision Makers.* New York: The Bobbs-Merrill Co., Inc., 1963.

ALLPORT, G. W., and H. S. ODBERT. "Trait Names: A Psycho-Lexical Study," *Psychological Monographs,* No. 211 (1936).

ARBUCKLE, D. S. "Counselor-Parent Interactions," *Guidance Journal,* V (Winter 1967).

———. *Pupil Personnel Services in the Modern School.* Boston: Allyn & Bacon, Inc., 1966.

BARRY, R., and B. WOLF. *Epitaph for Vocational Guidance.* New York: Columbia University Teachers College, 1962.

BAURENFEND, R. H. *Building a School Testing Program.* Boston: Houghton Mifflin Company, 1963.

BENDER, I. E., H. A. IMUS, and J. W. M. ROTHNEY. *Motivation and Visual Factors: Individual Studies of College Students.* Hanover, N.H.: Dartmouth College Publications, 1942.

BERGSTEIN, H. B. "The Parent and the School Counselor: An Emerging Relationship," *Vocational Guidance Quarterly,* XIII (Summer 1965).

BISCHOF, L. J. *Interpreting Personality Theories* (2nd ed.). New York: Harper & Row, Publishers, 1970.

BOROW, H., ed. *Man in a World of Work.* Boston: Houghton Mifflin Company, 1964.

BREWER, J. M. *Education as Guidance.* New York: The Macmillan Company, 1932.

BUROS, O. *Mental Measurements Yearbooks.* Highland Park, N.J.: Gryphon Press, 1965 and other years.

BYRNE, R. H. *The School Counselor*. Boston: Houghton Mifflin Company, 1963.

CALIA, V. F. "The Culturally Deprived Client: A Reformulation of the Counselor's Role," *Journal of Counseling Psychology*, XIII (1966).

CAMP, W. L., and J. W. M. ROTHNEY. "Parental Response to Counselors' Suggestions," *The School Counselor*, XVII (1970).

CAMPBELL, J., and M. D. DUNNETTE. "Effectiveness of T Group Experiences in Managerial Training and Development," *Psychological Bulletin*, LXXIX (1968).

CONANT, J. B. *Slums and Suburbs*. New York: McGraw-Hill Book Company, 1961.

CREMIN, L. A. "The Progressive Heritage of the Guidance Movement," *Harvard Educational Review*, III (1964).

CRONBACH, L. J. *Essentials of Psychological Testing*. New York: Harper & Row, Publishers, 1960.

DEARBORN, W. F., and J. W. M. ROTHNEY. *Predicting the Child's Development* (2nd ed.). Cambridge, Mass.: Sci-Art Publishers, 1963.

FAUST, V. *The Counselor-Consultant in the Elementary School*. Boston: Houghton Mifflin Company, 1968.

————. *History of Elementary School Counseling*. Boston: Houghton Mifflin Company, 1968.

FITZGIBBON, F. J. "The Ethical and Legal Position of the Counselor in Divulging Test Information," *Measurement and Evaluation in Guidance*, I (Spring 1968).

GAZDA, G. M., ed. *Basic Approaches to Group Psychotherapy and Group Counseling*. Springfield, Ill.: Charles C Thomas, Publisher, 1968.

GINZBERG, E. "Guidance—Limited or Unlimited?" *Personnel and Guidance Journal*, XXXVIII (1960).

————, and D. W. BRAY. *The Uneducated*. New York: Columbia University Press, 1953.

————, and J. L. HERMA. *Talent and Performance*. New York: Columbia University Press, 1964.

GOLDMAN, L. *Using Tests in Counseling*. New York: Appleton-Century-Crofts, 1961.

GORDON, E. W., ed. "Education for Socially Disadvantaged Children," *Review of Educational Research*, XL (1970).

GOSLIN D. A., Conference Chairman. *Guidelines for the Collection, Maintenance and Dissemination of Pupil Records*. New York: Russell Sage Foundation, 1969.

HANSEN, D. A., ed. *Explorations in Sociology and Counseling*. Boston: Houghton Mifflin Company, 1969.

HAYS, D. G., and J. W. M. ROTHNEY. "Educational Decision-making by Superior Secondary School Students and Their Parents," *Personnel and Guidance Journal*, XL (1961).

HENJUM, R. J., and J. W. M. ROTHNEY. "Parental Action on Counselors' Suggestions," *Vocational Guidance Quarterly*, VIII, No. 1 (1969).

HILGARD, E. R. *Theories of Learning*. New York: Appleton-Century-Crofts, 1966.

HILL, G. E., and E. B. LUCKEY. *Guidance for Children in Elementary Schools.* New York: Appleton-Century-Crofts, 1969.

HOPPOCK, R. *Occupational Information* (3rd ed.). New York: McGraw-Hill Book Company, 1967.

HOTT, I. "Counseling Youthful Drug Users," *Guidepost,* XII (1969).

HOYT, K. B. "What the School Has a Right to Expect of Its Counselor," *Personnel and Guidance Journal,* XL (1961).

———, and C. P. FROELICH. *Guidance Testing.* Chicago: Science Research Associates, Inc., 1959.

HULL, C. L. *Aptitude Testing.* Yonkers-on-Hudson, N.Y.: World Book Co., 1928.

JACKSON, R. M., and J. W. M. ROTHNEY. "A Comparative Study of the Mailed Questionnaire and the Interview in Follow-up Studies," *Personnel and Guidance Journal,* XXXIX (1961).

JESSELL, J. C., and J. W. M. ROTHNEY. "The Effectiveness of Parent-Counselor Conferences," *Personnel and Guidance Journal,* XLIX (1965).

JOHNSON, W. F., *et al. Pupil Personnel and Guidance Services.* New York: McGraw-Hill Book Company, 1961.

KATZ, M. R. "Theoretical Foundations of Guidance," *Review of Educational Research,* XXXIX, No. 2 (1969).

KENNEDY, D. A., and I. THOMPSON. "Use of a Reinforcement Technique with a First-Grade Boy," *Personnel and Guidance Journal,* XLVI, No. 4 (1967).

KRUMBOLTZ, J. D., ed. *Revolution in Counseling: Implications of Behavior Science.* Boston: Houghton Mifflin Company, 1966.

———, and C. E. THORESEN. *Behavioral Counseling: Cases and Techniques.* New York: Holt, Rinehart and Winston, Inc., 1969.

LAZARUS, A. "Relationship Therapy: Often Necessary but Usually Insufficient," *Journal of Counseling Psychology,* I (Summer 1969).

LINDEN, J. D., S. C. STONE, and B. SHERTZER. "Development and Evaluation of an Inventory for Rating Counseling," *Personnel and Guidance Journal,* XXXVIII (September 1965).

MATHEWSON, R. H. *Guidance Policy and Practice.* New York: Harper & Row, Publishers, 1962.

MICHAEL, J., and L. MEYERSON. "A Behavioral Approach to Counseling and Guidance," *Harvard Educational Review,* XXXII, No. 4 (Fall 1962).

MILLARD, C. V., and J. W. M. ROTHNEY. *The Elementary School Child: A Book of Cases.* New York: Holt, Rinehart and Winston, Inc., 1957.

MILLER, C. *Foundations of Guidance.* New York: Harper & Row, Publishers, 1961.

MITCHELL, Joyce S. "Social Visibility and College Choice," *Personnel and Guidance Journal,* XLVIII (1970).

MORGAN, G. D. *The Ghetto College Student.* Iowa City, Iowa: American College Testing Program, 1970.

MOWRER, O. H. *The New Group Therapy.* Princeton, N.J.: Van Nostrand Reinhold Company, 1964.

MUELLER, W. J., and J. W. M. ROTHNEY. "Comparisons of Selected Descriptions and Predictive Statements of Superior Students, Their Parents, and Their Teachers," *Personnel and Guidance Journal,* XXXVIII (1960).

MYRICK, R. D. "The Counselor-Consultant and the Effeminate Boy," *Personnel and Guidance Journal,* XLVIII (1970).

OGG, Elizabeth. *The Rehabilitation Counselor.* Public Affairs Pamphlet No. 392A. New York: Russell Sage Foundation, 1970.

OHLSEN, M. M. *Group Counseling.* New York: Holt, Rinehart and Winston, Inc., 1970.

PARSONS, F. *Choosing a Vocation.* Boston: Houghton Mifflin Company, 1909.

PATTERSON, C. H. *Theories of Counseling and Psychotherapy.* New York: Harper & Row, Publishers, 1966.

———, *et al.* "A Current View of Client-Centered or Relationship Therapy," *Counseling Psychologist,* I, No. 2 (Summer 1969).

PERRONE, P. A., T. A. RYAN, and F. R. ZERAN. *Guidance and the Emerging Adolescent.* Scranton, Pa.: International Textbook Co., 1970.

———, M. L. WEIKING, and E. H. NAGEL. "The Counseling Function as Seen by Students, Parents and Teachers," *Journal of Counseling Psychology,* XII (1965).

PETERS, H. J., and G. F. FARWELL. *Guidance: A Developmental Approach.* Chicago: Rand McNally & Co., 1967.

Review of Progress, Title V—A National Defense Education Act. Washington, D.C.: Bureau of Elementary and Secondary Education, U.S. Office of Education (February 1969).

RICCIO, A. C. "Me Change—Are You Joking?" *Guidepost,* XII (1970).

ROEBER, E. C., G. WALZ, and G. E. SMITH. *A Strategy for Guidance.* New York: The Macmillan Company, 1969.

ROGERS, C. R. *Client-Centered Therapy.* Boston: Houghton Mifflin Company, 1951.

———. *Counseling and Psychotherapy.* Boston: Houghton Mifflin Company, 1942.

———. "The Interpersonal Relationship: The Core of Guidance," *Harvard Educational Review,* XXXII, No. 4 (Fall 1962).

———. "The Necessary and Sufficient Conditions for Therapeutic Change," *Journal of Counseling Psychology,* XXI (1957).

———. *On Becoming a Person.* Boston: Houghton Mifflin Company, 1961.

———, and R. DYMOND. *Psychotherapy and Personality Change.* Chicago: University of Chicago Press, 1954.

———, and B. F. SKINNER. "Some Issues Concerning the Control of Human Behavior," *Science,* No. 124 (1956).

ROSEN, H. "Vocational Guidance: Room for Improvement," *Guidepost,* XII (1969).

ROTHNEY, J. W. M. *Educational, Vocational and Social Performances of Counseled and Uncounseled Youth Ten Years After High School.* Cooperative Research Project SAE 9231. Washington, D.C.: U.S. Office of Education, 1963.

———. *Evaluating and Reporting Pupil Progress.* No. 7 of the series, "What Research Says to the Teacher." Washington, D.C.: National Education Association, 1963.

———. *Guidance of American Youth.* Cambridge, Mass.: Harvard University Press, 1951.

ROTHNEY, J. W. M. *Guidance Practices and Results*. New York: Harper & Row, Publishers, 1958.

————. *The High School Student*. New York: Holt, Rinehart and Winston, Inc. 1953.

————. "Improving Reports to Parents," *National Elementary Principal*, XLV (1966).

————. *Methods of Studying the Individual Child: The Psychological Case Study*. Waltham, Mass.: Ginn/Blaisdell, 1968.

————. "Review of the Strong Vocational Interest Blank and the Minnesota Vocational Interest Inventory," *Journal of Counseling Psychology*, XIV, No. 2 (1967).

————. "School Counselors: Do They Make a Difference?" *Guidelines*, State Department of Public Instruction, Madison, Wisconsin, IV (1966).

————. "Who Gets Counseled for What?" in *1971 Yearbook of the Association for Supervision and Curriculum Development*. Washington, D.C.: The Association for Supervision and Curriculum Development.

————, and N. KOOPMAN. "Guidance of the Gifted," in *Fifty-Seventh Yearbook of the National Society for the Study of Education*. Washington, D.C.: 1958.

ROTHNEY, J. W. M., and C. W. LEWIS. "Use of Control Groups in Studies of Guidance," *Personnel and Guidance Journal*, XLVII, No. 5 (January 1969).

ROTHNEY, J. W. M., and B. A. ROENS. *Counseling the Individual Student*. New York: William Sloane Associates, 1949.

ROTHNEY, J. W. M., and M. P. SANBORN. *Identifying and Educating Superior Students in Wisconsin High Schools*. Madison: University of Wisconsin Research and Guidance Laboratory for Superior Students, 1967.

————. "Wisconsin's Research Through Guidance Programs for Superior Students," *Personnel and Guidance Journal*, XLIV (March 1966).

ROTHNEY, J. W. M., P. J. DANIELSON, and R. A. HEIMANN. *Measurement for Guidance*. New York: Harper & Row, Publishers, 1959.

RULON, P. J. "On the Concepts of Growth and Ability," *Harvard Educational Review*, XVII (1947).

SCHWIRIAN, K. P. "Testing at Issue: A Case Study of School and Community Conflict," in D. A. Hansen, ed. *Explorations in Sociology and Counseling*. Boston: Houghton Mifflin Company, 1969.

SEWELL, W. H. "Community of Residence and College Plans," *American Sociological Review*, XXIX (1964).

————. "Community of Residence and Occupational Choice," *American Journal of Sociology*, LXX (1965).

SMITH, P. M., JR., ed. "What Guidance for Blacks?" *Personnel and Guidance Journal*, XLVIII (1970).

STEFFLRE, B. *Theories of Counseling*. New York: McGraw-Hill Book Company, 1965.

STEWART, L., and O. F. WARMATH. *The Counselor and Society: A Cultural Approach*. Boston: Houghton Mifflin Company, 1965.

TELFORD, C. W., and J. M. SAUREY. *The Exceptional Individual: Psycho-

logical and Educational Aspects. Englewood Cliffs, N.J.: Prentice-Hall, Inc., 1967.

THORESEN, C. E. "The Counselor as an Applied Behavior Scientist," *Personnel and Guidance Journal,* XLVII (1969).

———. "Relevance and Research in Counseling," *Review of Educational Research,* XXXIX, No. 2 (1969).

TRAXLER, A. E., and R. D. NORTH. *Techniques of Guidance.* New York: Harper & Row, Publishers, 1966.

TRUAX, C. B., and R. R. CARKUFF. "Experimental Manipulation of Therapeutic Conditions," *Journal of Counseling Psychology,* XXIX (1955).

———. *Recent Advances in the Study of Behavior Change.* Montreal: McGill University Press, 1963.

———. *Toward Effective Counseling and Therapy.* Chicago: The Aldine Press, 1967.

TYLER, Leona E. *The Psychology of Individual Differences.* New York: Appleton-Century-Crofts, 1965.

———. *The Work of the Counselor.* New York: Appleton-Century-Crofts, 1969.

ULLMAN, L. P., and L. KRASNER. *Case Studies in Behavior Modification.* New York: Holt, Rinehart and Winston, Inc., 1965.

VAN HOOSE, W. H., and J. J. PIETROFESA, eds. *Counseling and Guidance in the Twentieth Century: Reflections and Formulations.* Boston: Houghton Mifflin Company, 1970.

WARTERS, Jane. *Techniques of Counseling.* New York: McGraw-Hill Book Company, 1964.

WESMAN, A. G. "Intelligent Testing," *American Psychologist,* XXIII, No. 4 (1968).

WILLIAMSON, E. G. *Vocational Counseling: Some Historical, Philosophical and Theoretical Perspectives.* New York: McGraw-Hill Book Company, 1965.

WRENN, C. G. *The Counselor in a Changing World.* Washington, D.C.: The American Personnel and Guidance Association, 1962.

subject index

189

author index